Advanced Excel Success

A Practical Guide to Mastering Excel

Alan Murray

apress®

Advanced Excel Success: A Practical Guide to Mastering Excel

Alan Murray
Ipswich, UK

ISBN-13 (pbk): 978-1-4842-6466-9   ISBN-13 (electronic): 978-1-4842-6467-6
https://doi.org/10.1007/978-1-4842-6467-6

Managing Director, Apress Media LLC: Welmoed Spahr
Acquisitions Editor: Smriti Srivastava
Development Editor: Matthew Moodie
Coordinating Editor: Shrikant Vishwakarma

Cover designed by eStudioCalamar

Cover image designed by Pexels

Distributed to the book trade worldwide by Springer Science+Business Media LLC, 1 New York Plaza, Suite 4600, New York, NY 10004. Phone 1-800-SPRINGER, fax (201) 348-4505, e-mail orders-ny@springer-sbm.com, or visit www.springeronline.com. Apress Media, LLC is a California LLC and the sole member (owner) is Springer Science + Business Media Finance Inc (SSBM Finance Inc). SSBM Finance Inc is a **Delaware** corporation.

For information on translations, please e-mail booktranslations@springernature.com; for reprint, paperback, or audio rights, please e-mail bookpermissions@springernature.com.

Apress titles may be purchased in bulk for academic, corporate, or promotional use. eBook versions and licenses are also available for most titles. For more information, reference our Print and eBook Bulk Sales web page at http://www.apress.com/bulk-sales.

Any source code or other supplementary material referenced by the author in this book is available to readers on GitHub via the book's product page, located at www.apress.com/978-1-4842-6466-9. For more detailed information, please visit http://www.apress.com/source-code.

Printed on acid-free paper

To my children, George and Lily

Table of Contents

About the Author

 **Alan** is a Microsoft MVP, Excel trainer, YouTuber, and freelance writer. He has been helping people in Excel for over 20 years. He loves training and the joy he gets from knowing he is making people's working lives easier.

Alan runs his own blog – Computergaga – and writes for multiple other websites. His YouTube channel has over 500 videos and over 24 million views. He organizes a monthly Excel meetup in London where the Excel community learns, shares, and enjoys each other's company.

About the Technical Reviewer

Mark Proctor is a senior finance professional, qualified accountant, and blogger who has been applying spreadsheet-based solutions to solve real-world problems for the last 20 years. He has built a variety of Excel-based reporting, predictive, decision-making, and automation tools for achieving process efficiency in multinational companies in the media, food, retail, and manufacturing sectors. He is also the owner of Excel Off The Grid (`https://exceloffthegrid.com`), one of the most popular Excel blogs on the Internet, which focuses on teaching intermediate and advanced Excel techniques.

Acknowledgments

Firstly, a thank you to everyone at Apress who was involved with this book. A special thanks to Smriti Srivastava, the acquisitions editor, for the opportunity. Writing a book is a challenge, but a rewarding one. And also Shrikant Vishwakarma, the coordinating editor, for his assistance and putting up with my many emails.

Thank you to Mark Proctor, the technical editor for this book. He is a good friend and a super smart Excel dude. He has provided encouragement at every step and was there when I needed someone to talk to.

My gratitude goes to the excellent Excel community. They inspire and help me. I massively appreciate everybody who subscribes to my blog and YouTube channel and attends my Excel meetups. Your feedback, love, and support are greatly valued.

Thank you to Tea Kuseva, my co-organizer of the London Excel Meetup. She has a lot of faith in me, provides encouragement for my endeavors, and has become a good friend.

Finally, a thank you to my children George and Lily. They are my support and my best friends. They are a motivation to me, more than they know.

Introduction

The aim of this book is to show the advanced Excel skills you need to be a success in the workplace. It is full of Excel techniques, formula examples, and uses of Excel features that I have learned over the last 20 years of teaching and consulting in Excel and want to share with you now.

Microsoft Excel is utilized by businesses all over the world to manage, analyze, and share data. However, most users are taught how to use the tools and formulas of Excel in a very narrow way. They have typically learned them from a colleague or through Google. They perform the steps and it does a job, but they often do not know how it returned that result. *Advanced Excel Success* will uncover some of the secrets that you are not told and use Excel tools in a way that you did not realize was possible.

This book will benefit anyone who works with Excel regularly, no matter the profession or their requirements from Excel.

Advanced Excel Success is divided into six chapters:

- **Chapter 1:** This chapter focuses on Excel tricks to boost productivity – tricks and innovative ways of using Excel features that I have learned over the years.

- **Chapter 2:** This chapter is all about formulas and some of the best functions in Excel. It takes a deep dive into Excel formulas to understand them in a way you may not have done before. It then focuses on some of Excel's best functions to analyze data and produce dynamic reports with "real-world" examples.

- **Chapter 3:** This chapter will look at advanced formatting techniques to add more meaning to your data. It starts with some advanced Conditional Formatting techniques. And then it takes formatting up another step with some very creative uses and unleashes the power of custom formatting.

- **Chapter 4:** This chapter will cover a variety of advanced charting tricks. These include automatically changing the color of key metrics, dynamically sorting chart data, and how to build creative chart labels.

- **Chapter 5:** This chapter is a guide to Power Query, one of the most important upgrades in Excel history. The chapter walks through several examples using Power Query to streamline common data tasks and prepare data for analysis.

- **Chapter 6:** This chapter is a guide to Power Pivot, a feature that goes beyond the Excel spreadsheet. With Power Pivot, we can store huge volumes of data, model it, and perform powerful calculations. This is all covered in the chapter.

Download the Example Files

You are encouraged to download the example files used by me throughout the book to practice on. The best way of learning is by doing. Follow along, explore, and this experience will benefit your learning greatly.

You can download the example files from the book's Apress web page (`www.apress.com/gp/book/9781484264669`).

The files are organized into folders that match the chapters of this book.

CHAPTER 1

Excel Tricks and Data Tools

Everybody loves an Excel trick. I certainly do. I love picking up new shortcuts and secret tips and learning innovative ways of using tools that I never thought to try. We are always learning.

When trying to accomplish an Excel task, sometimes the solution can come from an unexpected source. It could be from a tool that you thought you knew very well. And suddenly a clever new trick has opened your mind to new possibilities. You find yourself eagerly thinking of other ways you can use this new knowledge. I love that feeling.

This chapter will explore some of the tricks that I have learned over the years. I am indebted to my friends, my students, and occasionally my own endeavor in Excel to learning these. I hope these tips become a reference you can refer to again and again.

Fill Techniques

Let us begin with some fill techniques. It is one of the first techniques that you learn in Excel, but there are options that many are not aware of.

Generate a Number Series

When you generate a simple series of numbers, for a ranking list, for instance, you may know that entering one number is not enough. By default, Excel repeats the same number.

1. Enter the first number of the series (1 in this example), select the cell, and position your cursor over the fill handle until you see the skinny black cross. Figure 1-1 shows the fill handle.

© Alan Murray 2021
A. Murray, *Advanced Excel Success*, https://doi.org/10.1007/978-1-4842-6467-6_1

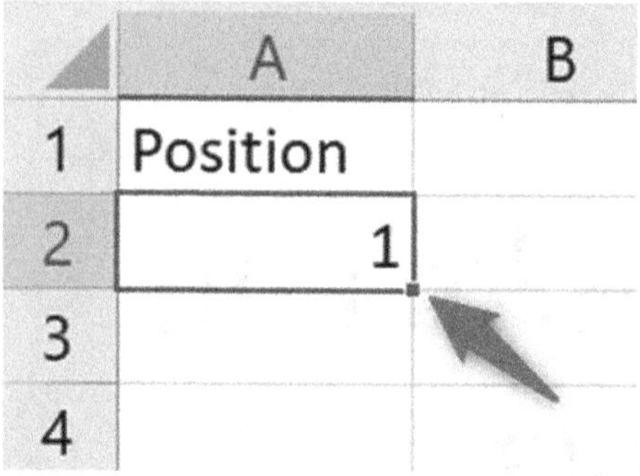

Figure 1-1. *Using the fill handle to generate a series of numbers*

2. Click and drag down the number of rows you want to generate a number series for.

The same number is repeated for every row (Figure 1-2).

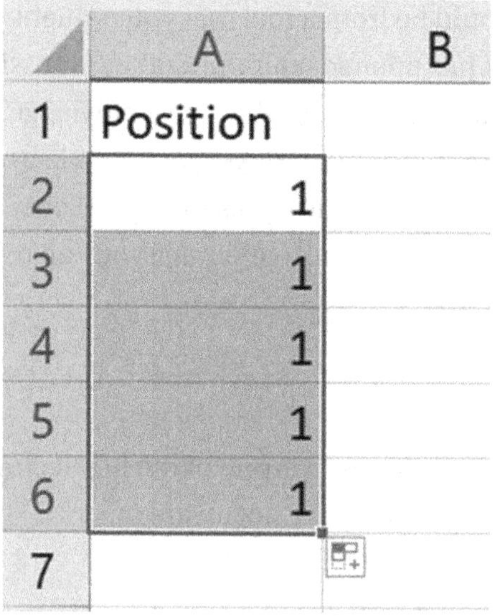

Figure 1-2. *Same number is repeated when you fill down a single number*

By entering a second number, you can get a sequence (Figure 1-3).

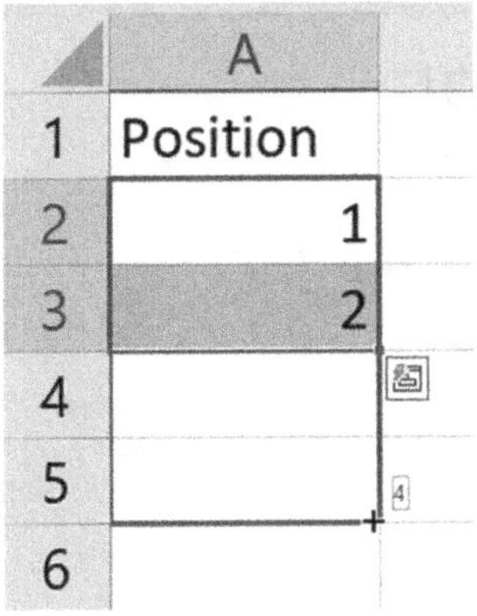

Figure 1-3. *Using two numbers to generate the series*

But you do not need to go through that hassle. There are a couple of neat tricks to generate the series. Simply type the first number and hold the **Ctrl** key down as you fill to generate the sequence.

An alternative method is to use the magic square to the right. Select the square in addition to the one containing the number and fill down (Figure 1-4).

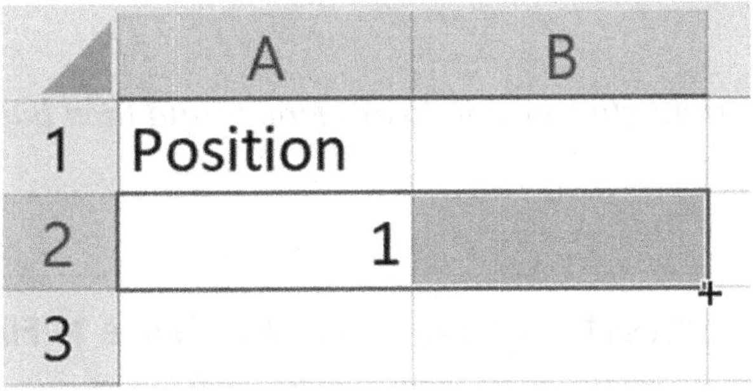

Figure 1-4. *Using the magic square to generate a series of numbers*

Additional Series Options

You can access additional series options by dragging the fill handle away and then back with the right button depressed. On releasing the right button, a menu appears (Figure 1-5). Click **Series**.

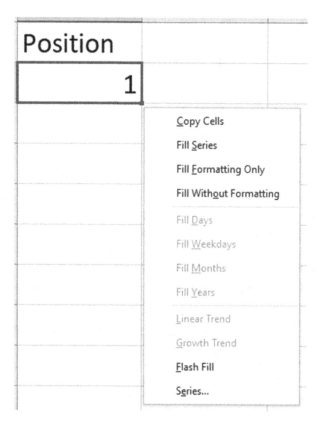

Figure 1-5. *Use the right-click button to drag away and then back to unlock secret options*

Note   You can also access these options by clicking **Home ➤ Fill ➤ Series**.

The Series window (Figure 1-6) provides some brilliant options such as to fill along rows or down columns, if you want to step values and at what value to stop.

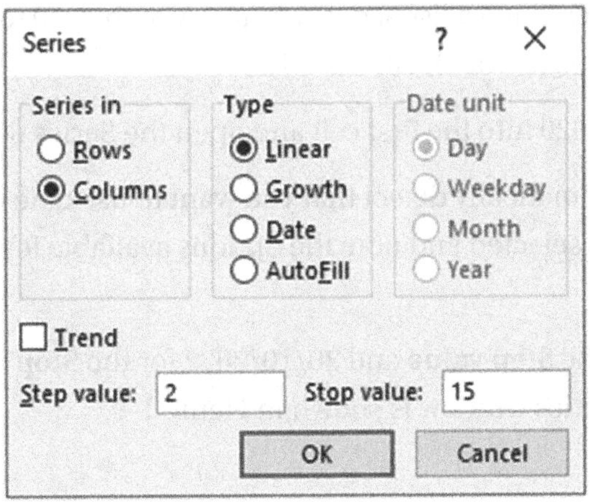

Figure 1-6. *Additional options in the Series window*

In this example, I have set it to step by 2 and to stop at number 15. The list is created with minimum fuss (Figure 1-7).

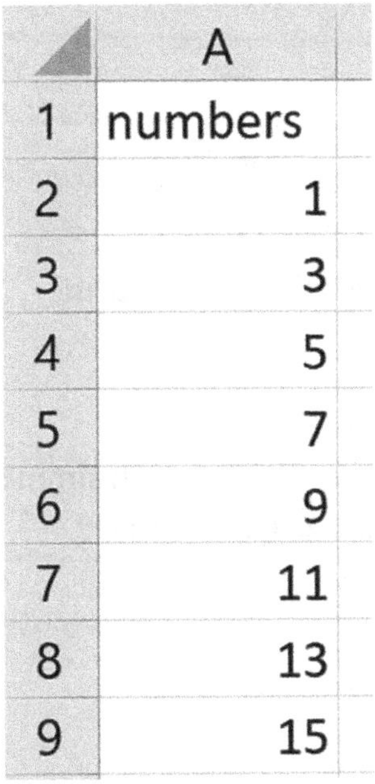

Figure 1-7. *A list from 1 to 15 stepping by 2*

This is just one example of what is available. But let us look at a far more realistic scenario.

We are tasked with creating a list of dates from 3 March 2020 to 30 October 2022, and we want every other week (3 March 2020 is a Tuesday).

1. Type 03/03/2020 into the first cell and open the Series window.

2. It should automatically detect that you want to use date values. Ensure this is selected and note the options available for date units.

3. Enter 14 for the **Step value** and 30/10/2022 for the **Stop value**. The completed Series window is shown in Figure 1-8.

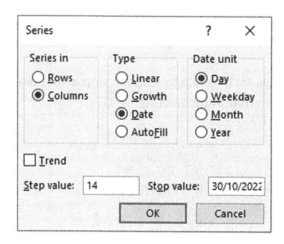

Figure 1-8. *Setting a date series with a stop value*

4. Click **OK**.

The list is generated (Figure 1-9). This is much simpler than typing two dates and dragging down cells until you reach 30 October 2022.

	A
1	**Dates**
2	03/03/2020
3	17/03/2020
4	31/03/2020
5	14/04/2020
6	28/04/2020

Figure 1-9. *Schedule of dates every 14 days from 3 March 2020*

In this scenario, the list stops at 25 October 2022 because that is the final Tuesday in the series.

The Incredible Flash Fill

Flash Fill is a tool that arrived with Excel 2013, and the day I first used it, I could not sleep that night. Along with the more important Power Query (Chapter 5), these tools make easy what was once a frustrating task.

Let us look at a couple of examples of what Flash Fill can do and how. These examples just give an insight, and you should further explore what else it can do.

File   flash-fill.xlsx

For the first example, we have people's first names in column A and their last names in column B. In column C, we want to combine the two together.

Type the full name of the first person and press Enter. Start typing the name of the second person, and Flash Fill appears offering to complete the rest for you (Figure 1-10). Press **Enter** to confirm and fill in every full name.

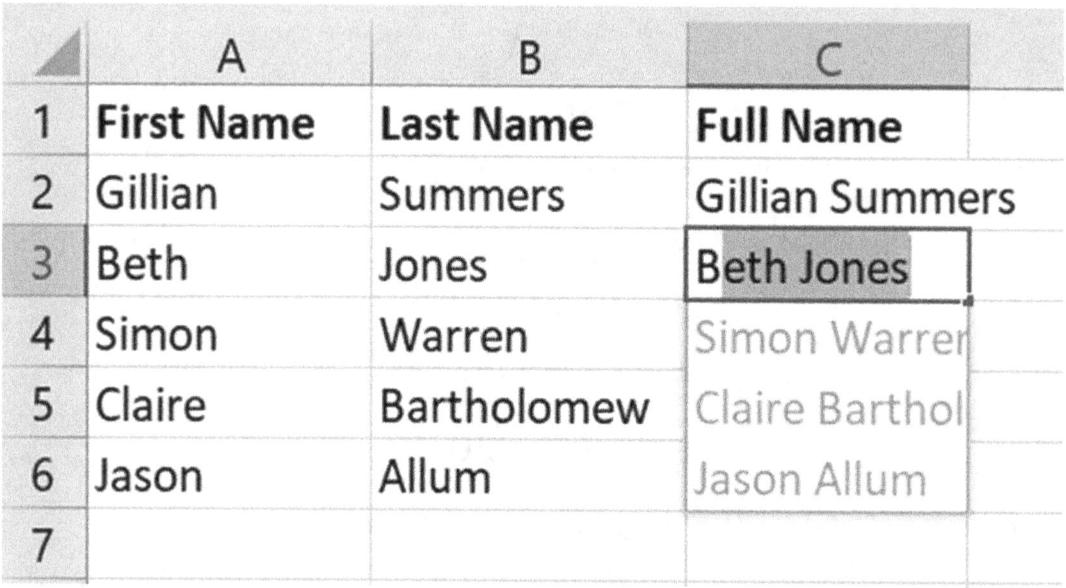

◢	A	B	C
1	**First Name**	**Last Name**	**Full Name**
2	Gillian	Summers	Gillian Summers
3	Beth	Jones	Beth Jones
4	Simon	Warren	Simon Warren
5	Claire	Bartholomew	Claire Barthol
6	Jason	Allum	Jason Allum
7			

Figure 1-10. *Flash Fill automatically picking up a data entry pattern*

So easy to combine hundreds or thousands of names and without any formula.

Note   You can disable this automatic Flash Fill from Excel Options if you do not like this behavior.

For a second example, we have the codes in Figure 1-11, and we want to extract the letters from between the two hyphens (-). They also need to be displayed in uppercase.

This would be a complicated formula, but with Flash Fill it is simple.

	A	B
1	Code	Area
2	13-Jh-829	
3	5-MMP-217	
4	23-YGE-04	
5	44-Pac-115	
6	6-XXF-814	

Figure 1-11. *A list of codes with information we want to extract*

1. Click cell B2 and type "JH", the first area code in uppercase.

2. Press **Ctrl + Enter** to confirm your entry but stay on cell B2.

3. Press **Ctrl + E**. This is the Flash Fill shortcut.

As easy as that, we have the data we want for further analysis (Figure 1-12).

Note   You can also run Flash Fill by clicking **Home ➤ Fill ➤ Flash Fill** or **Data ➤ Flash Fill**.

	A	B
1	Code	Area
2	13-Jh-829	JH
3	5-MMP-217	MMP
4	23-YGE-04	YGE
5	44-Pac-115	PAC
6	6-XXF-814	XXF

Figure 1-12. *Completed Flash Fill solution for the area codes*

Take Advantage of Custom Lists

When you enter the name of a month or day of the week in Excel and fill to other cells, a series is automatically created (Figure 1-13). This is possible because Excel has these series stored as custom lists.

	A
1	**Day of the Week**
2	Monday
3	Tuesday
4	Wednesday
5	Thursday
6	Friday
7	Saturday
8	Sunday

Figure 1-13. *The day of the week series in Excel*

You can create your own custom lists in Excel. This can improve the speed and accuracy of entering a series of data. This is very useful.

Another scenario for using custom lists is for sorting data effectively. You can sort lists using a custom list, but what if the items are not in the correct order?

Take this scenario. We have a Slicer connected to a table or PivotTable for filtering. It has the days of the week and is sorted in order (Figure 1-14). But, maybe, for you the first day of the week is not Monday, but Sunday. So, you would prefer this to be at the top when sorted.

File   custom-lists.xlsx

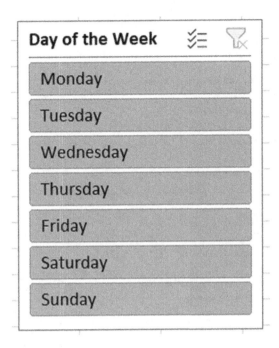

Figure 1-14. *Slicer with the days of the week sorted using the standard custom list*

To create a custom list:

1. Click **File ➤ Options ➤ Advanced ➤ Edit Custom Lists**
    (Figure 1-15).

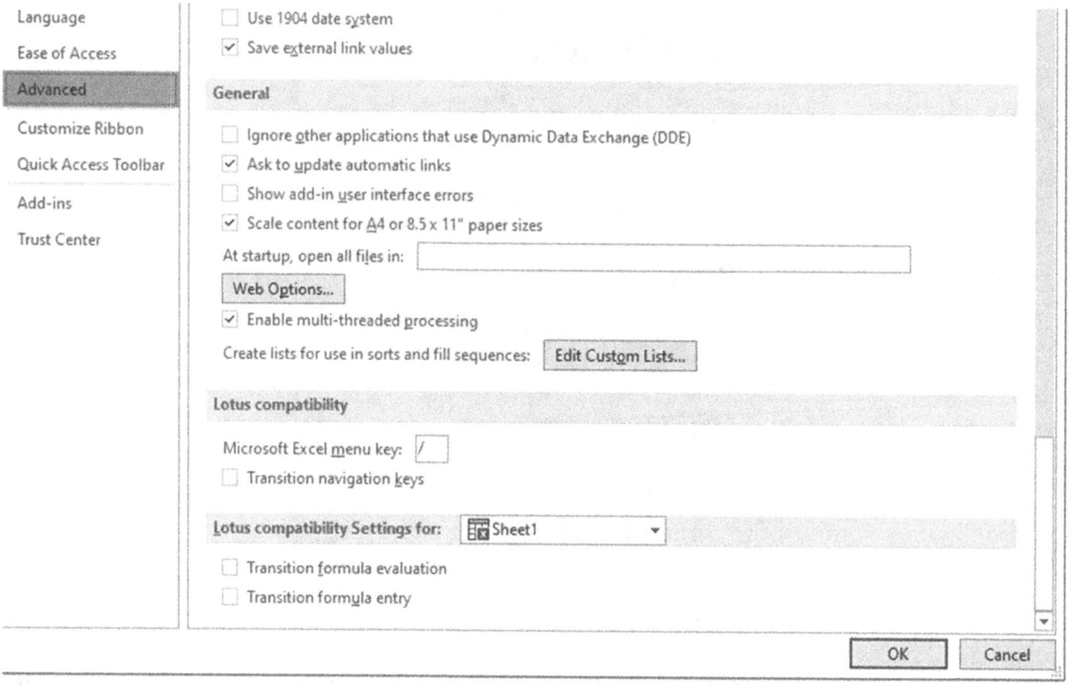

Figure 1-15. *Edit Custom Lists button in the Advanced options*

2. You cannot edit the built-in custom lists, so we will need to create a new one. With NEW LIST selected, type the days of the week into the **List entries** box in the order that you want. Press **Enter** after each one (Figure 1-16).

3. Click **Add** to add the new list to the Custom lists on the left, then click *OK* to close the window.

Note   You can also import a list from a range of cells.

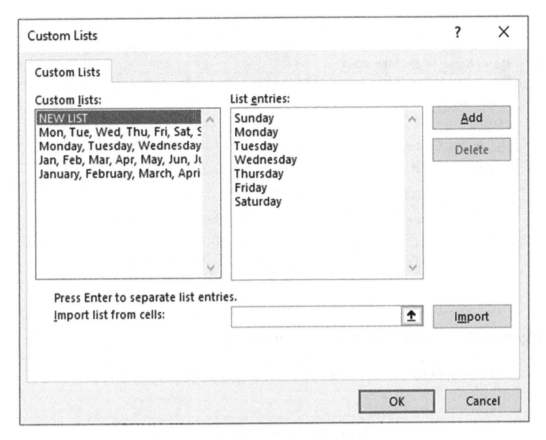

Figure 1-16. *Creating a new day of the week custom list*

This list can now be used to sort the Slicer.

1. Select the Slicer, then click **Slicer ➤ Slicer Settings**.

2. Ensure the **Use Custom Lists when sorting** box is checked
    (Figure 1-17). You may need to sort it in descending order and
    then switch back to ascending to get the new custom list to take
    control.

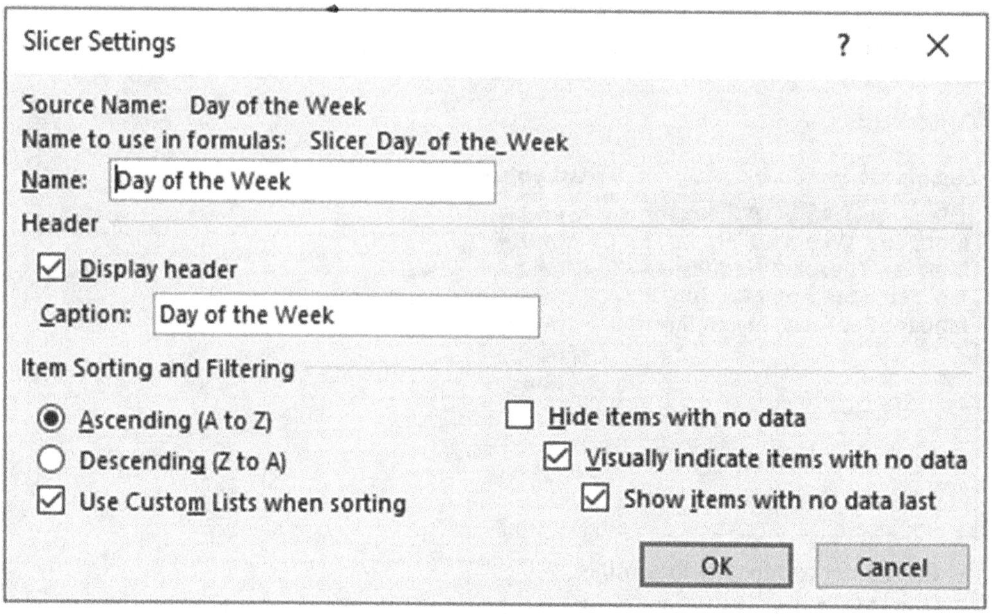

Figure 1-17. *Use Custom Lists when sorting a Slicer*

The Slicer options are now sorted correctly (Figure 1-18).

Figure 1-18. *Slicer sorted using the new custom list*

Creating your own version of these month name and day of week custom lists is a typical example. Different scenarios may call for a different "first month."

You can get creative with this for other work scenarios. Imagine we have many store locations used in a Slicer (or a table or a PivotTable) that we want sorted. But two are our flagship stores (Germany and Switzerland), and we would like to see them at the top of the list for quicker access.

Creating a custom list and then sorting using that list can create the desired order (Figure 1-19).

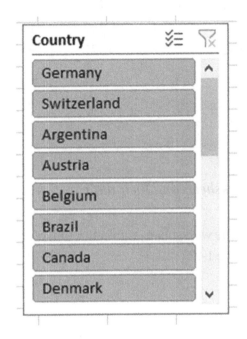

Figure 1-19. *Custom List to specify the order of countries in a Slicer*

Change Multiple Worksheets at the Same Time

Occasionally, you may need to make the same change to multiple worksheets at one time. This could be deleting columns, formatting cells, or writing a formula. By grouping worksheets, this task is simple.

File   group-worksheets.xlsx

In the workbook *group-worksheets.xlsx,* there are five worksheets, each with the quarterly sales of products. Each worksheet represents a store, and some modifications need to be made to them. This is shown in Figure 1-20.

▲	A	B	C	D	E	F	G
1		Qtr 1	Qtr 2	Qtr 3	Qtr 4		
2	Coffee	534	1631	1526	1694		
3	Tea	1875	1471	1928	1175		
4	Cake	1703	1472	787	924		
5	Pastries	812	1164	793	1178		
6	Pizza	1132	792	1477	1931		
7							
8							
21							

Euston | Victoria | Holborn | Edmonton | Paddington | ⊕

Figure 1-20. *The five worksheets and their data*

To make changes to all the worksheets, right-click one of the worksheet tabs and click **Select All Sheets** (Figure 1-21).

Figure 1-21. *Select all the sheets in a workbook*

The sheets are now grouped, and this is identified by the word *Group* in the Title bar next to the workbook's name (Figure 1-22).

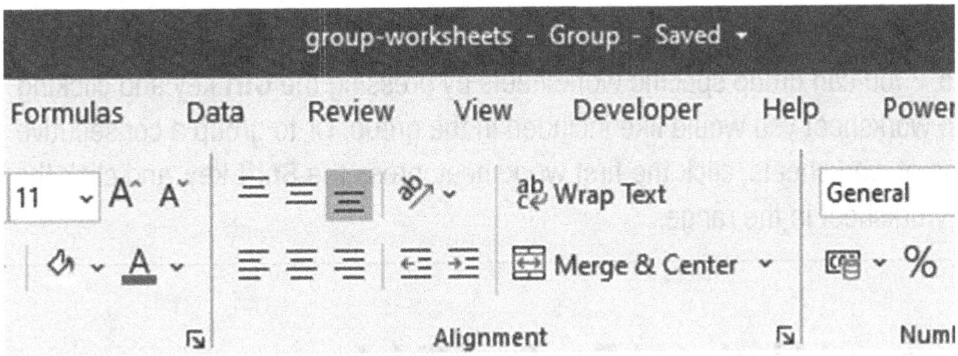

Figure 1-22. *Group in the Excel Title bar*

We can now begin to make some changes, and those changes will be replicated on all the sheets.

In this example, the quarter headers were formatted bold, in row 8 a SUM function was used to total the quarter's sales, and those cells were formatted with a top and bottom border and number formatting applied (Figure 1-23).

	A	B	C	D	E
1		**Qtr 1**	**Qtr 2**	**Qtr 3**	**Qtr 4**
2	Coffee	534	1631	1526	1694
3	Tea	1875	1471	1928	1175
4	Cake	1703	1472	787	924
5	Pastries	812	1164	793	1178
6	Pizza	1132	792	1477	1931
7					
8		6,056	6,530	6,511	6,902
9					

Figure 1-23. *Formatting and a formula applied to the grouped sheets*

To ungroup the sheets, simply click a different sheet tab to the currently active sheet.

Note   You can group specific worksheets by pressing the **Ctrl** key and clicking each worksheet you would like included in the group. Or to group a consecutive range of worksheets, click the first worksheet, press the **Shift** key, and click the last worksheet in the range.

Advanced Find and Replace Tricks

Find and Replace is an often-forgotten hero of data manipulation. It has been around for such a long time and is hidden away on the far end of the Home tab of the Ribbon – leading people to forget about it.

Sometimes, these methods are still the best. Fancy formulas, Power Query, and macros are all great. Occasionally though, you just need to get the job done. Here are some examples of when Find and Replace can come to the rescue.

File   find-and-replace.xlsx

Find and Replace in the Entire Workbook

Let us begin with a huge time saver, being able to replace, format, or remove values from an entire workbook with a few clicks of a button.

We have three worksheets: *North East, North West,* and *South* (of course, it could be many more), and we need to make some changes to data across all these sheets.

For this first example, we want to change the name of a product from "Supreme Pizza" to "Mega Pizza." We need to change every instance of this name and for all worksheets.

1. Open the Find and Replace window by using the **Ctrl + H** keyboard shortcut or clicking **Home ➤ Find & Select ➤ Replace**.

2. Type "Supreme Pizza" in the **Find what** box and "Mega Pizza" in the **Replace with** box.

3. Click the **Options** button to expand the dialog window.

4. Change the **Within** setting from Sheet to Workbook. The completed steps are shown in Figure 1-24.

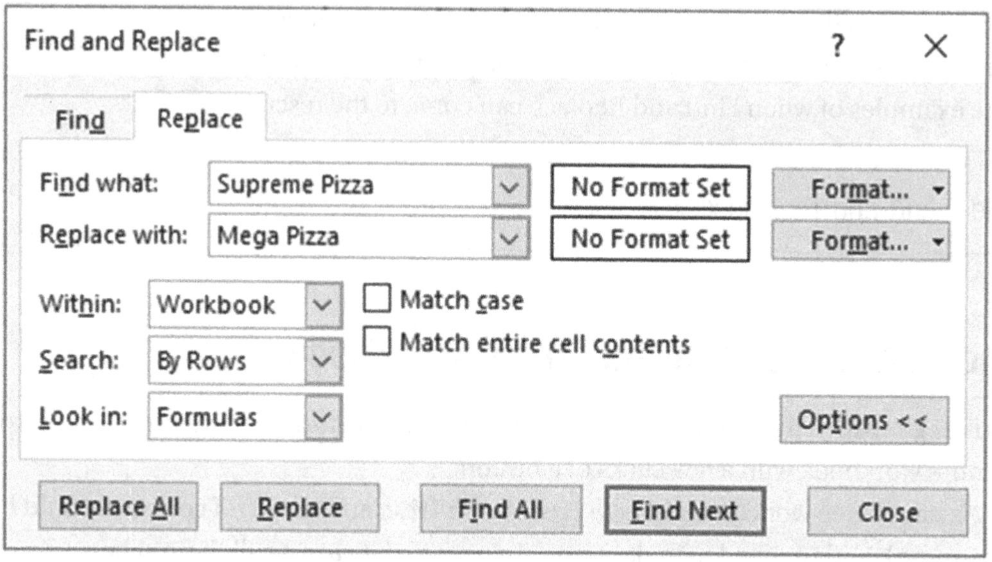

Find and Replace   ?   ✕

Find   Replace

Find what: Supreme Pizza   ⌄   No Format Set   Format... ▾
Replace with: Mega Pizza   ⌄   No Format Set   Format... ▾

Within: Workbook   ⌄   ☐ Match case
Search: By Rows   ⌄   ☐ Match entire cell contents
Look in: Formulas   ⌄   Options < <

Replace All   Replace   Find All   Find Next   Close

Figure 1-24. *Replace all instances of Supreme Pizza for the entire workbook*

5. Click **Replace All**.

All instances of "Supreme Pizza" have been replaced. A message is shown confirming the number of replacements made (Figure 1-25). If this is more than expected, you can undo the operation and refine your search criteria.

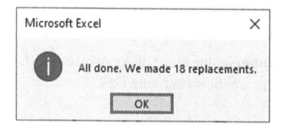

Microsoft Excel   ✕

ⓘ   All done. We made 18 replacements.

OK

Figure 1-25. *Completion message confirming the number of replacements made*

Note   Find and Replace is incredibly powerful, and therefore some care should be taken. The word "Pizza" is included in the search to protect against changing other uses of "Supreme" outside of the one intended.

Edit Your Formulas Fast

The Find and Replace tool is set to look in formulas by default. This setting can be extremely useful for editing many formulas quickly.

On the same three worksheets, *North East, North West,* and *South,* formulas have been used to analyze the sales data. An example of one of these formulas is

```
=SUMIFS($C$2:$C$21,$A$2:$A$21,E3)
```

They are using sheet references. $C$2:$C$21 refers to the sales values on that sheet.

The ranges on these sheets are now being formatted as tables, and because of these we want to quickly update all formulas to use the table references instead, as this is more efficient.

Each table is named as *NorthEast, NorthWest,* and *South* (spaces cannot be used in table names). A sample of the *NorthEast* table is shown in Figure 1-26.

	A	B	C
1	Product	Period	Sales
2	Supreme Pizza	1	4,181
3	Spicy Chicken	1	3,181
4	Tomato Heaven	1	4,060
5	Big Broccoli Bake	1	3,718
6	Supreme Pizza	2	3,611
7	Spicy Chicken	2	2,453

Figure 1-26. *The NorthEast table with the Sales column*

Let us look at changing all references to the sales values.

1. Open the Find and Replace window.

2. Enter $C$2:$C$21 in the **Find what** box and NorthEast[Sales] in the **Replace with** box.

3. Change the **Within** setting to Sheet. We need to edit each sheet individually as the tables have different names.

4. Ensure that the **Look in** setting is set to Formulas. The completed steps are shown in Figure 1-27.

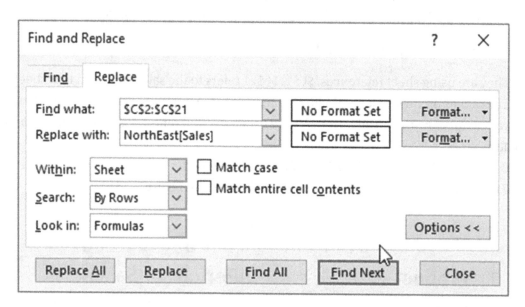

Figure 1-27. *Edit all formulas on the worksheet quickly with Find and Replace*

5. Click **Replace All**.

Note   Find and Replace settings are retained. This is useful if you perform that technique regularly on a workbook, but also something to be wary of. Be sure to clear previous settings as you work along with the book examples.

Change Cell Formatting

Yes, it is true. Find and Replace can even be used to locate, replace, or remove based on the cell formatting.

The formulas on the *North East, North West,* and *South* worksheets all have a specific formatting applied to them. This is a good idea as it makes the cells containing formulas instantly recognizable to users.

If the formatting of these cells needs to change, Find and Replace makes this a simple task.

1. Open the Find and Replace window.

2. Click the **Options** button to make the formatting options available.

3. Next to the **Find what** box, click the **Format** button arrow, select **Choose Format From Cell** (Figure 1-28), and click one of the formula cells.

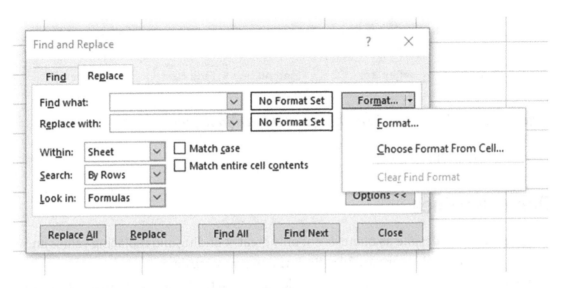

Figure 1-28. *Choose format from a cell*

4. Next to the **Replace with** box, click the **Format** button arrow and either click **Format** to specify the formatting to use or **Choose Format From Cell** if the formatting to use is already applied to a cell.

5. Select Workbook from the **Within** list to change the formatting on all worksheets (Figure 1-29).

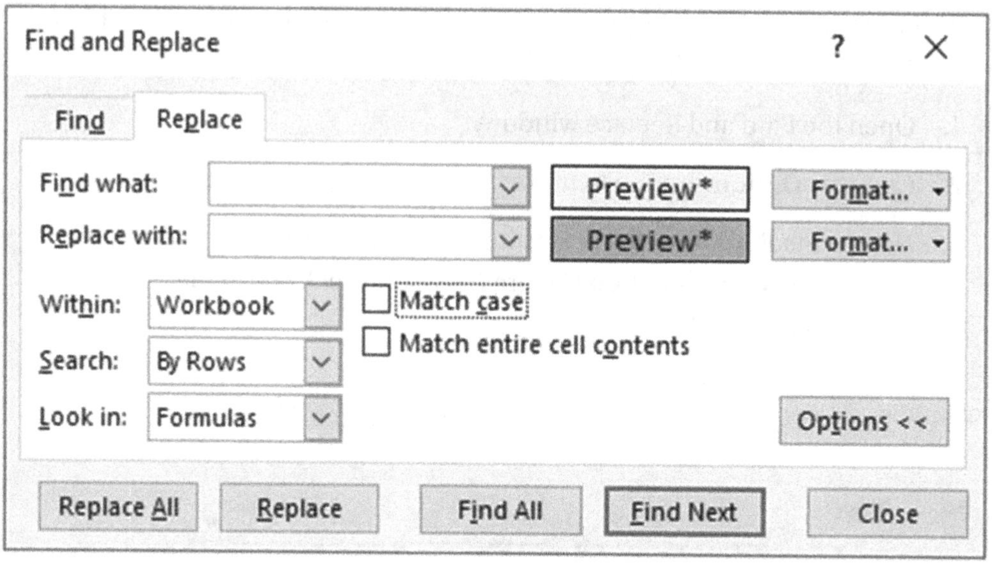

Figure 1-29. *Change cell formatting with Find and Replace*

    6.   Click **Replace All**.

Remove Values

Find and Replace, despite its name, is not only great at finding and replacing values and formatting. But it is also very useful at finding and removing data.

Figure 1-30 shows the first ten rows of sales data with total rows inserted into the range. For a more efficient analysis, we will remove these total rows.

	A	B
1	**Product**	**Sales**
2	Supreme Pizza	2422
3	Spicy Chicken	3961
4	Tomato Heaven	1645
5	Big Broccoli Bake	3297
6	Total	11325
7	Supreme Pizza	3077
8	Spicy Chicken	3634
9	Tomato Heaven	1485
10	Big Broccoli Bake	1030
11	Total	9226

Figure 1-30. *Sample data with total rows that need removing*

1. Open the Find and Replace window.

2. Type "Total" into the **Find what** box.

3. Select Sheet from the **Within** list.

4. Click the **Match entire cell contents** box. We want to be sure that the found cells only contain the word "Total".

5. Click **Find All**. A list of all the found cells including information such as the cell address is shown. The completed steps are shown in Figure 1-31.

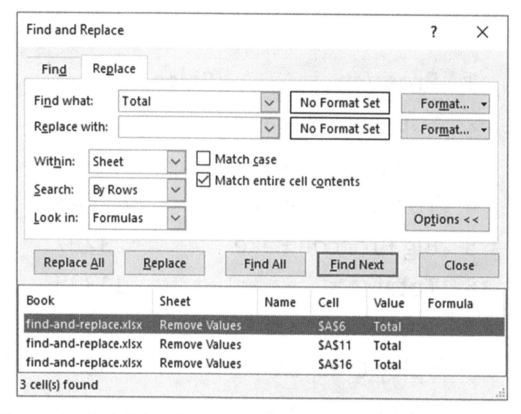

Figure 1-31. *Find all the cells with "Total" as the entire cell content*

6. Ensure the area with the list of found cells is active and press **Ctrl + A** to select all the cells (Figure 1-32).

7. Click **Close**.

▲	A	B	C	D	E	F
1	**Product**	**Sales**				
2	Supreme Pizza	2422				
3	Spicy Chicken	3961				
4	Tomato Heaven	1645				
5	Big Broccoli Bake	3297				
6	Total	11325				
7	Supreme Pizza	3077				
8	Spicy Chicken	3634				
9	Tomato Heaven	1485				
10	Big Broccoli Bake	1030				
11	Total	9226				
12	Supreme Pizza	1621				

Find and Replace dialog:

Find what: Total — No Format Set — Format...
Replace with: — No Format Set — Format...

Within: Sheet   ☐ Match case
Search: By Rows   ☑ Match entire cell contents
Look in: Formulas   Options <<

Replace All   Replace   Find All   Find Next   Close

Book	Sheet	Name	Cell	Value	Formula
find-and-replace.xlsx	Remove Values		$A$6	Total	
find-and-replace.xlsx	Remove Values		$A$11	Total	
find-and-replace.xlsx	Remove Values		$A$16	Total	

3 cell(s) found

Figure 1-32. *Select all the found cells*

8. Click **Home ➤ Delete ➤ Delete Sheet Rows** to remove the rows that were found (Figure 1-33).

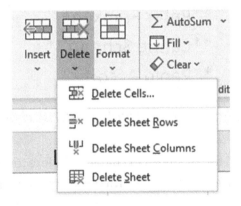

Figure 1-33. *Delete the selected rows on the sheet*

Remove Asterisks from a Range

There are two main wildcard characters that can be used in your search criteria. These are the question mark (?) and the asterisk (*).

These wildcard characters can be used in place of characters you are unsure of. The question mark can be used in place of a single character. For example, A?an would find both Adam and Alan. And the asterisk can be used in place of any number of characters. For example, L*n would find both London and Linton.

If the asterisk and question mark are wildcards, how would you look for those characters specifically if needed?

Let us look at the scenario shown in Figure 1-34. A data import has positioned asterisks around the names in a list, and we need to remove them.

	A
1	**Names**
2	**Roland Mendel**
3	**Aria Cruz**
4	**Diego Roel**
5	**Martine Rancé**
6	**Maria Larsson**
7	**Peter Franken**
8	**Carine Schmitt**
9	**Paolo Accorti**

Figure 1-34. *List of imported names including asterisk characters*

In this scenario, we can use the tilde (~) character before the asterisk in the **Find what** box (Figure 1-35). Leave the **Replace with** box empty to replace them with nothing and click **Replace All**.

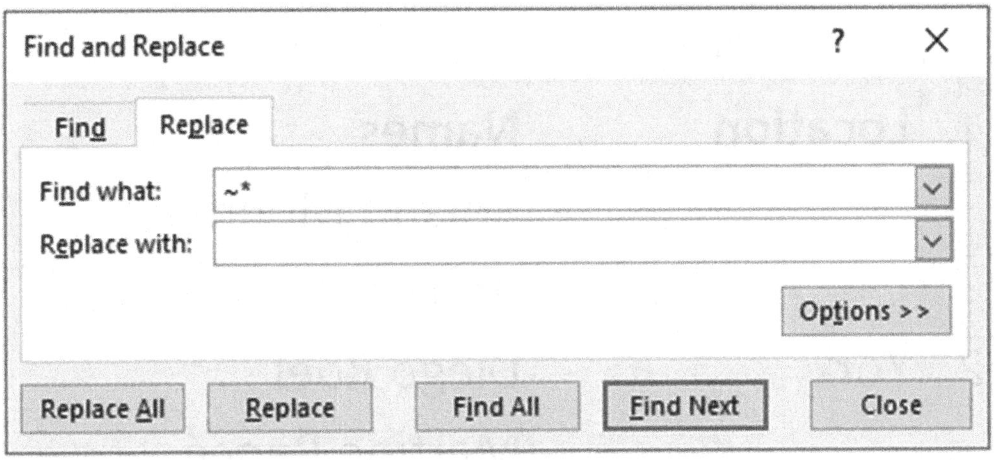

Figure 1-35. *Using the tilde to find the asterisk characters*

The tilde informs the Find and Replace tool that the following character should be used as the search criteria and not as a wildcard.

Note   This can also be used to replace or remove the question mark. If you need to replace or remove a tilde, use two tildes (~~) in the Find what box.

Replace Line Breaks Easily

Line breaks are another type of nasty character that you can find yourself removing from Excel spreadsheets, especially when you are getting data from external sources. Once again, though, this is easy with Find and Replace.

In Figure 1-36, line breaks have been used to separate the names.

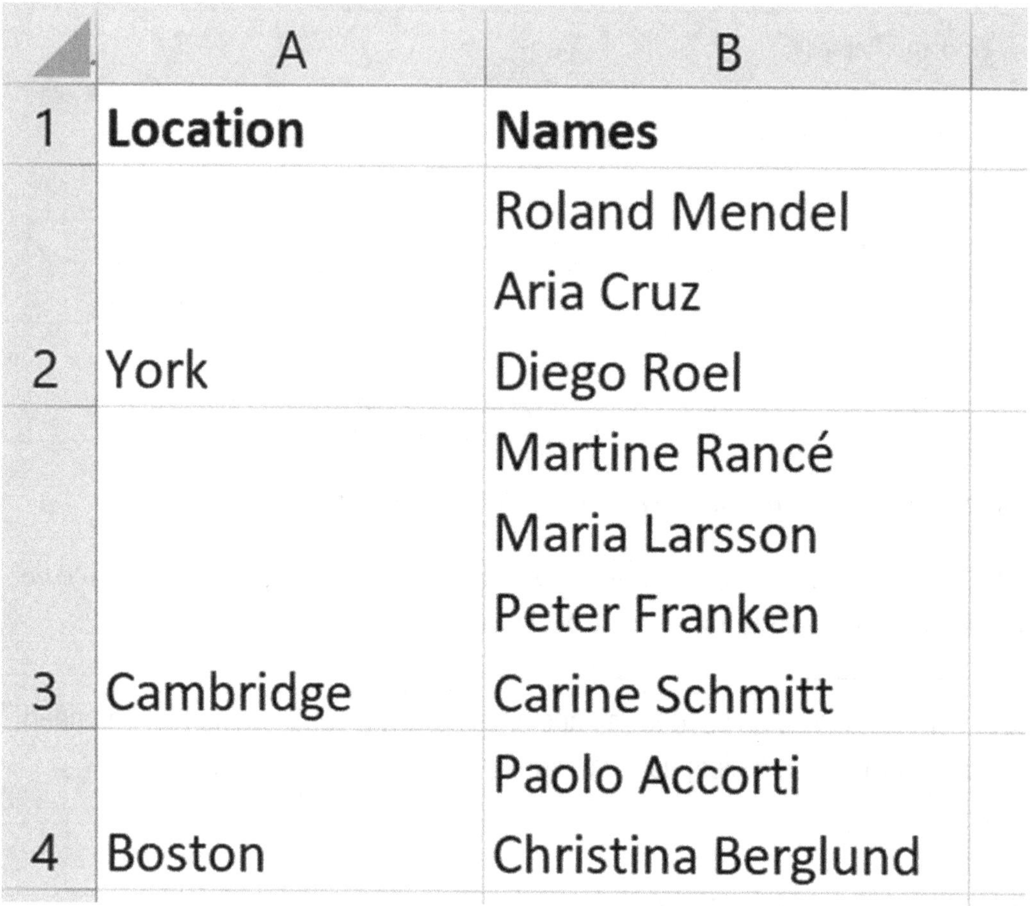

	A	B
1	**Location**	**Names**
2	York	Roland Mendel Aria Cruz Diego Roel
3	Cambridge	Martine Rancé Maria Larsson Peter Franken Carine Schmitt
4	Boston	Paolo Accorti Christina Berglund

Figure 1-36. *Line breaks separate the names in column B*

1. Select the range of names and open the Find and Replace window.

2. In the **Find what** box, press **Ctrl + J** on the keyboard. This shortcut inserts a line break for the search criteria (it may not be visible).

3. In the **Replace with** box, type a comma and a space (,)
   (Figure 1-37).

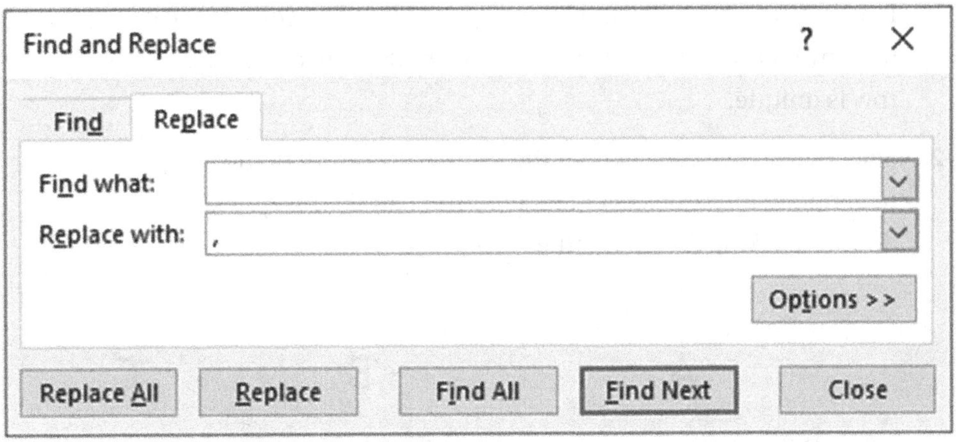

Figure 1-37. *Replace line breaks with Find and Replace*

4. Click **Replace All** to replace all the line breaks.

5. Click the **Wrap Text** button on the **Home** tab to remove the text wrapping enforced by the line breaks.

Note   The line break is character 10 on Windows and 13 on a Mac. You can also replace the line breaks using the CHAR function with the appropriate character code within the SUBSTITUTE function if you wanted a formula solution.

Delete Every Nth Row Quickly

At times we need to be inventive, and if we cannot search directly for the text we need, a helper column can be created.

In this example, we have a list of sales data with total rows inserted into the range which we want to remove. The total rows are labeled with the region name so we do not have consistent text that we can use as search criteria, but they do occur in every fifth row.

To get around this, we will create a column with a series of characters and use a unique character for every fifth row (Figure 1-38).

1. In column C, type the characters into the first five cells. You can use any characters you want; just ensure that the one in the fifth row is unique.

2. Select these five cells and fill the list to the bottom of the range to generate the series of characters. You can do this quickly by double-clicking the fill handle.

	A	B	C
1	**Product**	**Sales**	
2	Supreme Pizza	2422	-
3	Spicy Chicken	3961	-
4	Tomato Heaven	1645	-
5	Big Broccoli Bake	3297	-
6	North East	11325	@
7	Supreme Pizza	3077	-
8	Spicy Chicken	3634	-
9	Tomato Heaven	1485	-
10	Big Broccoli Bake	1030	-
11	North West	9226	@

Figure 1-38. Generate a series of characters to identify the rows we need

3. In the Find and Replace window, type the unique character in the **Find what** box. Click **Find All** to list the cells containing that character.

4.   Press **Ctrl + A** to select all the cells (Figure 1-39).

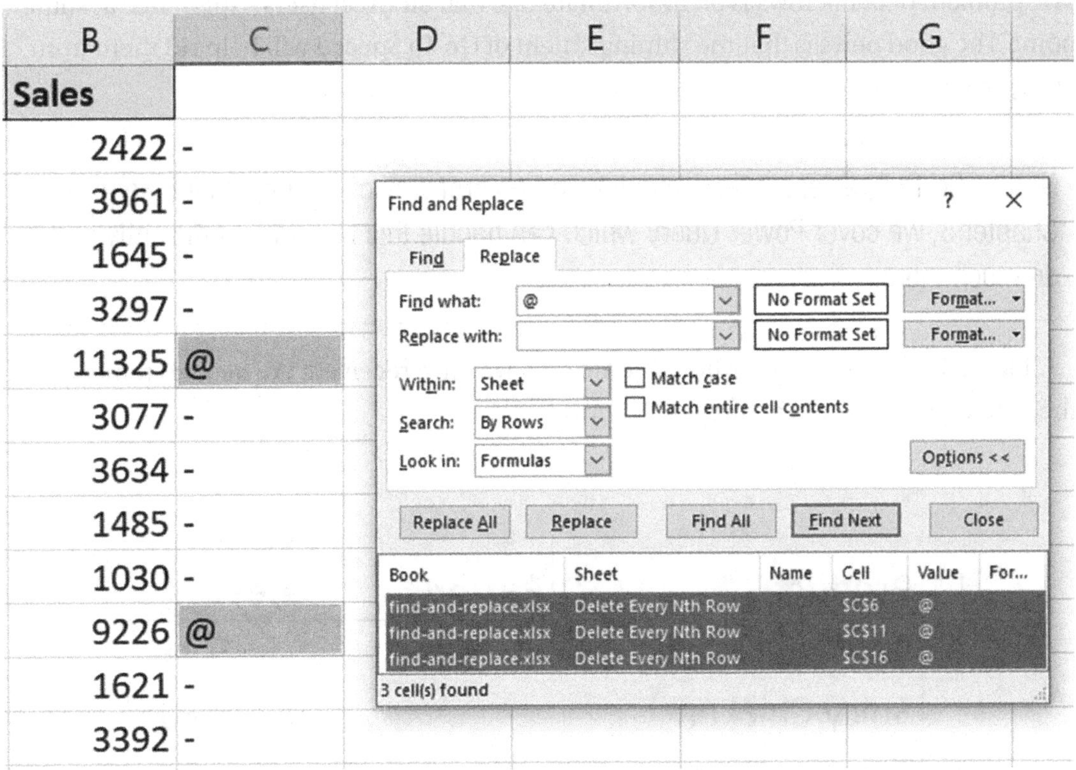

Figure 1-39. *Select all the cells with that unique character*

5.   Click **Home ➤ Delete ➤ Delete Sheet Rows** to remove every fifth row.

Quickly Find All Cells That Meet Criteria

The Go To Special tool is incredibly useful and enables us to select all cells that meet specific criteria easily. It is fantastic for auditing spreadsheets and performing quick no-nonsense tasks.

File   go-to-special.xlsx

Remove Blank Rows

The problem of blank rows is an unfortunate tale that all Excel users experience at some point. The good news is that the shining knight of Go To Special will help rid them from our spreadsheets.

Note   Go To Special provides a quick and no fluff way of getting the job done. In Chapter 5, we cover Power Query which can handle this task more efficiently and do much more.

Figure 1-40 shows a snapshot of some data we have received. We need to remove all the blank rows that appear after each period.

	A	B	C
1	**Product**	**Period**	**Sales**
2	Supreme Pizza	1	5,182
3	Spicy Chicken	1	5,613
4	Tomato Heaven	1	4,399
5	Big Broccoli Bake	1	4,677
6			
7	Supreme Pizza	2	3,449
8	Spicy Chicken	2	2,927
9	Tomato Heaven	2	3,139
10	Big Broccoli Bake	2	1,702
11			
12	Supreme Pizza	3	3,867

Figure 1-40. *Blank rows in a spreadsheet. Bad news!*

1. Select the range to search for blanks. In this example, I will select column A as that is sufficient to identify a blank row.

2. Press **F5** to open the Go To window and click **Special**, or click **Home ➤ Find & Select ➤ Go To Special** to open the Go To Special window.

3. Select **Blanks** (Figure 1-41) and click **OK**.

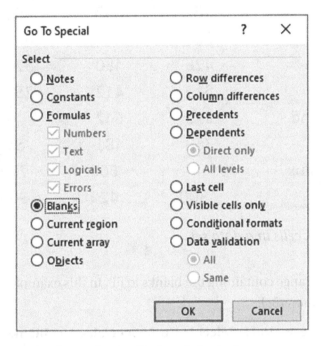

Figure 1-41. *Select Blanks in the Go To Special window*

All the blank cells in the given range are selected. We can now move on to removing them.

4. Click **Home ➤ Delete ➤ Delete Sheet Rows**.

Note   To open the Go To Special window, you can use either the **F5** or **Ctrl + G** shortcuts followed by **Alt + S**.

Fill Blank Cells with 0

In addition to blank rows to remove, there is the other common issue of blank cells.

Figure 1-42 shows a sample of data with blank cells scattered within the range. We want to fill those cells with a value. In this example, we will fill them with 0.

Product	North	East	South	West
Maria Anders	262	432	490	456
Ana Trujillo	388		663	343
Antonio Moreno	426	480	525	552
Thomas Hardy	515	412	257	645
Christina Berglund	323	642		457
Hanna Moos	369	481	55	187
Frédérique Citeaux		660	779	254
Martín Sommer	300	429	303	499

Figure 1-42. *Blank cells in a data set*

1. Select the range containing the blanks to fill. In this example, I will select columns B:E.

2. Click **Home ➤ Find & Select ➤ Go To Special**, select **Blanks,** and click **OK**.

3. All the blank cells in the range are selected. The first one is the active cell (Figure 1-43).

36

B	C	D	E
North	**East**	**South**	**West**
262	432	490	456
388		663	343
426	480	525	552
515	412	257	645
323	642		457
369	481	55	187
	660	779	254
300	429	303	499
781	592	477	

Figure 1-43. *Quickly select all the blank cells in a range*

4. Type 0. This will appear in the active cell only. Press **Ctrl + Enter**
   to apply to all the other selected cells (Figure 1-44).

B	C	D	E
North	**East**	**South**	**West**
262	432	490	456
388	0	663	343
426	480	525	552
515	412	257	645
323	642	0	457
369	481	55	187
0	660	779	254
300	429	303	499
781	592	477	0

Figure 1-44. *Zero in all blank cells*

Fill Blank Cells with the Cell Value Above

Exporting reports from other systems into Excel often leaves us with data that is awkward to analyze further. Take the example in Figure 1-45 which has blank cells under the labels in the first two columns.

We will fill those cells with the value from the cell above.

	A	B	C	D
1	Country	Category	Product	Value
2	Germany	Food	Pizza	1,960
3			Hot Dogs	757
4			Burger	3,374
5		Beverage	Coffee	1,274
6			Juice	3,509
7	USA	Food	Pizza	1,651
8			Hot Dogs	1,015
9			Burger	2,743
10		Beverage	Coffee	2,535
11			Juice	2,680

Figure 1-45. *Exported report containing blank cells*

1. Select the range containing the blanks to fill. In this example, I will select columns A:B.

2. Click **Home ➤ Find & Select ➤ Go To Special,** select **Blanks,** and click **OK.**

3. The blank cells are selected. Type = and click the cell above the active cell. In Figure 1-46, that is cell B2.

4. **Press Ctrl + Enter.**

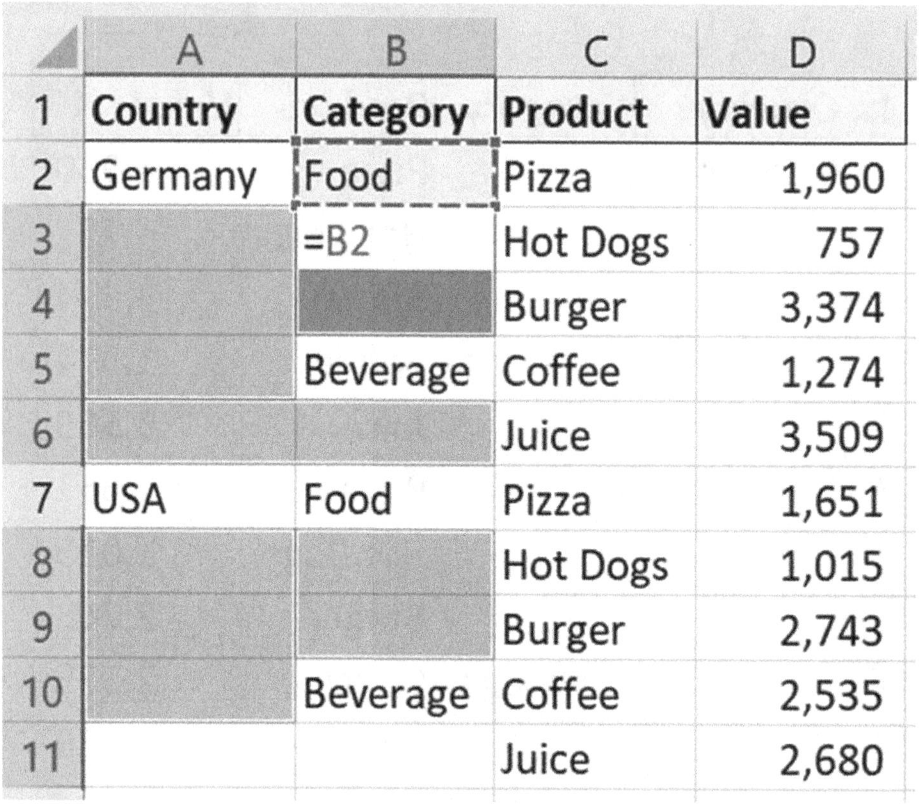

	A	B	C	D
1	Country	Category	Product	Value
2	Germany	Food	Pizza	1,960
3		=B2	Hot Dogs	757
4			Burger	3,374
5		Beverage	Coffee	1,274
6			Juice	3,509
7	USA	Food	Pizza	1,651
8			Hot Dogs	1,015
9			Burger	2,743
10		Beverage	Coffee	2,535
11			Juice	2,680

Figure 1-46. *Fill the blanks with the value from the cell above*

All the blank cells are populated with the content from the cell above (Figure 1-47).

	A	B	C	D
1	Country	Category	Product	Value
2	Germany	Food	Pizza	1,960
3	Germany	Food	Hot Dogs	757
4	Germany	Food	Burger	3,374
5	Germany	Beverage	Coffee	1,274
6	Germany	Beverage	Juice	3,509
7	USA	Food	Pizza	1,651
8	USA	Food	Hot Dogs	1,015
9	USA	Food	Burger	2,743
10	USA	Beverage	Coffee	2,535
11	USA	Beverage	Juice	2,680

Figure 1-47. *Completed Excel range with blanks filled from the cell value above*

Format All Cells Containing Formulas

When creating models and reports in Excel, it can be awkward to remember which cells contain input values or which contain formulas.

Doing something simple such as formatting these cells differently will give them that distinction so that it is no longer a headache in the future.

If you have many formulas on a spreadsheet, this may sound a tedious task to find and select them all to format. Let us get Go To Special to do it for us.

1. Open the Go To Special window.

2. Click the **Formulas** option. You can be more specific and select the formulas that return numbers, text, logicals, or errors, if needed. We will select all (Figure 1-48).

3. With the formulas selected, they can now be formatted how you want.

Figure 1-48. *The formulas options in the Go To Special window*

Compare Two Columns by Identifying Row Differences

When auditing spreadsheets, you may need to highlight inconsistencies between values in different columns. Go To Special has an option to quickly identify these differences.

Figure 1-49 shows a list of invoices and the amount paid which we want to compare for this example.

◢	A	B	C
1	ID	Amount Inv	Amount Paid
2	511	1,472	1,472
3	512	471	350
4	513	502	502
5	514	400	400
6	515	1,103	803

Figure 1-49. *Data with columns to compare*

1. Select the range of cells to compare. In this example, this is B2:C6.

2. Open the Go To Special window by pressing **F5** followed by
    Alt + S, or click **Home ➤ Find & Select ➤ Go To Special**.

3. Click the **Row differences** option (Figure 1-50) and click **OK**.

Figure 1-50. *Row differences option in the Go To Special window*

With the cells containing a different value to its adjacent column selected, we can format the cells so that they are easily identified (Figure 1-51).

	A	B	C
1	ID	Amount Inv	Amount Paid
2	511	1,472	1,472
3	512	471	350
4	513	502	502
5	514	400	400
6	515	1,103	803

Figure 1-51. *Formatting applied to identify the row differences*

The Secrets of Text to Columns

The Text to Columns feature is very well known in Excel, but it does have some secret abilities that you may not be aware of.

File   text-to-columns.xlsx

Convert Text to Number

Text to Columns is one of the fastest no-nonsense ways to convert data. Many users do not realize this because its name implies that it will split data into columns. But you do not have to.

In this example, we have a classic scenario of converting numbers stored as text to numbers.

1. Select the range of text you want to convert to numbers.

2. Click **Data ➤ Text to Columns** to open the Text to Columns wizard.

3. Leave the first step as Delimited and click **Next**.

4. Remove all delimiter options in step 2. We are not interested in splitting columns. Click **Next**.

5. Ensure **General** is selected as the format (Figure 1-52). This will convert numbers and dates if it recognizes them. Click **Finish**.

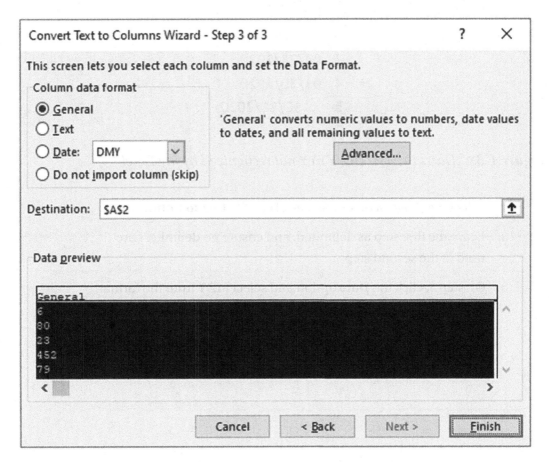

Figure 1-52. *Convert text to numbers with Text to Columns*

Converting Date Formats

Excel can sometimes have trouble recognizing dates. This could be that they have come from a country with a different format to the regional settings of your Excel. For example, I am based in the UK, so dates formatted as MM/DD/YYYY are not recognized as a date.

Figure 1-53 shows dates in the MM/DD/YYYY formats. Two of the dates are stored as text, and two have been stored as dates. Excel thinks it understands two of them, but the dates are wrong as they do not follow the expected DD/MM/YYYY format.

Text to Columns will take care of this.

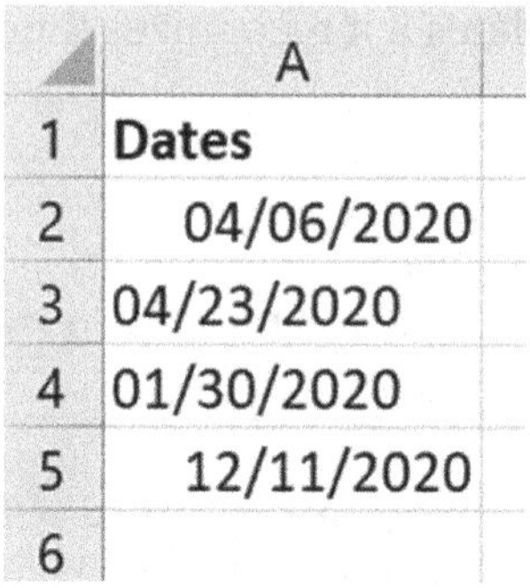

	A
1	**Dates**
2	04/06/2020
3	04/23/2020
4	01/30/2020
5	12/11/2020
6	

Figure 1-53. *Dates in MM/DD/YYYY not recognized by my Excel*

1. Select the range of dates and click **Data ➤ Text to Columns**.

2. Leave the first step as delimited, and ensure no delimiters are used in the second step.

3. On step 3, click the **Date** option and select **MDY** from the format list (Figure 1-54). Click **Finish**.

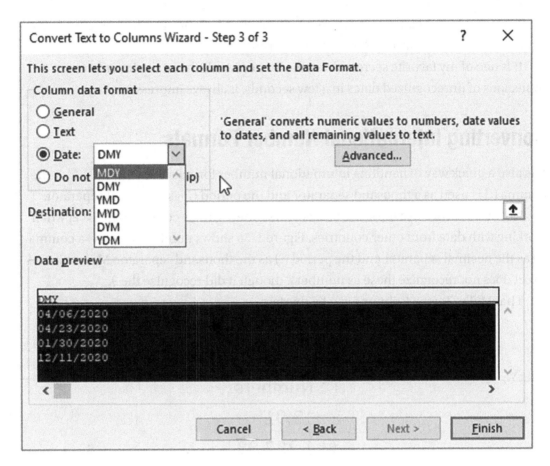

Figure 1-54. *Select the format that the dates are using*

The dates are now recognized and stored correctly (Figure 1-55).

	A
1	**Dates**
2	06/04/2020
3	23/04/2020
4	30/01/2020
5	11/12/2020

Figure 1-55. *MM/DD/YYYY dates successfully converted to DD/MM/YYYY*

Text to Columns can be used to convert from any date format. This could be dates stored as text or dates using a YYYYMMDD format.

It is one of my favorite secrets about the feature. And when I use it to resurrect thousands of unrecognized dates in a few seconds, it always impresses.

Converting International Number Formats

It is also a quick way of handling international number formats. I live in the UK, so the comma (,) is used as a thousand separator and the period (.) as a decimal separator.

Not all countries use the same characters so there can be confusion in Excel when working with data from other countries. Figure 1-56 shows numbers that use a comma (,) as the decimal separator and the period (.) as the thousand separator. My version of Excel does not recognize these as numbers, though it did recognize the 9.

Thankfully, Text to Columns can fix this fast.

	A
1	Numbers
2	13,91
3	1.782,08
4	9
5	20,10

Figure 1-56. International numbers not recognized by Excel

1. Select the range of numbers to convert and click **Data ➤ Text to Columns**.

2. Leave the first step as delimited, and ensure no delimiters are used in the second step.

3. In step 3, click the **Advanced** button.

4. Change the **Decimal separator** and the **Thousands separator** to the ones used by the data (Figure 1-57).

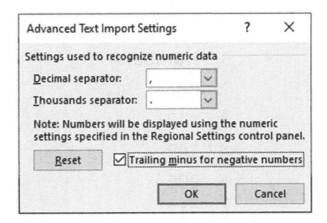

Figure 1-57. *Advanced settings for converting text to numbers*

5. Click **OK** to close the advanced settings and then **Finish**.

The numbers are successfully converted (Figure 1-58).

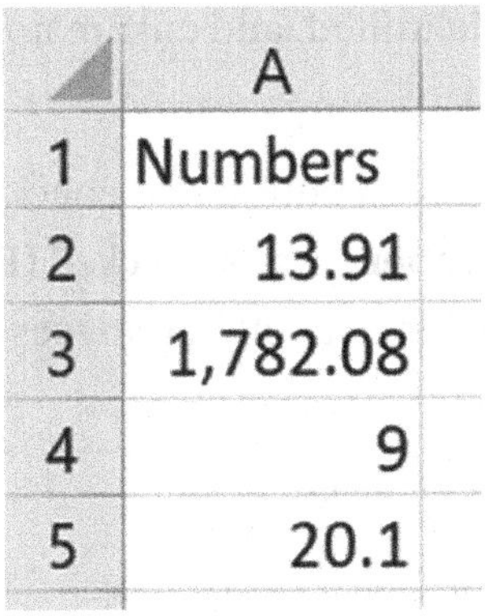

	A
1	Numbers
2	13.91
3	1,782.08
4	9
5	20.1

Figure 1-58. *International numbers successfully converted*

Convert Values with a Trailing Minus Sign

Let us look at how Text to Columns can easily handle the scenario of trailing minus signs as shown in Figure 1-59.

	A
1	**Numbers**
2	86-
3	179-
4	149-
5	206-
6	217-

Figure 1-59. Numbers with a trailing minus sign

1. Select the range you need to convert and click **Data ➤ Text to Columns**.

2. Leave the first step as delimited, and ensure no delimiters are used in the second step.

3. In step 3, click the **Advanced** button and check that the **Trailing minus for negative numbers** box is checked (Figure 1-60). By default, it should be so this is an often unnecessary check.

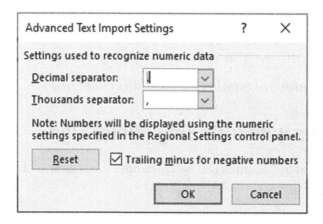

Figure 1-60. Trailing minus for negative numbers check box in advanced settings

4. Click **OK** and then **Finish**.

The text values have been successfully converted to negative numbers (Figure 1-61).

	A
1	**Numbers**
2	-86
3	-179
4	-149
5	-206
6	-217

Figure 1-61. *Text values converted to negative number values*

What Is So Special About Paste Special?

Paste Special is an incredible tool for quickly manipulating data. It is very helpful for simple but brilliant time-saving data formatting and other transformations.

File   paste-special.xlsx

Convert Positive Values to Negative

Using Paste Special, we can easily convert positive values to negative or vice versa.

1. Type **-1** into a vacant cell.

2. Copy that cell value by pressing **Ctrl + C**.

3. Select the range of cells you want to convert and click **Home ➤ Paste** arrow ➤ **Paste Special** or use the **Ctrl + Alt + V** shortcut.

4. In the Paste Special window, select **Values** and **Multiply** (Figure 1-62).

Multiplying the values by –1 converts them to negative. The same technique converts negative values to positive.

These operations in Paste Special are extremely useful. We can perform fast mathematical operations without having to use a cell formula and then copy the results.

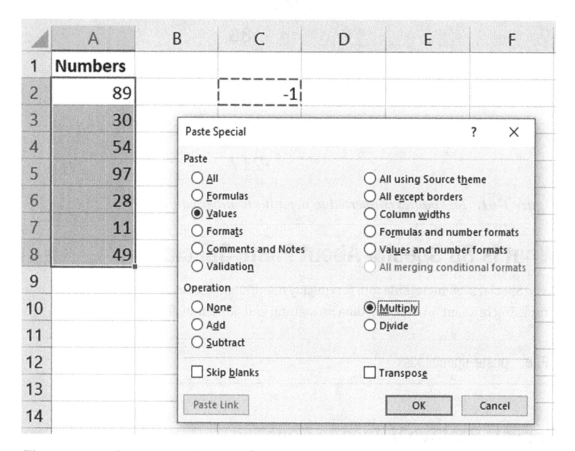

Figure 1-62. *Convert positive numbers to negative with Paste Special*

Remove Formulas from a Cell

Pasting values only to remove the formulas from a cell is probably the most common use of Paste Special.

Instead of achieving this through the Paste Special options, let us look at one of my favorite shortcuts – the right-click wiggle.

1. Select the range containing the formulas you want to replace with values only.

2. Position your cursor on the edge of the selected range, right-click and drag away from the selection, then back again and release the mouse.

3. A menu appears with some useful paste options (Figure 1-63). Click **Copy Here as Values Only**.

Miles	Expense
104	£ 36.40
60	£ 21.00
25	£ 8.75
240	£ 84.00
55	£ 19.25

B2:B6

Move Here

Copy Here

Copy Here as Values Only

Copy Here as Formats Only

Link Here

Create Hyperlink Here

Shift Down and Copy

Shift Right and Copy

Shift Down and Move

Shift Right and Move

Cancel

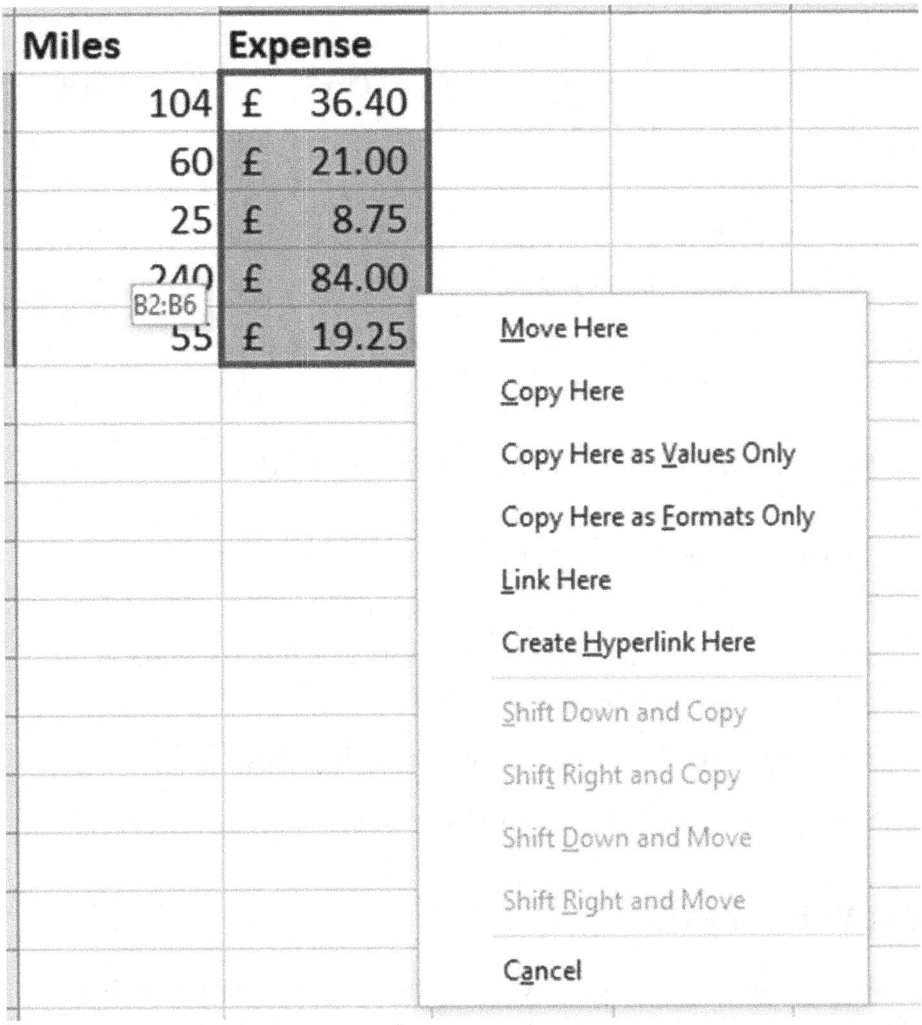

Figure 1-63. *Right-click wiggle to paste as values only*

Repeat Column Widths

This is a question I get a lot on my beginner's classes in Excel. How can we make each column the same width quickly?

Figure 1-64 shows four columns, and the "Qtr3" column is clearly wider than the other three. Also, how do we know the other three are the same width?

Let us repeat the width of the "Qtr1" column to the other three to be sure they are all the same.

	A	B	C	D
1	Qtr1	Qtr2	Qtr3	Qtr4
2	£ 1,500	£ 1,750	£ 1,500	£ 2,700
3	£ 3,560	£ 3,000	£ 1,700	£ 2,000
4	£ 4,500	£ 4,000	£ 3,500	£ 3,700
5	£ 3,250	£ 2,725	£ 3,000	£ 3,250
6	£ 2,520	£ 2,000	£ 2,500	£ 2,700
7	£ 1,500	£ 1,700	£ 1,800	£ 2,000

Figure 1-64. *Column C is wider than the other three columns*

1. Click a cell in column A ("Qtr1" column) and press **Ctrl + C** to copy.

2. Select cells in columns B:D. Just some cells in all three columns is enough; you do not need to select the entire column.

3. Press **Ctrl + Alt + V** to open the Paste Special options.

4. Select **Column Widths** and click **OK**.

Pasting with Charts

Paste Special can also be used to quickly copy formatting between charts. In this example, we want to repeat the formatting from the "Income" chart on the left to the "Expenses" chart on the right (Figure 1-65).

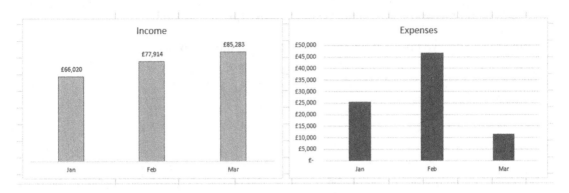

Figure 1-65. *Two charts with different formatting*

1. Select the chart with the format you want to copy and
    press **Ctrl + C**.

2. Click the chart you want to paste the formatting to.

3. Click **Home ➤ Paste** arrow ➤ **Paste Special** to open the window
    shown in Figure 1-66.

Figure 1-66. *Paste Special options for charts*

4. Select **Formats**. We do not want to paste the data as well.

Job done! The two charts have the same format (Figure 1-67).

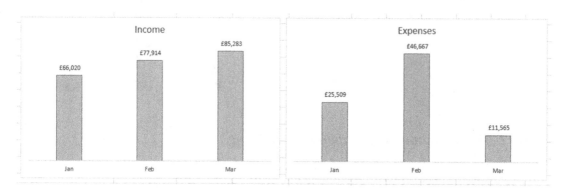

Figure 1-67. *Same formatting applied quickly between two charts*

CHAPTER 2

The Ten Power Functions of Excel

I love using formulas in Excel. They are the heartbeat of a spreadsheet.

They turn a static spreadsheet into a dynamic and interactive spreadsheet that can make decisions, change over time, and react to user requests.

Excel has many tools now to create powerful reports including Power Query, VBA, and Power Pivot. However, formulas are still the heartbeat of a smart spreadsheet.

Many users learn to use a function to complete a specific task at work. And they will often learn this from a colleague or from a Google (or Bing) search. This is great! I do it too 😊.

However, to achieve advanced success with formulas, you need to understand exactly how these functions work and why.

There are too many functions in Excel to go through each one in detail. So, in this chapter, I will go into intimate detail on the ten power functions of Excel for dynamic, interactive reports and models. The ten functions covered in this chapter are

1. SUMPRODUCT

2. UNIQUE

3. SORT

4. SORTBY

5. FILTER

6. INDEX

7. CHOOSE

8. XLOOKUP

© Alan Murray 2021
A. Murray, *Advanced Excel Success*, https://doi.org/10.1007/978-1-4842-6467-6_2

9.   INDIRECT

10.   SWITCH

This is not to discredit the incredible functions outside of these ten, such as FIND, SUM, ABS, VALUE, TEXT, and so on. These power functions cannot do it alone.

However, they are the real driving force behind dynamic spreadsheets. Therefore, I have labeled them the power functions.

Functions Are Beautiful

There are many Excel functions. Each has its own purpose and method of achieving that purpose.

A worksheet function returns something. It cannot delete or format values. We need tools such as Power Query, VBA, or Conditional Formatting for those needs.

Some functions can return ranges, and others only return values (text, numbers, logical). Some can return an array and others aggregate. Functions are diverse. All of them are beautiful.

These differences can be confusing and overwhelming to the less experienced user. Once you understand how a function wants to be used, it gets easier.

Using Tables

Many of the formula examples in this book reference data in a table. Although it is not necessary, tables offer many advantages compared to sheet ranges.

Let us look at how to create a table in Excel and then detail some of the reasons you should be using them.

Format a Range as a Table

Formatting a range as a table is quick and simple.

File   tables-and-das.xlsx

---

1. Click within the range of cells you want to format as a table.
    Click **Insert ➤ Table** or press **Ctrl + T.**

2. Ensure the range used in the Create Table window is correct
    and that the **My table has headers** box is checked (Figure 2-1).
    Click **OK.**

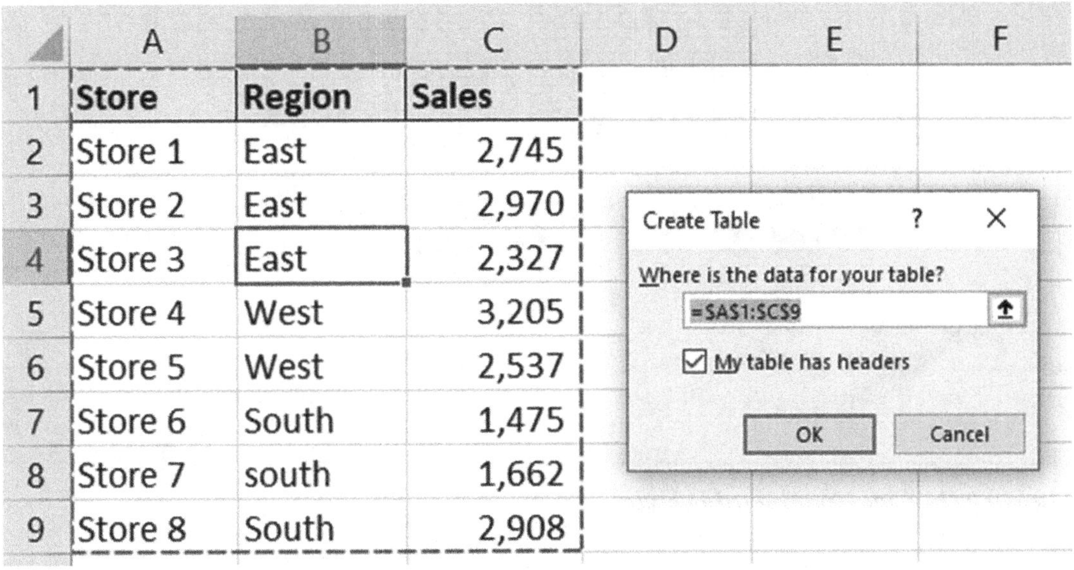

	A	B	C	D	E	F
1	**Store**	**Region**	**Sales**			
2	Store 1	East	2,745			
3	Store 2	East	2,970			
4	Store 3	East	2,327			
5	Store 4	West	3,205			
6	Store 5	West	2,537			
7	Store 6	South	1,475			
8	Store 7	south	1,662			
9	Store 8	South	2,908			

Create Table   ? ×

Where is the data for your table?

=SAS1:SCS9

☑ My table has headers

OK   Cancel

Figure 2-1. *Ensure the range is correct and headers box checked*

The range has now been converted to a table. After creating a table, I then perform two more steps.

The next step is to clear the formatting. This is optional. There are many styles you can use for your table, and you can also create your own. I like to clear it.

Click a cell within the table, click the **Table Design** tab, expand the Table Styles gallery, and click **Clear** (Figure 2-2).

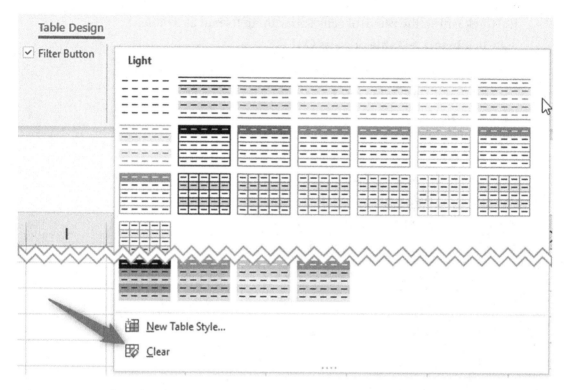

Figure 2-2. *Clearing the table style*

The next step to perform is very important. You must name your table something meaningful. This name will be used by formulas, PivotTables, Slicers, and anything else connected to it.

Enter a useful name into the **Table Name** box on the **Table Design** tab (Figure 2-3).

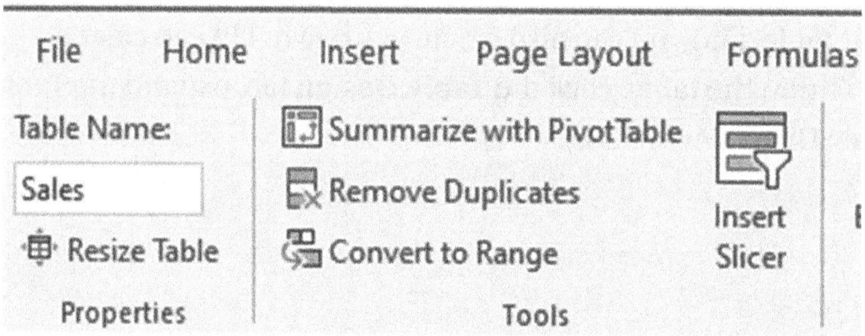

Figure 2-3. *Enter a meaningful name for the table*

Data imported into Excel is automatically formatted as a table. And tables will be used by the power tools (Power Query and Power Pivot) in the last two chapters of this book.

Advantages to Using Tables

The formulas we use will not just be returning a result for now but also the future. If data is added, removed, or changed, the formulas need to continue to return the correct results.

Tables are dynamic and so provide us with this future proofing. They automatically expand and contract when data is added or removed.

Tables also provide simple, meaningful, and consistent references for our formulas. Here is a SUMIFS function referencing the columns of a table:

=SUMIFS(Sales[Sales],Sales[Region],E3)

And this is the alternative formula referencing the ranges on a sheet:

=SUMIFS(C2:C9,B2:B9,E3)

There is a clear winner. The table references are more meaningful and much easier to enter in the formula.

When typing the formula, when you enter the table name followed by a square bracket ([), a list of the table elements appears (Figure 2-4). This makes it simple to reference the header row, entire table, or a specific column.

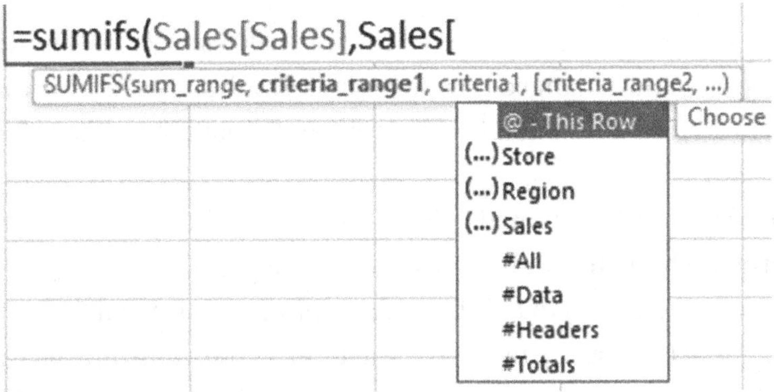

Figure 2-4. *Drop-down of table elements*

When referencing cells in a table from a formula, the column name is shown if the cell is on the same row as the formula (Figure 2-5). The @ character is used to indicate that the cell or cells are on this row, and not the entire column.

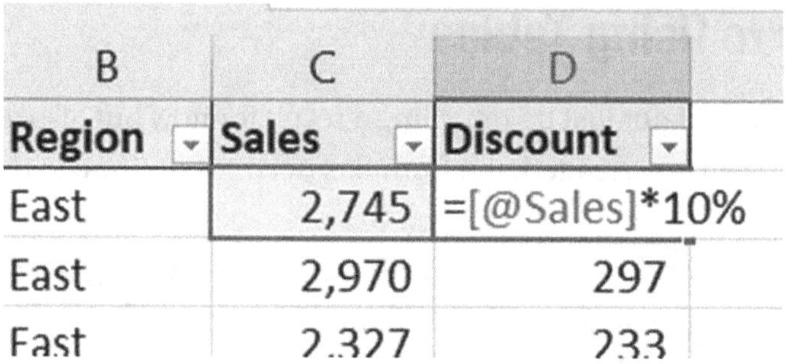

Figure 2-5. *Referencing cells on the same row*

This is clearer than the classic sheet references of the column letter and row number. The formula is also consistent for all rows of the table and automatically fills down if more rows are added to the table.

If you select cell(s) on a different row to the formula, then a sheet range is used, that is, D3 or B2:D2.

OK, we need to move on. This was just a quick lesson and insight on the importance and use of tables.

Dynamic Arrays – The Game Has Changed

Dynamic array formulas started to arrive for Microsoft 365 subscribers in November 2019 and have significantly changed how we write formulas. Dynamic arrays are not available to users of Excel 2019 or earlier. They are only available to Excel for Microsoft 365 users.

These new formulas will automatically fill into the neighboring cells if multiple values are returned. This behavior is known as "spilling."

Array formulas are not new to Excel, but there have been several limitations to their use in the past. These include the user needing to select the entire output range for the values and to press Ctrl + Shift + Enter to run them. This led to the name CSE formulas.

Dynamic arrays can be written just like any other formula and ends the need to use Ctrl + Shift + Enter when writing array formulas.

The ability to reference arrays easily within formulas is incredible. And their facility to dynamically resize with data is a game changer. Dynamic arrays are here.

Let us look at a simple example of their use.

File   tables-and-das.xlsx

Figure 2-6 shows the SUMIFS function being used on the Sales table we just created. It references cell E3 for the criteria and now needs to be filled down to the other cells where we need a result.

F3		✕ ✓	f_x	=SUMIFS(Sales[Sales],Sales[Region],E3)	

◢	A	B	C	D	E	F
1	**Store** ▾	**Region** ▾	**Sales** ▾			
2	Store 1	East	2,745		**Region**	**Total**
3	Store 2	East	2,970		East	8,042
4	Store 3	East	2,327		South	
5	Store 4	West	3,205		West	
6	Store 5	West	2,537			
7	Store 6	South	1,475			
8	Store 7	South	1,662			
9	Store 8	South	2,908			

Figure 2-6. *SUMIFS function that requires filling down*

With dynamic arrays, we can now reference the entire criteria range of E3:E5, and the formula will spill to include all the results.

```
=SUMIFS(Sales[Sales],Sales[Region],E3:E5)
```

This is shown in Figure 2-7. A blue border is used to identify the spill range.

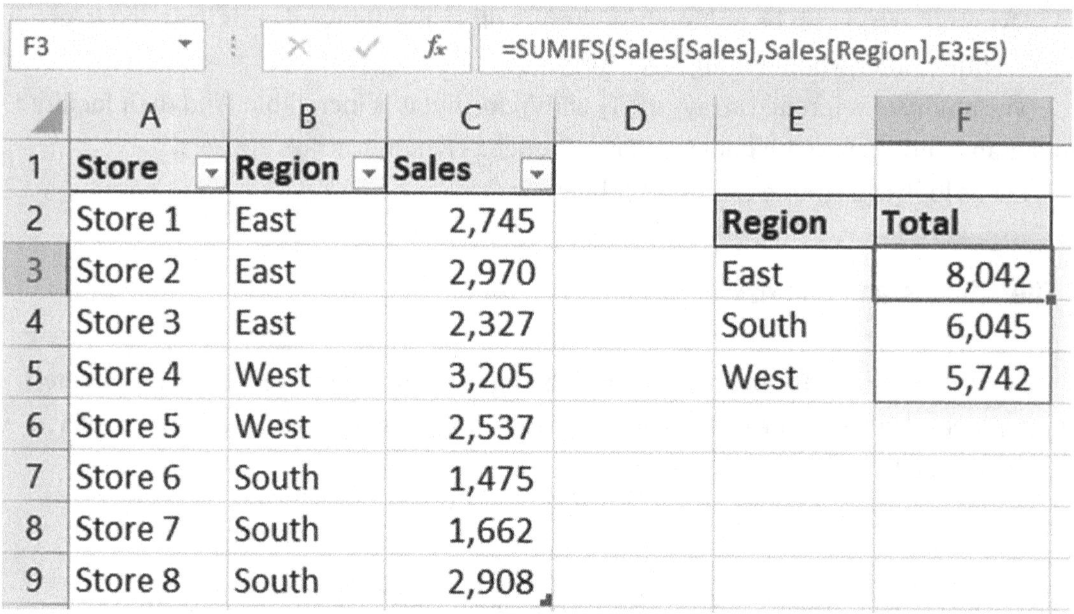

| F3 | ▾ | : | ✕ | ✓ | *fx* | =SUMIFS(Sales[Sales],Sales[Region],E3:E5) |

◢	A	B	C	D	E	F
1	Store ▾	Region ▾	Sales ▾			
2	Store 1	East	2,745		**Region**	**Total**
3	Store 2	East	2,970		East	8,042
4	Store 3	East	2,327		South	6,045
5	Store 4	West	3,205		West	5,742
6	Store 5	West	2,537			
7	Store 6	South	1,475			
8	Store 7	South	1,662			
9	Store 8	South	2,908			

Figure 2-7. *SUMIFS function with a spill range*

This formula is not completely dynamic as it uses the E3:E5 reference. This is OK for this first example. To be truly dynamic though, a formula should be referencing a table or a spill range. We will see many examples in this chapter.

There are a few key things to know about dynamic array formulas:

- A #SPILL! error is shown if the range that a formula attempts to spill into is blocked (Figure 2-8). This is fixed by moving or removing the content blocking the spill range.

	A	B	C	D	E	F	G
1	Store	Region	Sales				
2	Store 1	East	2,745		Region	Total	
3	Store 2	East	2,970		East	#SPILL!	
4	Store 3	East	2,327		South		
5	Store 4	West	3,205		West	I shouldn't be here	
6	Store 5	West	2,537				
7	Store 6	South	1,475				
8	Store 7	South	1,662				
9	Store 8	South	2,908				

Figure 2-8. #SPILL! error caused by the text in cell F5

- Dynamic array formulas cannot be used within tables. This will also cause a #SPILL! error. However, using them on table data is encouraged.

- The formula exists in the first cell only and spills to the others. It cannot be edited from any cell except the first one.

- To reference a spill range, the hash or pound operator (#) is used (Figure 2-9). This makes it easy to run other formulas and Excel features off dynamic spill ranges.

f_x	=SUM(F3#)			
	E	F	G	H
	Region	Total		Total
	East	8,042		19,829
	South	6,045		
	West	5,742		

Figure 2-9. Referencing a spill range

- If a workbook containing dynamic array formulas is opened by a user on a previous version, it is shown as a legacy array formula with the curly braces.

  `{=SUMIFS(Sales[Sales],Sales[Region],E3:E5)}`

- The @ character is used to indicate implicit intersection. In the following formula, the range B2:B15 is used so the @ character implies the use of the value in the cell on the same row as the formula. The @ character is also used in table references to indicate implicit intersection.

  `=IF(@'Due Dates'!$B$2:$B$15<TODAY(),"yes","no")`

When sharing workbooks with users without the Excel for Microsoft 365 version, it is recommended to avoid the use of dynamic arrays.

SUMPRODUCT

Availability: All versions

File   sumproduct.xlsx

The first power function on the list is SUMPRODUCT. This function is incredibly versatile and was my favorite function prior to the introduction of dynamic arrays.

Dynamic arrays have replaced the need for SUMPRODUCT. However, this remains an incredibly useful function for those using or sharing spreadsheets with others on versions outside of Excel for Microsoft 365.

The most popular uses of SUMPRODUCT are to sum and count values with complex criteria beyond what SUMIFS and COUNTIFS can handle and to use it as an alternative to array formulas.

The SUMPRODUCT function multiplies the values from corresponding ranges/arrays and then sums those results. Does not sound like much but wait till you see what it can do.

The syntax for the SUMPRODUCT function is

`=SUMPRODUCT(array1, [array2], [array3], ...)`

Simple Example of SUMPRODUCT

Let us start with a simple example to understand how the SUMPRODUCT function works.

We have some products with a column of the quantity sold and the product price. To find the total, we could multiply the quantity by the price for each product and then sum the results. But with SUMPRODUCT, we can do this in one formula (Figure 2-10).

```
=SUMPRODUCT(product_sales[Qty],product_sales[Price])
```

The formula will multiply the first product quantity and price, then the second product quantity and price, and so on. These results are then summed.

E3	▼ : × ✓ ƒx	=SUMPRODUCT(product_sales[Qty],product_sales[Price])

	A	B	C	D	E
1	**Product**	**Qty**	**Price**		
2	Coffee	58	£ 2.10		**Total**
3	Tea	42	£ 1.40		£551.60
4	Cake	56	£ 2.00		
5	Pastry	24	£ 3.30		
6	Pizza	29	£ 6.20		

Figure 2-10. *A simple example of using SUMPRODUCT*

In Excel 365 with the dynamic array formulas, we can simply multiply the quantity and price columns in a SUM function.

```
=SUM(product_sales[Qty]*product_sales[Price])
```

Sum and Count with Multiple Criteria

Moving on from that simple example, let us look at some of the real reasons people use and love SUMPRODUCT.

There are many functions in Excel that help us sum and count values based on criteria being met. The most used are the SUMIFS and COUNTIFS functions. These functions are brilliant, but they are limited in that they can only handle AND logic between their conditions.

Using the table shown in Figure 2-11, we would like to return the number of sales from the regions *North* and *South*.

	A	B	C	D
1	**Region**	**Category**	**Product**	**Total**
2	East	Food	Pizza	291
3	North	Beverages	Coffee	113
4	East	Food	Burger	284
5	North	Food	Pizza	121
6	East	Food	Burger	463
7	East	Food	Hot Dogs	481
8	North	Food	Burger	342
9	East	Food	Burger	234
10	South	Food	Pizza	426
11	South	Beverages	Water	266
12	North	Beverages	Coffee	250

Figure 2-11. *Sample data for SUMPRODUCT with multiple criteria*

The COUNTIFS function cannot handle OR logic, so it would need to use two functions and add them together.

```
=COUNTIFS(Sales[Region],"North")+COUNTIFS(Sales[Region],"South")
```

Note   There is a trick using array constants so COUNTIFS and SUMIFS can handle OR logic, but it is awkward and limited in its ability.

SUMPRODUCT provides a much simpler way to complete this, especially when you have more than two conditions. It does take some practice though to get familiar with it.

The following formula will return the number of sales for the regions *North* and *South* (Figure 2-12):

```
=SUMPRODUCT((Sales[Region]="North")+(Sales[Region]="South"))
```

Each condition is enclosed in brackets, and the plus operator (+) is used for OR logic.

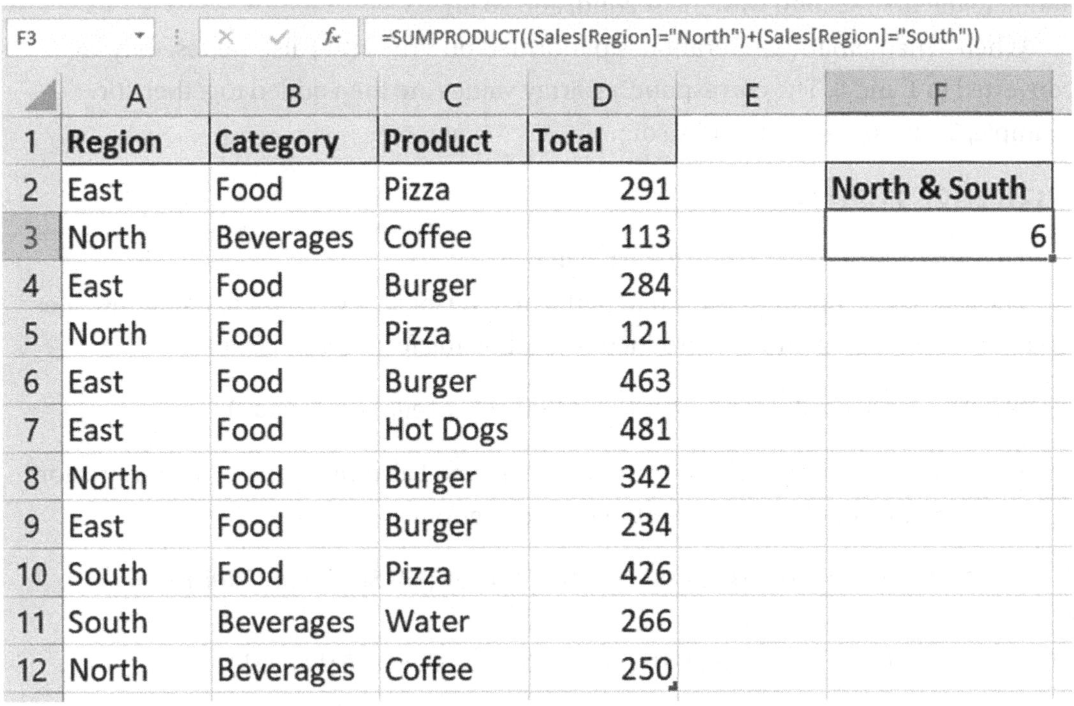

	A	B	C	D	E	F
	Region	Category	Product	Total		
1	**Region**	**Category**	**Product**	**Total**		
2	East	Food	Pizza	291		**North & South**
3	North	Beverages	Coffee	113		6
4	East	Food	Burger	284		
5	North	Food	Pizza	121		
6	East	Food	Burger	463		
7	East	Food	Hot Dogs	481		
8	North	Food	Burger	342		
9	East	Food	Burger	234		
10	South	Food	Pizza	426		
11	South	Beverages	Water	266		
12	North	Beverages	Coffee	250		

F3 — `=SUMPRODUCT((Sales[Region]="North")+(Sales[Region]="South"))`

Figure 2-12. *SUMPRODUCT with multiple OR conditions*

Note   The * operator is used for AND logic between conditions.

Understanding the Logic

Let us break down how this works before we explore further examples.

In Excel, the number 0 is False, and any number other than 0 is True.

The SUMPRODUCT function evaluates the two conditions and returns TRUE or FALSE. The first array in the following is the results for North and the second array is South:

{FALSE;TRUE;FALSE;TRUE;FALSE;FALSE;TRUE;FALSE;FALSE;FALSE;TRUE}
+
{FALSE;FALSE;FALSE;FALSE;FALSE;FALSE;FALSE;FALSE;TRUE;TRUE;FALSE})

The values from the relative position in each array are added together. So, the first is added to the first, second with the second, and so on.

When a mathematical operation is performed on True and False values, they are converted to 1 and 0. The corresponding array values are then added together, for example, 0 + 0 = 0; 1 + 0 = 1; and so on.

{0;1;0;1;0;0;1;0;1;1;1}

This is then summed to return the result of 6.

The asterisk (*) operator is used to perform AND logic. If we want to count the sales from the *North* region for *Food* products, the following formula can be used:

=SUMPRODUCT((Sales[Region]="North")*(Sales[Category]="Food"))

The two arrays when evaluated produce True and False values. The first array is for the *North* region and the second for the *Food* category.

{FALSE;TRUE;FALSE;TRUE;FALSE;FALSE;TRUE;FALSE;FALSE;FALSE;TRUE}
*
{TRUE;FALSE;TRUE;TRUE;TRUE;TRUE;TRUE;TRUE;TRUE;FALSE;FALSE})

The array values are then multiplied, converting them to 1 and 0 and performing the operation, for example, 0 * 1 = 0; 1 * 0 = 0; and so on.

{0;0;0;1;0;0;1;0;0;0;0}

By using the * operator, a 1 is returned only if both arrays result in 1 (or True), as 1 * 1 = 1.

This array is then summed to produce the result of 2.

Note   This same logic is used with the FILTER function later in this chapter.

More Complex Examples

Let us expand on those SUMPRODUCT examples by using cell values for the criteria instead of typing values such as "North" and "Food" into the formula. We need to also look at summing values and using both AND and OR criteria in one formula.

To sum values using multiple conditions in SUMPRODUCT, we multiply by the range of values we want to sum.

Suppose we want to sum the total sales for the regions of *North* and *South*. The following SUMPRODUCT formula can be used (Figure 2-13):

```
=SUMPRODUCT(((Sales[Region]=F3)+(Sales[Region]=G3))*Sales[Total])
```

Each condition is enclosed in brackets, and then brackets also surround the two OR conditions to force the + operation to occur before the * operation.

F5	▼ : × ✓ *fx*	=SUMPRODUCT(((Sales[Region]=F3)+(Sales[Region]=G3))*Sales[Total])					
◢	A	B	C	D	E	F	G
1	**Region**	**Category**	**Product**	**Total**			
2	East	Food	Pizza	291		**Regions**	
3	North	Beverages	Coffee	113		North	South
4	East	Food	Burger	284		**Total**	
5	North	Food	Pizza	121		1518	
6	East	Food	Burger	463			
7	East	Food	Hot Dogs	481			
8	North	Food	Burger	342			
9	East	Food	Burger	234			
10	South	Food	Pizza	426			
11	South	Beverages	Water	266			
12	North	Beverages	Coffee	250			

Figure 2-13. *Sum values with multiple criteria using SUMPRODUCT*

This time, cell values (F3 and G3) were used instead of entering *North* and *South* into the formula. The regions can be changed easily by editing the cell values.

For a final example, we need to return the total sales for the regions *North* and *South* only for the product *Pizza* (Figure 2-14).

```
=SUMPRODUCT(
    ((Sales[Region]=F3)+(Sales[Region]=G3))*
    (Sales[Product]=F5)*
    Sales[Total]
)
```

This formula has been split onto different lines using **Alt + Enter** to make it easier to digest. This is optional. The formula bar needs to be expanded and resized to see all the formula.

F7	▼	⋮	×	✓	ƒx	=SUMPRODUCT(
						((Sales[Region]=F3)+(Sales[Region]=G3))*
						(Sales[Product]=F5)*
						Sales[Total]
						)

	A	B	C	D	E	F	G
1	Region	Category	Product	Total			
2	East	Food	Pizza	291		Regions	
3	North	Beverages	Coffee	113		North	South
4	East	Food	Burger	284		Product	
5	North	Food	Pizza	121		Pizza	
6	East	Food	Burger	463		Total	
7	East	Food	Hot Dogs	481			547
8	North	Food	Burger	342			
9	East	Food	Burger	234			
10	South	Food	Pizza	426			
11	South	Beverages	Water	266			
12	North	Beverages	Coffee	250			

Figure 2-14. *Using AND and OR logic in a SUMPRODUCT formula*

Note   With the dynamic array formulas in Excel 365, you can do all this in a SUM function. However, it is important to stress the use of SUMPRODUCT for compatibility for those on other versions.

Alternative to Array Formulas

The other great strength of SUMPRODUCT is that it can handle arrays without the need to press Ctrl + Shift + Enter.

Take this example; we have a list of dates and values of transactions on those dates. We want to find the total for a specific month.

Most users would create an additional column to extract the month before then writing a SUMIFS function. SUMPRODUCT can do this in one formula (Figure 2-15).

```
=SUMPRODUCT((MONTH(Monthly_Sales[Date])=D3)*Monthly_Sales[Total])
```

A True is returned whenever there is a match between the result of the MONTH function and the value in cell D3. This is then converted to 1 and 0, multiplied by the corresponding total value and summed.

| E3 | ▾ | ⋮ | ✕ | ✓ | fx | =SUMPRODUCT((MONTH(Monthly_Sales[Date])=D3)*Monthly_Sales[Total]) |

◢	A	B	C	D	E
1	**Date**	**Total**			
2	26/03/2020	500		**Month**	**Total Sales**
3	23/04/2020	640		5	1,102.00
4	28/06/2020	186			
5	18/06/2020	678			
6	22/05/2020	717			
7	11/05/2020	172			
8	15/02/2020	101			
9	08/06/2020	725			
10	27/04/2020	161			
11	24/05/2020	213			
12	28/01/2020	419			

Figure 2-15. *SUMPRODUCT as an array alternative for non-Excel 365 users*

Let us look at another example; this time, we have asked a bunch of people for their favorite three colors. We now want to count the occurrences of a specific color in the list.

The following SUMPRODUCT function is used (Figure 2-16). It includes the FIND function which will return the index number position of the word, if it finds it, and ISNUMBER to convert that number to a True value.

```
=SUMPRODUCT(--(ISNUMBER(FIND(C2,Colours[Favourite Colours],1))))
```

The double unary (--) is used to convert the True and False values to 1 and 0 so that they can be summed.

Instead of the double unary, we could have performed a mathematical operation to convert them. The following example multiplies the array values by 1 to convert them:

```
=SUMPRODUCT((ISNUMBER(FIND(C2,Colours[Favourite Colours],1)))*1)
```

| D2 | ▼ | : | × | ✓ | f_x | =SUMPRODUCT(--(ISNUMBER(FIND(C2,Colours[Favourite Colours],1)))) |

▲	A	B	C	D	E
1	**Favourite Colours**		**Colour**	**Total**	
2	Green, Blue, Black		Green	3	
3	Red, Pink, Blue				
4	Red, Green, Yellow				
5	Grey, Black, Purple				
6	Pink, Green, Yellow				

Figure 2-16. *Counting the occurrences of a word in a column with SUMPRODUCT*

UNIQUE

Availability: Excel for Microsoft 365 only

File   unique.xlsx

The UNIQUE function returns a list of distinct or unique values from a range or array. The syntax for the UNIQUE function is

`=UNIQUE(array, [by_col], [exactly_once])`

- **array:** The range or array you want to return unique values from.

- **[by_col]:** This is a logical value (True/False). The default is False to compare rows against each other and return unique rows. Use True to compare and return unique columns.

- **[exactly_once]:** A logical value. The default value is False which returns a distinct list of the values. Using True returns a list of the unique values (those that only occur once).

Note   Function arguments enclosed in square brackets are optional. For example, [by_col].

Create a Distinct List

The UNIQUE function is brilliant for generating a distinct list of items for other formulas or Excel features to use.

In this example, we want to create a distinct list (a list with duplicate values removed) of the food products we have sold. We can then use SUMIFS to generate a quick and dynamic analysis of sales by product.

The following UNIQUE function is used in cell F6 and spills to the cells below to list each product (Figure 2-17):

```
=UNIQUE(Sales[Product])
```

We only need to provide the array in this example, as the UNIQUE function defaults to generating a distinct list (exactly_once argument is set to False).

F6			fx	=UNIQUE(Sales[Product])		
	A	B	C	D	E	F	G
1	Region	Category	Product	Total			
2	East	Food	Pizza	291			
3	North	Beverages	Coffee	113		Total	
4	East	Food	Burger	284			
5	North	Food	Pizza	121		Products	Total
6	East	Food	Burger	463		Pizza	
7	East	Food	Hot Dogs	481		Coffee	
8	North	Food	Burger	342		Burger	
9	East	Food	Burger	234		Hot Dogs	
10	South	Food	Pizza	426		Water	
11	South	Beverages	Water	266			
12	North	Beverages	Coffee	250			

Figure 2-17. *Generate a distinct list of products*

This result is dynamic. If more rows are added to the *Sales* table with new products, the UNIQUE function will automatically add them to the spill range.

We can now write a SUMIFS function in cell G6 that uses this spill range (Figure 2-18).

```
=SUMIFS(Sales[Total],Sales[Product],F6#)
```

F6 is the cell containing the UNIQUE function, and the # operator is used to reference the spill range.

G6			× ✓ *fx*	=SUMIFS(Sales[Total],Sales[Product],F6#)		

	A	B	C	D	E	F	G
1	**Region**	**Category**	**Product**	**Total**			
2	East	Food	Pizza	291			
3	North	Beverages	Coffee	113		**Total**	
4	East	Food	Burger	284			
5	North	Food	Pizza	121		**Products**	**Total**
6	East	Food	Burger	463		Pizza	838
7	East	Food	Hot Dogs	481		Coffee	363
8	North	Food	Burger	342		Burger	1,323
9	East	Food	Burger	234		Hot Dogs	481
10	South	Food	Pizza	426		Water	266
11	South	Beverages	Water	266			
12	North	Beverages	Coffee	250			

Figure 2-18. *SUMIFS using the UNIQUE function spill range*

Dynamic List for Data Validation

The UNIQUE function is very useful for providing a dynamic distinct list of items for a Data Validation list.

In this example, we will use the same table (this time named *Food_Sales)*, and we will generate a drop-down list of products in cell F3 (Figure 2-19).

	A	B	C	D	E	F	G
1	Region	Category	Product	Total			
2	East	Food	Pizza	291		Product	Total
3	North	Beverages	Coffee	113			-
4	East	Food	Burger	284			
5	North	Food	Pizza	121			
6	East	Food	Burger	463			
7	East	Food	Hot Dogs	481			
8	North	Food	Burger	342			
9	East	Food	Burger	234			
10	South	Food	Pizza	426			
11	South	Beverages	Water	266			
12	North	Beverages	Coffee	250			

Figure 2-19. *Food Sales table with space for a drop-down list in cell F3*

Unfortunately, the dynamic array formulas cannot be used directly in a Data Validation rule. So, in this example, we have used the following UNIQUE function in cell I1 (Figure 2-20). We can then reference this spill range from the Data Validation window.

```
=UNIQUE(Food_Sales[Product])
```

1. Select cell F3 and click **Data ➤ Data Validation** to open the Data Validation window.

2. Select **List** and enter =**$I$1#** into the *Source* box.

Figure 2-20. *Referencing a spill range in a Data Validation rule*

The drop-down list is in cell F3. A SUMIFS function is returning the total sales of the selected product in cell G3 (Figure 2-21).

If new products appear in the *Food_Sales* table, they are automatically added to this list.

	A	B	C	D	E	F	G
1	**Region**	**Category**	**Product**	**Total**			
2	East	Food	Pizza	291		**Product**	**Total**
3	North	Beverages	Coffee	113		Burger	1,323
4	East	Food	Burger	284		Pizza	
5	North	Food	Pizza	121		Coffee	
6	East	Food	Burger	463		Burger	
7	East	Food	Hot Dogs	481		Hot Dogs	
8	North	Food	Burger	342		Water	
9	East	Food	Burger	234			
10	South	Food	Pizza	426			
11	South	Beverages	Water	266			
12	North	Beverages	Coffee	250			

Figure 2-21. *Dynamic Data Validation list from formula spill range*

Count of Distinct and Unique Entries

For a final example of the UNIQUE function, we have a list of attendee names in a table named *Attendees (*Figure 2-22*)*. There are duplicate names because some people have attended more than once.

We need to find out how many people only attended once (unique names) and how many distinct people have attended.

◢	A	B	C	D	E
1	**Names**				
2	Rita Müller		**Unique**		**Distinct**
3	Liu Wong				
4	Karin Josephs				
5	Mary Saveley				
6	Anabela Domingues				
7	Anabela Domingues				
8	Paul Henriot				
9	Mary Saveley				
10	Liz Nixon				
11	Miguel Angel Paolino				
12	Mary Saveley				
13	Rita Müller				
14	Miguel Angel Paolino				

Figure 2-22. *Attendees table with a list of names*

In cell C3, the following UNIQUE function can be used to return the list of names that only attended once (Figure 2-23):

```
=UNIQUE(Attendees[Names],,TRUE)
```

The *by_col* argument has been ignored, and True has been set for the *exactly_once* argument.

f_x	=UNIQUE(Attendees[Names],,TRUE)

	C	D	E	F
	Unique		**Distinct**	
	Liu Wong			
	Karin Josephs			
	Paul Henriot			
	Liz Nixon			

Figure 2-23. *Unique list of names that only attended once*

This is great, but we are not interested in their names; we just want to know how many. The COUNTA function can be used to count the items in the array returned by UNIQUE.

=COUNTA(UNIQUE(Attendees[Names],,TRUE))

We can then do the same in cell E3, though this time we want a distinct count and so will ignore the last two arguments of the UNIQUE function (Figure 2-24).

=COUNTA(UNIQUE(Attendees[Names]))

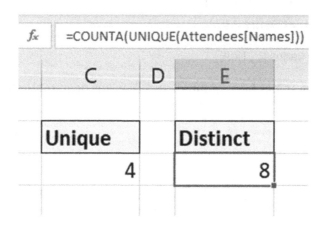

f_x	=COUNTA(UNIQUE(Attendees[Names]))

	C	D	E
	Unique		**Distinct**
	4		8

Figure 2-24. *Unique and distinct count formulas*

SORT and SORTBY

Availability: Excel for Microsoft 365 only

File   sort-and-sortby.xlsx

The sort functions were a terrific addition to Excel. Sorting data is a very popular feature of Excel, and now there are two functions in Excel 365 that will dynamically sort a range or array.

SORT Function

Let us begin with the SORT function. Its syntax is

=SORT(array, [sort_index], [sort_order], [by_col])

- **array:** The range or array of data you want to sort.

- **[sort_index]:** An index number which represents the row or column number of the array to sort by. If omitted, the first row or column is used.

- **[sort_order]:** Enter 1 to sort in ascending order or –1 for descending. If omitted, it will sort in ascending order.

- **[by_col]:** Logical value which specifies whether to sort by row or by column. The default value is False, which sorts by row (vertical sort). Enter True to sort by column (horizontal sort).

Sort a Distinct List

We just looked at how the UNIQUE function can return a distinct range of values and that this is great for dynamic reports and feeding other features such as Data Validation lists.

We can take that a step further and automatically sort that list.

In this example, we show the total sales by product but have the products in ascending order by name. The following formula was used in cell F3 (Figure 2-25):

```
=SORT(UNIQUE(Sales[Product]))
```

Because the array is one column and we want it in ascending order, we do not need to provide any other arguments except the array to sort. In this example, that is the array returned by the UNIQUE function.

This same technique can also be used to ensure Data Validation lists are always in the correct order.

F3				fx	=SORT(UNIQUE(Sales[Product]))	

	A	B	C	D	E	F	G
1	Region	Category	Product	Total			
2	East	Food	Pizza	291		Products	Total
3	North	Beverages	Coffee	113		Burger	1,323
4	East	Food	Burger	284		Coffee	363
5	North	Food	Pizza	121		Hot Dogs	481
6	East	Food	Burger	463		Pizza	838
7	East	Food	Hot Dogs	481		Water	266
8	North	Food	Burger	342			
9	East	Food	Burger	234			
10	South	Food	Pizza	426			
11	South	Beverages	Water	266			
12	North	Beverages	Coffee	250			

Figure 2-25. Sorting the products in ascending order

Sort Multiple Columns

In that example, we only needed to sort one column. Let us see an example of sorting a multiple column array.

In this example, we have a table named *Scores* with names and exam scores. We want to sort the list of names and scores in descending order by scores.

The following SORT function has been used in cell D2 to accomplish this (Figure 2-26):

```
=SORT(Scores,2,-1)
```

It sorts the entire Scores table (you can select specific columns only in a table to return) by the second column (Scores). The –1 specifies to sort in descending order.

	A	B	C	D	E
1	Name	Scores		Name	Scores
2	Elizabeth Lincoln	75		Janine Labrune	97
3	Victoria Ashworth	83		Sven Ottlieb	96
4	Patricio Simpson	79		Francisco Chang	92
5	Francisco Chang	92		Pedro Afonso	85
6	Yang Wang	66		Victoria Ashworth	83
7	Pedro Afonso	85		Elizabeth Brown	83
8	Elizabeth Brown	83		Patricio Simpson	79
9	Sven Ottlieb	96		Elizabeth Lincoln	75
10	Janine Labrune	97		Yang Wang	66

D2 ... *fx* =SORT(Scores,2,-1)

Figure 2-26. *Sort the scores in descending order*

Two of the scores are the same (Victoria Ashworth and Elizabeth Brown). If scores are tied, we want a second sort to be ascending by the name.

This SORT function uses array constants to specify multiple columns to sort (Figure 2-27). These constants are enclosed in curly braces. The sort index is set to sort by column 2 and then column 1. The corresponding sort order array is set to descending first and then ascending.

```
=SORT(Scores,{2,1},{-1,1})
```

Elizabeth Brown and Victoria Ashworth are now correctly ordered.

| D2 | | ▼ | : | × | ✓ | fx | =SORT(Scores,{2,1},{-1,1}) |

▲	A	B	C	D	E
1	**Name**	**Scores**		**Name**	**Scores**
2	Elizabeth Lincoln	75		Janine Labrune	97
3	Victoria Ashworth	83		Sven Ottlieb	96
4	Patricio Simpson	79		Francisco Chang	92
5	Francisco Chang	92		Pedro Afonso	85
6	Yang Wang	66		Elizabeth Brown	83
7	Pedro Afonso	85		Victoria Ashworth	83
8	Elizabeth Brown	83		Patricio Simpson	79
9	Sven Ottlieb	96		Elizabeth Lincoln	75
10	Janine Labrune	97		Yang Wang	66

Figure 2-27. *Adding a second-level sort to order tied values*

SORTBY Function

Let us now look at the SORTBY function. With this function, you specify the range or array to sort by instead of using an index number. Also, the range or array to sort by does not need to be in the sorted array results.

```
=SORTBY(array, by_array1, [sort_order1], ...)
```

- **array:** The range or array that you want to sort.
- **by_array1:** The range or array to sort on.
- **[sort_order1]:** Enter 1 for ascending order and –1 for descending. If omitted, the array is sorted in ascending order.

Sort Multiple Columns with SORTBY

Let us repeat the previous example of sorting the *Scores* table descending by exam scores and then ascending by name, but this time with the SORTBY function.

The SORTBY function can handle multiple column ranges to sort so there is no need for array constants (Figure 2-28). This can make things easier.

```
=SORTBY(Scores,Scores[Scores],-1,Scores[Name],1)
```

D2	▼	:	×	✓	fx	=SORTBY(Scores,Scores[Scores],-1,Scores[Name],1)		

▲	A	B	C	D	E
1	**Name**	**Scores**		**Name**	**Scores**
2	Elizabeth Lincoln	75		Janine Labrune	97
3	Victoria Ashworth	83		Sven Ottlieb	96
4	Patricio Simpson	79		Francisco Chang	92
5	Francisco Chang	92		Pedro Afonso	85
6	Yang Wang	66		Elizabeth Brown	83
7	Pedro Afonso	85		Victoria Ashworth	83
8	Elizabeth Brown	83		Patricio Simpson	79
9	Sven Ottlieb	96		Elizabeth Lincoln	75
10	Janine Labrune	97		Yang Wang	66

Figure 2-28. *SORTBY function to sort by multiple columns*

Sort by Column Not in the Sorted Array

The biggest strength of the SORTBY function over SORT is that the array to sort by does not need to be included in the sorted array results.

To start with a simple example, let us repeat the sort by exam score and name example, but we will only return the name column.

This formula is the same as the last one except that the array only specifies the *Name* column to be returned. It can still sort by exam score even though it is not in the returned range (Figure 2-29).

```
=SORTBY(Scores[Name],Scores[Scores],-1,Scores[Name],1)
```

D2		▼	⋮	✕ ✓ fx	=SORTBY(Scores[Name],Scores[Scores],-1,Scores[Name],1)		

◢	A	B	C	D	E	F
1	**Name**	**Scores**		**Name**	**Scores**	
2	Elizabeth Lincoln	75		Janine Labrune		
3	Victoria Ashworth	83		Sven Ottlieb		
4	Patricio Simpson	79		Francisco Chang		
5	Francisco Chang	92		Pedro Afonso		
6	Yang Wang	66		Elizabeth Brown		
7	Pedro Afonso	85		Victoria Ashworth		
8	Elizabeth Brown	83		Patricio Simpson		
9	Sven Ottlieb	96		Elizabeth Lincoln		
10	Janine Labrune	97		Yang Wang		

Figure 2-29. *Sort by a column not included in the returned array*

Sort Products by Sales Totals

Let us go back to that first sort example with the total sales by product. We have changed our mind and wish to sort the list in descending order by the sales totals.

This example is complex. The range of products and the range of total sales values are separate spill ranges. So, we need SORTBY because we are sorting the products by a range outside of the sorted array.

Beginning with the total sales in cell G3, this formula sums the sales of each distinct product in the table and sorts the values in descending order:

```
=SORT(SUMIFS(Sales[Total],Sales[Product],UNIQUE(Sales[Product])),,-1)
```

Then in cell F3 (Figure 2-30), this formula sorts the distinct products array using the SUMIFS function for the by array argument:

```
=SORTBY(UNIQUE(Sales[Product]),SUMIFS(Sales[Total],Sales[Product],
UNIQUE(Sales[Product])),-1)
```

| F3 | ▼ | : | × | ✓ | *fx* | =SORTBY(UNIQUE(Sales[Product]),SUMIFS(Sales[Total],Sales[Product],UNIQUE(Sales[Product])),-1) |

◢	A	B	C	D	E	F	G	H
1	Region	Category	Product	Total				
2	East	Food	Pizza	291		Products	Total	
3	North	Beverages	Coffee	113		Burger	1,323	
4	East	Food	Burger	284		Pizza	838	
5	North	Food	Pizza	121		Hot Dogs	481	
6	East	Food	Burger	463		Coffee	363	
7	East	Food	Hot Dogs	481		Water	266	
8	North	Food	Burger	342				
9	East	Food	Burger	234				
10	South	Food	Pizza	426				
11	South	Beverages	Water	266				
12	North	Beverages	Coffee	250				

Figure 2-30. SORTBY products using the SUMIFS range

FILTER

Availability: Excel for Microsoft 365 only

File   filter.xlsx

The FILTER function will filter a range or array based on specified criteria. Along with the SORT function, this is a massive addition to Excel for creating powerful dynamic reports.

The filter feature found on the Home and Data tabs is one of the most popular in Excel, but it is let down by being a manual process. A user needs to reapply the filter every time they want to update the results.

However, there is now a function to automate your filtering and spill to a worksheet range or to feed another function.

This is the syntax for the FILTER function:

```
=FILTER(array, include, [if_empty])
```

- **array:** The range or array that you want to filter and return

- **include:** The filter criteria that determines which rows to return

- **[if_empty]:** The action to take if no results are returned by the filter

FILTER Function Example

OK, let us see it in action. We have a table named *Issues* with information about logged issues to a support team (Figure 2-31).

	A	B	C	D	E
1	Centre	Assigned To	Received	Level	Solved
2	Bedford Falls	Teresa	19/05/2020	3	Yes
3	Bedford Falls	Monica	16/05/2020	2	Yes
4	Springfield	Kyle	24/05/2020	3	No
5	Zion	Teresa	15/05/2020	2	Yes
6	Bedrock	Dawn	11/05/2020	2	No
7	Springfield	Teresa	12/05/2020	1	Yes
8	Bedford Falls	Kyle	24/05/2020	3	Yes
18	Zion	Monica	10/05/2020	2	Yes
19	Bedford Falls	Tammy	12/05/2020	1	No
20	Springfield	Kyle	07/05/2020	1	No
21	Bedrock	Monica	14/05/2020	2	No
22					

Figure 2-31. *Issues table with data about logged issues to a support team*

We want an automatic report that lists the unsolved issues by center, with the higher priority ones at the top of the list.

We have an output area ready for the FILTER function to be used in cell G8 and spill to the other cells (Figure 2-32). We want to return the *Assigned To, Received,* and *Level* information. Cell G5 contains a drop-down list for the user to select the center they want to filter by.

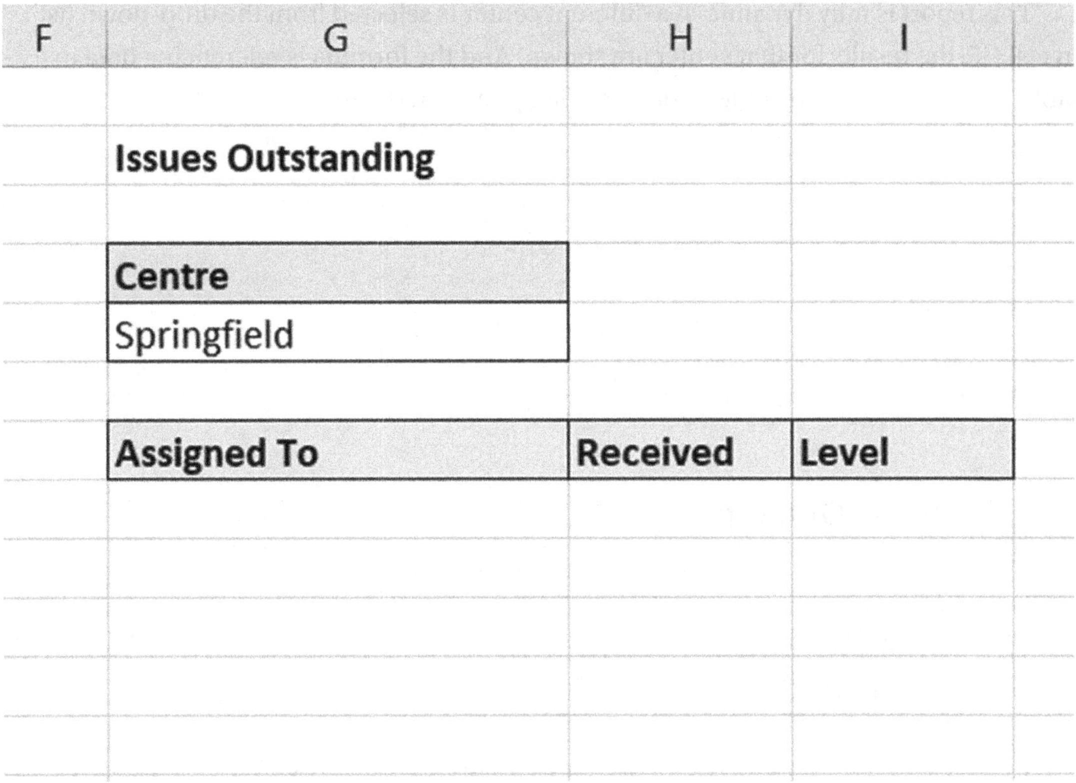

F	G	H	I
	Issues Outstanding		
	Centre		
	Springfield		
	Assigned To	**Received**	**Level**

Figure 2-32. *Range for the FILTER function output*

The following FILTER function returns the desired results (Figure 2-33). It has been broken up over multiple lines to make it more readable.

```
=FILTER(Issues[[Assigned To]:[Level]],
    (Issues[Solved]="no")*(Issues[Centre]=G5),
    "All issues resolved"
)
```

The formula uses two conditions shown in the second line. The issues column must be equal to "No" and the center equal to the one selected in cell G5. The asterisk (*) operator is used for AND logic.

The technique to writing the filter criteria is the same as what we discussed with the SUMPRODUCT function earlier in this chapter (see "Understanding the Logic").

If no results are returned, the text "All issues resolved" is shown.

This report is fully dynamic. If a different center is selected from the drop-down list in cell G5, the results for that center are shown. And the formula is referencing data in a table, so if more rows are added, the formula updates perfectly.

```
=FILTER(Issues[[Assigned To]:[Level]],
    (Issues[Solved]="no")*(Issues[Centre]=G5),
    "All issues resolved"
)
```

F	G	H	I
	Issues Outstanding		
	Centre		
	Springfield		
	Assigned To	**Received**	**Level**
	Kyle	24/05/2020	3
	Teresa	23/05/2020	2
	Kyle	07/05/2020	1

Figure 2-33. *Report on unresolved issues using the FILTER function*

Let us add to this function by sorting the results so that the higher priority issues are at the top. The higher the level number, the more important, so the list needs to be sorted in descending order by level.

In addition to this, if there are unresolved issues with the same level, then they should be sorted in ascending order by the received date so that those logged longer are higher in the list.

We can add the SORT function to the FILTER. We need two sort levels, so the sort index (3,2) and sort order (-1, 1) are entered into arrays in curly braces (Figure 2-34).

```
=SORT(FILTER(Issues[[Assigned To]:[Level]],
    (Issues[Solved]="no")*(Issues[Centre]=G5),
    "All issues resolved"),
    {3,2},{-1,1}
)
```

The Bedrock center is a good example. There are three level 2 issues unresolved, and they have been sorted in ascending order by date received.

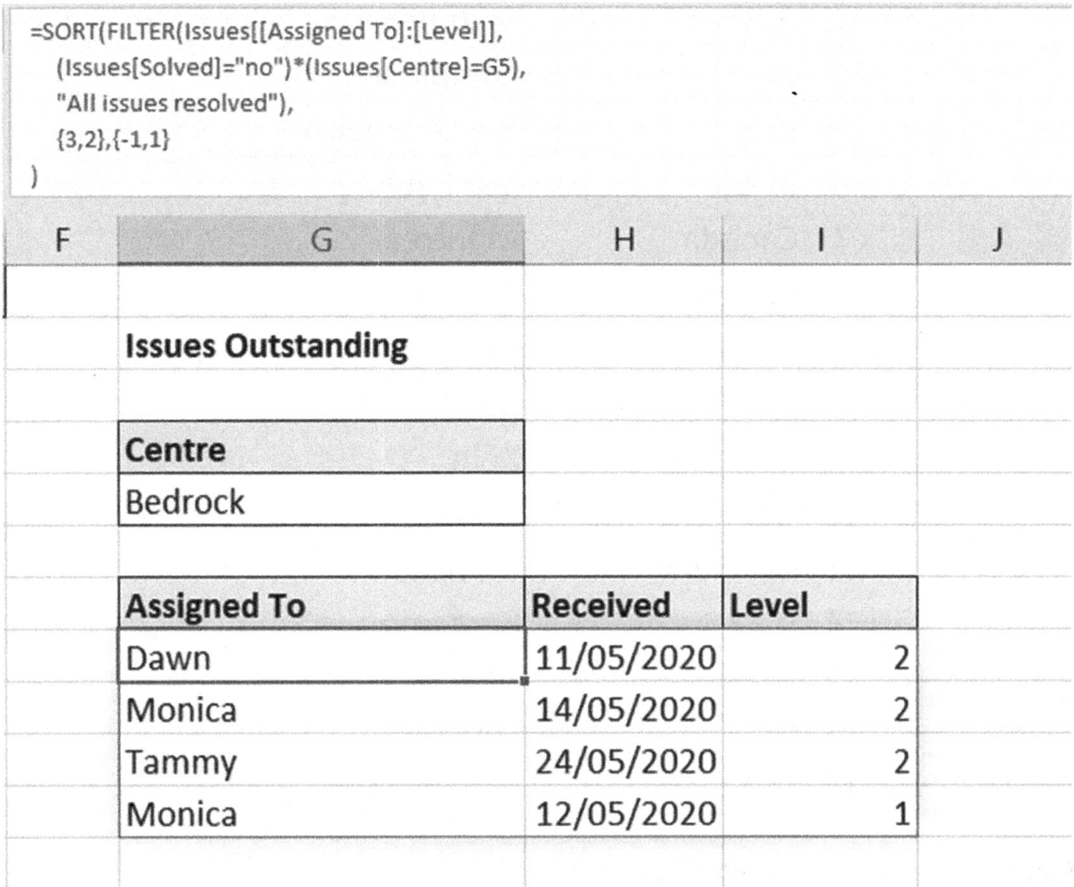

```
=SORT(FILTER(Issues[[Assigned To]:[Level]],
    (Issues[Solved]="no")*(Issues[Centre]=G5),
    "All issues resolved"),
    {3,2},{-1,1}
)
```

F	G	H	I	J
	Issues Outstanding			
	Centre			
	Bedrock			
	Assigned To	**Received**	**Level**	
	Dawn	11/05/2020	2	
	Monica	14/05/2020	2	
	Tammy	24/05/2020	2	
	Monica	12/05/2020	1	

Figure 2-34. *FILTER and SORT functions together to order the issues by priority*

Dependent Drop-Down List

The FILTER function is brilliant for making more advanced drop-down lists. In this example, we will use it to create a dependent drop-down list.

We have a table named *Cities*, which has a column with a country name and then another for a city (Figure 2-35).

	A	B
1	**Country**	**City**
2	Austria	Graz
3	Austria	Salzburg
4	Brazil	Campinas
5	Brazil	Rio de Janeiro
6	Brazil	São Paulo
7	Canada	Montréal
8	Canada	Toronto
9	Canada	Vancouver
10	Germany	Berlin
11	Germany	Köln
12	Germany	Leipzig
13	Germany	München
14	Italy	Bergamo
15	Italy	Torino
16	UK	London
17	UK	Manchester

Figure 2-35. *Table of countries and cities*

We would like to create a drop-down list to select a country and then a second list that only shows cities from the selected country.

For the first country drop-down list, we can use the same technique discussed earlier in the "UNIQUE" section of this chapter (see "Dynamic List for Data Validation").

The following formula is used in cell G1 to create a sorted and distinct list of country names (Figure 2-36):

```
=SORT(UNIQUE(Cities[Country]))
```

Note   The formulas that prepare the lists would normally be put on a different hidden sheet. They are only used on the same sheet here to keep them all in one place.

Then, in cell D2, a Data Validation rule is set up for the list using the source =$G$1#.

Figure 2-36. *Dynamic drop-down list of country names*

Now for the sexy dependent list part. In cell H1, the following formula is used. It returns the cities where the country is equal to that selected in cell D2, and if no city is selected, then it returns all of them (Figure 2-37).

```
=SORT(FILTER(Cities[City],Cities[Country]=D2,Cities[City]))
```

The SORT function is added to ensure that the cities are returned in ascending order.

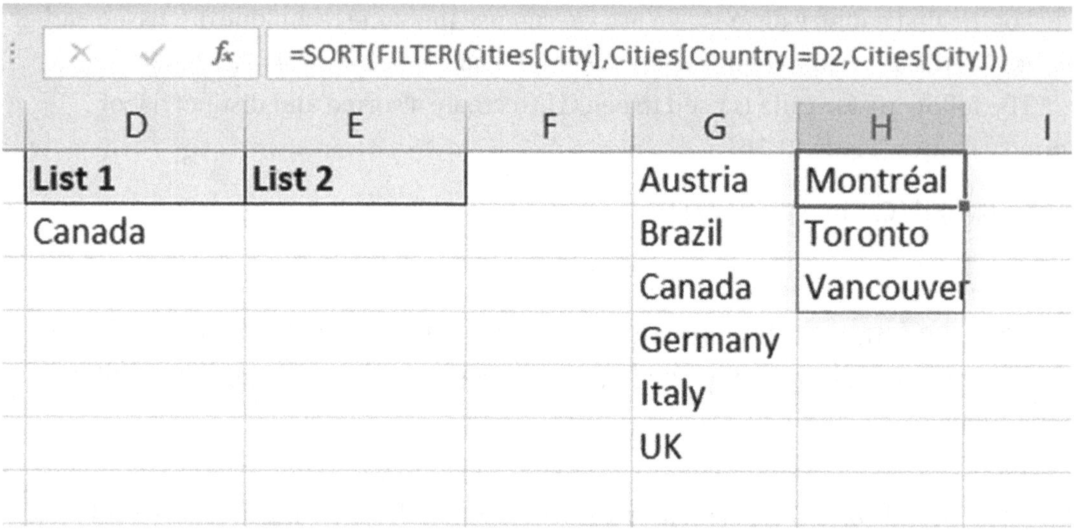

| | | fx | =SORT(FILTER(Cities[City],Cities[Country]=D2,Cities[City])) |

D	E	F	G	H	I
List 1	**List 2**		Austria	Montréal	
Canada			Brazil	Toronto	
			Canada	Vancouver	
			Germany		
			Italy		
			UK		

Figure 2-37. *FILTER function for the dependent list*

In cell E2, the Data Validation rule is set up using the =$H$1# spill range reference (Figure 2-38).

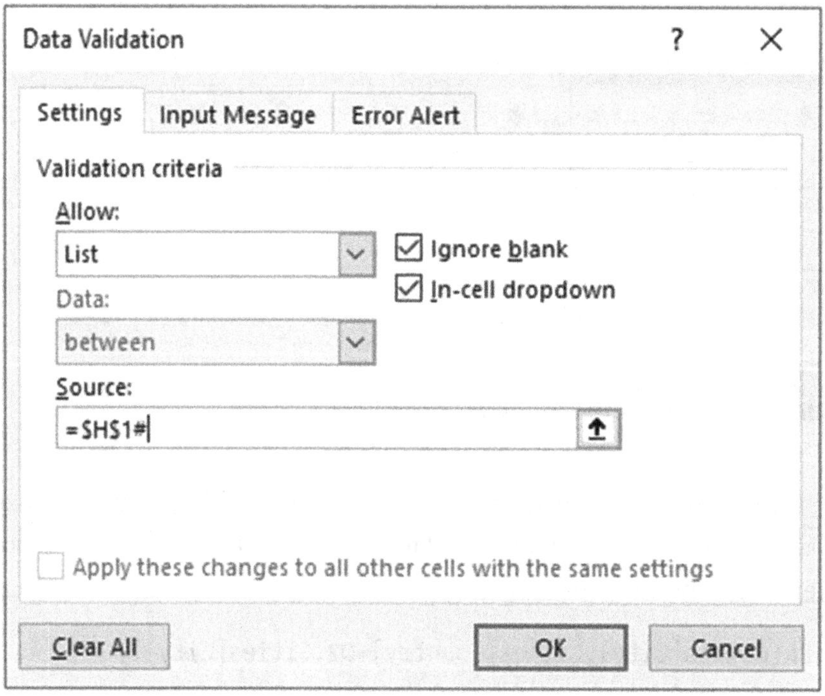

Figure 2-38. *City spill range used for the Data Validation list source*

The drop-down list successfully returns only the cities from the selected country (Figure 2-39).

D	E	F	G	H
List 1	**List 2**		Austria	Montréal
Canada			Brazil	Toronto
	Montréal		Canada	Vancouver
	Toronto		Germany	
	Vancouver		Italy	
			UK	

Figure 2-39. *City drop-down list dependent upon the selected country*

Shrinking Drop-Down List

In this second drop-down list example, the FILTER function will assist in creating a shrinking drop-down list.

We have a table named *Workers* and another table named *Tasks* with a list of tasks that we want to assign the workers to (Figure 2-40). We want to select a name from a drop-down list and have the list shrink (remove that name) as a worker cannot do more than one task.

	A	B	C	D
1	**Names**		**Task**	**This Week**
2	Elizabeth Lincoln		Task 1	
3	Victoria Ashworth		Task 2	
4	Patricio Simpson		Task 3	
5	Francisco Chang		Task 4	
6	Pedro Afonso		Task 5	
7	Elizabeth Brown		Task 6	
8	Sven Ottlieb		Task 7	
9				

Figure 2-40. *Table of workers to assign to tasks*

To achieve this, we will start with a COUNTIFS function in cell F2 (Figure 2-41).

```
=COUNTIFS(tasks[This Week],Workers[Names])
```

This function counts the occurrences of the names from the *Workers* table that have been used in the *This Week* column of the *Tasks* table. Francisco has been assigned to Task 2, and there is a 1 for his name in row 5.

F2			× ✓ *fx*	=COUNTIFS(tasks[This Week],Workers[Names])			
	A	B	C	D	E	F	
1	**Names**		**Task**	**This Week**		**Names Left**	
2	Elizabeth Lincoln		Task 1			0	
3	Victoria Ashworth		Task 2	Francisco Chang		0	
4	Patricio Simpson		Task 3			0	
5	Francisco Chang		Task 4			1	
6	Pedro Afonso		Task 5			0	
7	Elizabeth Brown		Task 6			0	
8	Sven Ottlieb		Task 7			0	
9							

Figure 2-41. *COUNTIFS function marking the workers that have been used*

The next step is to filter out the names that have been used. The FILTER function is perfect for this (Figure 2-42).

```
=SORT(FILTER(Workers[Names],COUNTIFS(tasks[This
Week],Workers[Names])=0,""))
```

The FILTER function returns only the names from the *Workers* table where the COUNTIFS result equals 0. This leaves us with the unused names. The SORT function is thrown in to order the names A to Z.

F2	▼ : × ✓ fx	=SORT(FILTER(Workers[Names],COUNTIFS(tasks[This Week],Workers[Names])=0,""))							
	A	B	C	D	E	F	G	H
1	Names		Task	This Week		Names Left		
2	Elizabeth Lincoln		Task 1			Elizabeth Brown		
3	Victoria Ashworth		Task 2	Francisco Chang		Elizabeth Lincoln		
4	Patricio Simpson		Task 3			Patricio Simpson		
5	Francisco Chang		Task 4			Pedro Afonso		
6	Pedro Afonso		Task 5			Sven Ottlieb		
7	Elizabeth Brown		Task 6			Victoria Ashworth		
8	Sven Ottlieb		Task 7					
9								

Figure 2-42. *FILTER function to only show the unused names*

The final step is to create the Data Validation list. Select the *This Week* column of the *Tasks* table and create a Data Validation list that uses =$F$2# as its source.

As names are selected from the list, they are removed (Figure 2-43). Next week the names can then be deleted from the *This Week* column, and the list will be complete again.

◢	A	B	C	D	E
1	**Names**		**Task**	**This Week**	
2	Elizabeth Lincoln		Task 1		
3	Victoria Ashworth		Task 2	Francisco Chang	
4	Patricio Simpson		Task 3	Pedro Afonso	
5	Francisco Chang		Task 4		
6	Pedro Afonso		Task 5		
7	Elizabeth Brown		Task	Elizabeth Brown	
8	Sven Ottlieb		Task	Elizabeth Lincoln	
9				Patricio Simpson	
10				Sven Ottlieb	
				Victoria Ashworth	

Figure 2-43. *Completed shrinking drop-down list*

Aggregate FILTER Results

The purpose of the FILTER function is to return values that meet specific filter criteria. All of the examples so far have returned the filtered range to a cell on a worksheet, but it could be returned to another function.

We looked at the SUMPRODUCT function earlier and how it can sum or count values dependent on complex criteria. And the way that we write the criteria is the same for FILTER.

Well, FILTER cannot sum or count values, but it can handle the complex criteria and then hand it over to another function for the aggregation.

In this example, we repeat the SUMPRODUCT example earlier but with FILTER and SUM. This formula returns the total sales for *pizza* in the *North* and *South* regions (Figure 2-44). It uses both OR and AND logic in the criteria.

```
=SUM(FILTER(Sales[Total],
    ((Sales[Region]=F3)+(Sales[Region]=G3))*(Sales[Product]=F5),
    0))
```

| F7 | ▾ | ⋮ | × | ✓ | fx | =SUM(FILTER(Sales[Total], ((Sales[Region]=F3)+(Sales[Region]=G3))*(Sales[Product]=F5), 0)) |

◢	A	B	C	D	E	F	G
1	Region	Category	Product	Total			
2	East	Food	Pizza	291		Regions	
3	North	Beverages	Coffee	113		North	South
4	East	Food	Burger	284		Product	
5	North	Food	Pizza	121		Pizza	
6	East	Food	Burger	463		Total	
7	East	Food	Hot Dogs	481		547	
8	North	Food	Burger	342			
9	East	Food	Burger	234			
10	South	Food	Pizza	426			
11	South	Beverages	Water	266			
12	North	Beverages	Coffee	250			

Figure 2-44. *FILTER function used for complex criteria to then aggregate*

The importance behind this example is that although the SUM function has been used, it could have been a different function. We could have used COUNTA, AVERAGE, LARGE, MEDIAN, or any other function that fulfills our objective.

INDEX

Availability: All versions

File   index.xlsx

The INDEX function is a very versatile function that can be used to return a value or a range. It is most often associated with the MATCH function to perform powerful lookups. It is also well known for creating dynamic ranges.

This is the syntax of the INDEX function:

```
=INDEX(array, row_num, [column_num])
```

- **array:** The range or array

- **row_num:** The row position in the range or array

- **[column_num]:** The column position in the range or array

---

Note   The INDEX function can also be used to return a range from an array of defined ranges. This technique has been ignored as there are better approaches to do this than INDEX.

Let us explore some interesting examples of why INDEX is one of the power functions.

INDEX and MATCH for Versatile Lookups

We are spoiled for choice nowadays for lookup techniques with XLOOKUP, FILTER, and Power Query, but the combination of the INDEX and MATCH functions remains one of the best ways to look up data.

Note   There is an XMATCH function in Excel 365 which is an improvement on the classic MATCH function. I have chosen to demonstrate with MATCH here to focus on a complete non-Excel 365 user's solution.

One of the biggest frustrations that initially lead users from VLOOKUP to an INDEX and MATCH lookup is the inability of VLOOKUP to look to the left.

Take this example (Figure 2-45) where we want to return the date and value of an invoice. The table is named *Invoices,* and the *Date* column is to the left of the *ID* column.

	A	B	C	D	E	F
1	**Date**	**ID**	**Value**			
2	11/07/2020	1305	555		**ID**	
3	18/07/2020	1298	1,037		1261	
4	11/07/2020	1291	581		**Date**	**Value**
5	22/07/2020	1297	581			
6	20/07/2020	1261	684			
7	14/07/2020	1272	229			
8	20/07/2020	1284	574			
9	14/07/2020	1304	240			

Figure 2-45. *Invoice data to look up with INDEX and MATCH*

Because INDEX and MATCH are two different functions, we can keep the lookup array and the return array separate.

Note   The XLOOKUP function can also be used for versatile lookups.

This formula in cell E5 (Figure 2-46) will look up the ID using the MATCH function and return the date using INDEX:

```
=INDEX(Invoices[Date],MATCH(E3,Invoices[ID],0))
```

E5		▼	:	×	✓	f_x	=INDEX(Invoices[Date],MATCH(E3,Invoices[ID],0))	

◢	A	B	C	D	E	F
1	Date	ID	Value			
2	11/07/2020	1305	555		ID	
3	18/07/2020	1298	1,037		1261	
4	11/07/2020	1291	581		Date	Value
5	22/07/2020	1297	581		20/07/2020	
6	20/07/2020	1261	684			
7	14/07/2020	1272	229			
8	20/07/2020	1284	574			
9	14/07/2020	1304	240			

Figure 2-46. *INDEX and MATCH to return data from the left*

This is great, but we do want to return the invoice value too. And it would be great if we could write one formula to handle both.

In the formula in Figure 2-46, the INDEX function was given one column (the *Date* column) as the array. This time, we will give it the entire table as the array and use another MATCH function to find the column to return from.

In this formula, the second MATCH function looks up the return column by looking for the cell values in E4 and F4 across the table headers (Figure 2-47).

```
=INDEX(Invoices,MATCH($E$3,Invoices[ID],0),MATCH(E4,Invoices[#Headers],0))
```

E5	▼	:	×	✓	fx	=INDEX(Invoices,MATCH($E$3,Invoices[ID],0),MATCH(E4,Invoices[#Headers],0))

	A	B	C	D	E	F	G	H
1	Date	ID	Value					
2	11/07/2020	1305	555		ID			
3	18/07/2020	1298	1,037		1261			
4	11/07/2020	1291	581		Date	Value		
5	22/07/2020	1297	581		20/07/2020	684		
6	20/07/2020	1261	684					
7	14/07/2020	1272	229					
8	20/07/2020	1284	574					
9	14/07/2020	1304	240					

Figure 2-47. *Two-way lookup with INDEX and MATCH*

An advantage INDEX has over XLOOKUP (discussed soon) is that it accepts index numbers for the row and column of the range or value to return. And we can do some awesome things with this.

In this example, a formula is used in cell C3 to return the last months value for the product selected in cell C2 (Figure 2-48).

The INDEX function uses the entire *Monthly_Sales* table as its array. MATCH is used to find the row number of the product in cell C2, and the COLUMNS function is used to return how many columns are in the *Monthly_Sales* table.

```
=INDEX(Monthly_Sales,
    MATCH(C2,Monthly_Sales[Product],0),
    COLUMNS(Monthly_Sales)
)
```

If more columns are added to the table, it will still return the value from the last column.

Note   There is a ROWS function to return the number of rows in a table or range.

C3	▼ :	× ✓ *fx*	=INDEX(Monthly_Sales, MATCH(C2,Monthly_Sales[Product],0), COLUMNS(Monthly_Sales))

	A	B	C	D	E
1					
2		Product	Hot Dog		
3		Last Month	176		
4					
5	Product	Jan	Feb	Mar	Apr
6	Pizza	140	394	691	514
7	Cookies	484	580	687	230
8	Pineapple	284	327	427	339
9	Hot Dog	663	264	519	176
10	Apple Juice	697	427	590	233
11	Crisps	227	559	197	344

Figure 2-48. *Return the value from the last column*

Return the Last X Values from a Row/Column

The INDEX function has always been the most efficient way to create dynamic references to use in other functions and features such as charts.

In this example, we have a table named Week_Data with weekly sales of products (Figure 2-49). Every week another column is added, and we want to return the last x number of week values.

	A	B	C	D	J	K	
1	**Product**	**Wk 1**	**Wk 2**	**Wk 3**	**Wk 9**	**Wk 10**	
2	Pizza	140	394	69	408	357	
3	Cookies	484	580	68	315	1,055	
4	Pineapple	284	327	42	869	646	
5	Hot Dog	663	264	51	354	805	
6	Apple Juice	697	427	59	780	751	
7	Crisps	227	559	19	675	1,135	
8							
9							

Figure 2-49. *The Week_Data table with weekly sales of products*

In this formula entered in cell C5, a user enters a value in cell C2 for the number of weeks they want to return values (Figure 2-50):

```
=SUM(
    INDEX(Week_Data,MATCH(B5,Week_Data[Product],0),COLUMNS
    (Week_Data)-$C$2+1)
    :
    INDEX(Week_Data,MATCH(B5,Week_Data[Product],0),COLUMNS(Week_Data))
)
```

There is a lot going on in this formula. The range operator (:) is the most important aspect.

The first INDEX function returns the first cell of the range, the second one returns the last cell, and they are joined to form a range.

The MATCH function finds the row of the product, and the COLUMNS function returns how many columns are in the table. In the first INDEX function, you can see -$C$2+1 used to go back from the end of the table to find the start of the range.

This range is given to a SUM function to then total the last X number of week sales for each product.

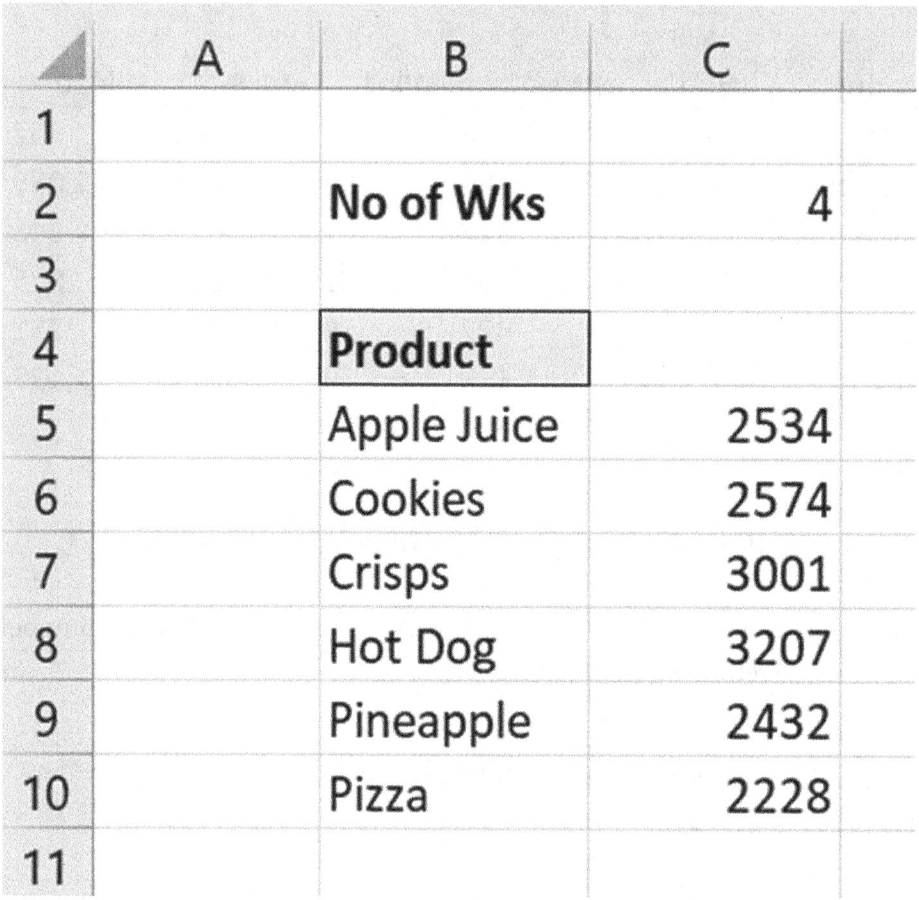

◢	A	B	C
1			
2		**No of Wks**	4
3			
4		**Product**	
5		Apple Juice	2534
6		Cookies	2574
7		Crisps	3001
8		Hot Dog	3207
9		Pineapple	2432
10		Pizza	2228
11			

Figure 2-50. *Sum the last X column values number*

The returned values could also be spilled to a range on a worksheet using the dynamic array formula engine. This is also possible in versions outside of Excel 365, but without the dynamic arrays, it is cumbersome to make it dynamic.

To do this, we just need to remove the SUM function from the formula. Without the aggregation, the array is returned and spilled to the worksheet (Figure 2-51).

```
=INDEX(Week_Data,MATCH(B5,Week_Data[Product],0),COLUMNS(Week_Data)-$C$2+1)
    :
    INDEX(Week_Data,MATCH(B5,Week_Data[Product],0),COLUMNS(Week_Data))
)
```

To get the dynamic week headers in row 4, the following formula was used in cell C4. It uses the table headers for the INDEX array, and the row number is simply 1 as there is no product to find.

```
=INDEX(Week_Data[#Headers],1,COLUMNS(Week_Data)-$C$2+1)
    :
    INDEX(Week_Data[#Headers],1,COLUMNS(Week_Data)
)
```

◢	A	B	C	D	E	F	G	H
1								
2		**No of Wks**	6					
3								
4		**Product**	Wk 5	Wk 6	Wk 7	Wk 8	Wk 9	Wk 10
5		Apple Juice	1018	468	627	376	780	751
6		Cookies	781	918	599	605	315	1055
7		Crisps	351	574	449	742	675	1135
8		Hot Dog	630	1129	1054	994	354	805
9		Pineapple	1060	777	417	500	869	646
10		Pizza	371	680	325	1138	408	357
11								

Figure 2-51. *Returned range spilled to the worksheet*

CHOOSE

Availability: All versions

File   choose.xlsx

The CHOOSE function is a brilliant lookup function in Excel that does not seem to get the credit that it should. Most users have never heard of it.

It does a very simple job, which is to choose a value or action from a list based on a selected index number.

This is the CHOOSE function syntax:

```
=CHOOSE(index_num, value1, [value2], ...)
```

- **index_num:** The selected index number which specifies the value that CHOOSE should return from the list
- **value1, [value2]:** A list of values, cell ranges, formulas, defined names, or tables from which CHOOSE selects

The beauty of the CHOOSE function is in its simplicity. It provides a simple way to do something very powerful. And this is to return a formula, range, or value from a user selection.

It is awkward to use with large lists so leave those for other lookup functions, but with smaller lists, it is very easy to understand and set up.

Let us look at some examples to see why CHOOSE is brilliant.

Pick a Formula from a List

The CHOOSE function returns a value or action from a list when given an index number. So, we need something to give it an index number.

A clever use of the CHOOSE function is therefore with form controls. In Figure 2-52, there is a simple table of product values named *Sales*. And there are three options. These have been inserted from the Developer tab in Excel. We will not go into how to do that here.

◢	A	B	C	D
1				
2			Result	
3				
4		◯ Total	**Product Name**	**Values**
5		◯ Average	Apple Juice	417
6			Cookies	153
7		◯ Max	Crisps	452
8			Hot Dog	138
9			Pineapple	271
10			Pizza	463
11				

Figure 2-52. *Select a formula from option buttons*

We want each option button to perform a different formula. So, a user can select if they want the total, the average, or the max of the values.

Option buttons (like most form controls) return an index number to distinguish which one was selected. This makes them the perfect partner for the CHOOSE function.

We need to link the option buttons to a cell, so that when an option button is clicked, the index number is returned to that cell.

Right-click an option button and click **Format Control**. Click the **Cell link** box and then click a cell on a worksheet to link to (Figure 2-53). This is normally on a different hidden sheet, but in this example, we will use $A$1.

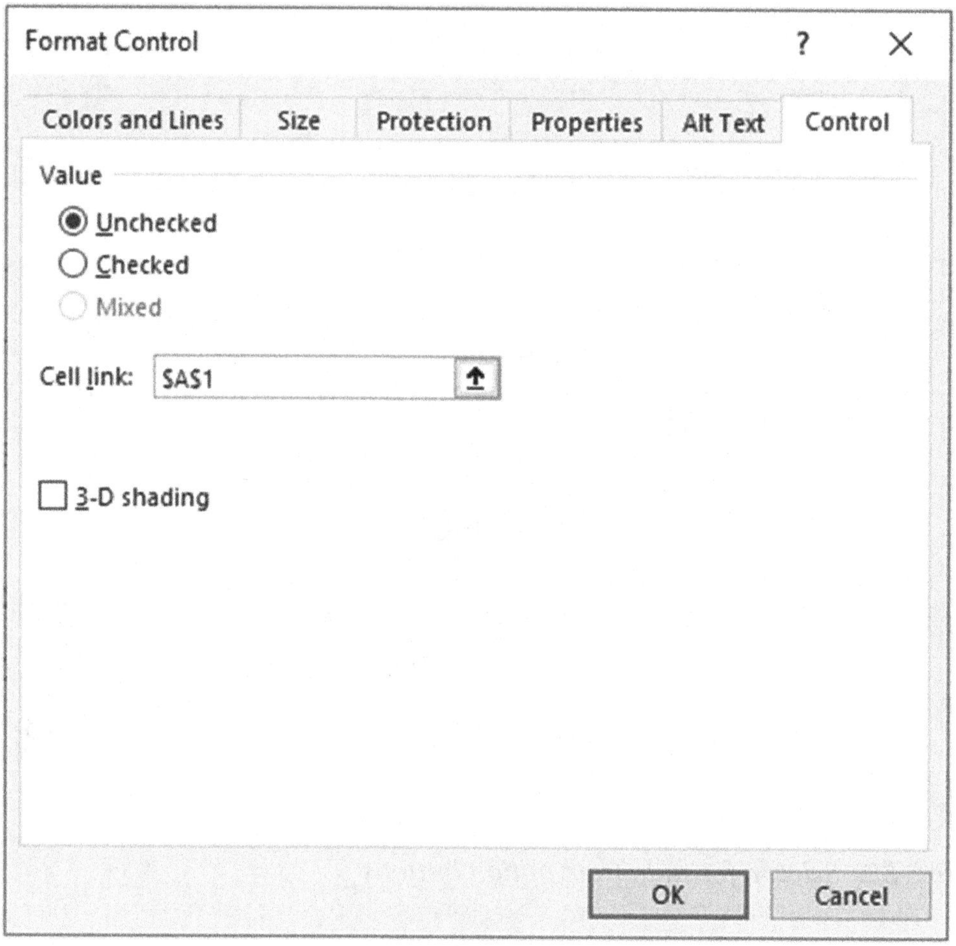

Figure 2-53. *Link the option buttons to a cell*

When the option buttons are used, Total returns 1, Average returns 2, and Max is 3.

In cell D2, the following formula is used to run a different formula based on the user selection (Figure 2-54):

```
=CHOOSE(A1,
    SUM(sales[Values]),
    AVERAGE(sales[Values]),
    MAX(sales[Values])
)
```

The CHOOSE function uses cell A1 for the index number, then picks from the three different formulas in its list. Simple, yet incredibly cool.

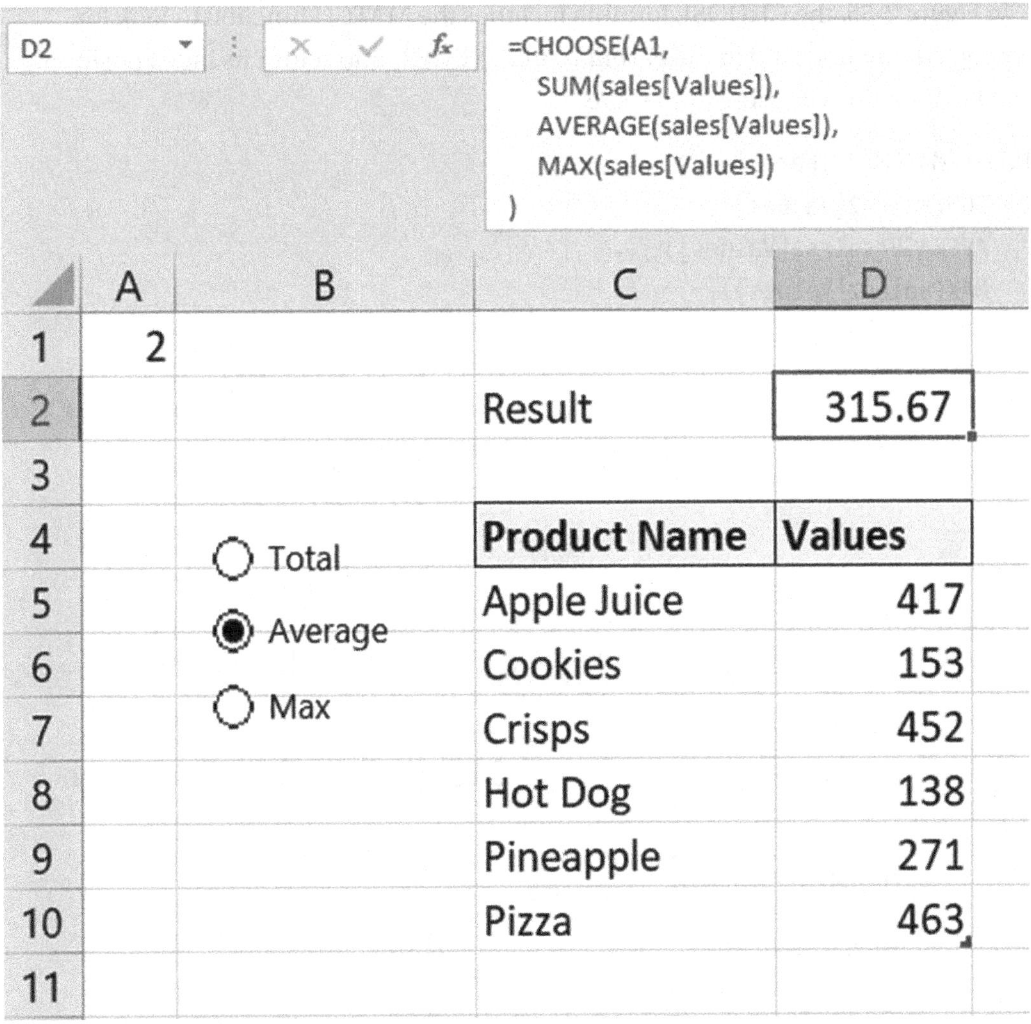

D2	▼	:	×	✓	fx	=CHOOSE(A1,
						SUM(sales[Values]),
						AVERAGE(sales[Values]),
						MAX(sales[Values])
						)

	A	B	C	D
1	2			
2			Result	315.67
3				
4		◯ Total	**Product Name**	**Values**
5		◉ Average	Apple Juice	417
6			Cookies	153
7		◯ Max	Crisps	452
8			Hot Dog	138
9			Pineapple	271
10			Pizza	463
11				

Figure 2-54. *CHOOSE formula running a formula based on user selection*

Let us see an example of running the CHOOSE function of a Data Validation list instead of using form controls.

If we create a Data Validation list with the options Sum, Average, and Max, it will return those values when selected. CHOOSE requires an index number. So, the two cannot communicate directly.

In Figure 2-55, the CHOOSE formula includes the MATCH function to look for the selected function (B2) in the *Formulas* table (E1:E3) and return its index position. CHOOSE then does its thing from there.

```
=CHOOSE(MATCH(B2,Formulas,0),
    SUM(sales2[Values]),
    AVERAGE(sales2[Values]),
    MAX(sales2[Values]),
)
```

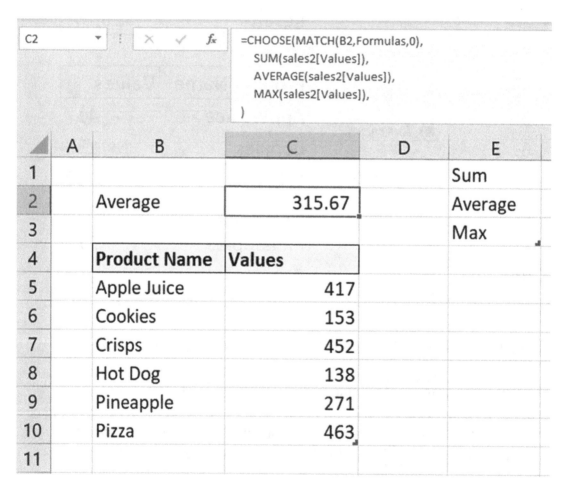

Figure 2-55. *CHOOSE working of a Data Validation list*

These examples are small to help understand the concept, but we could use any formula we want in the list for CHOOSE to pick from.

For example, we could add it to the INDEX function example in the previous chapter when we summed the last X number of week values.

CHOOSE Specific Columns for FILTER

Another scenario you may see CHOOSE being used is to reverse the order of the columns for VLOOKUP. It was a neat little trick to get VLOOKUP returning data to its left. Quite cool, but in truth not that useful. You should use XLOOKUP or INDEX and MATCH instead.

A better example of this technique is with the FILTER function. This function is awesome, but one limitation is that the columns of the array that it returns must be consecutive.

For example, if we wanted to use the FILTER function on the *Employees* table in Figure 2-56, and return the columns *First Name, Last Name, Age,* and *Salary*, the FILTER function alone could not do this.

◢	A	B	C	D	E	F
1	**First Name**	**Last Name**	**Department**	**Age**	**Start Date**	**Salary**
2	June	Foster	Sales	47	11/12/2011	41,936
3	Brett	Jones	IT	46	26/05/2017	23,669
4	Maurine	Krieger	IT	26	03/12/2017	30,978
5	Jerri	Ebron	Admin	28	17/09/2012	41,813
6	Li	Xi	Sales	40	17/06/2019	23,559
7	Eliza	Fekete	Admin	47	16/02/2010	41,820
8	Jean	Shagall	Admin	37	02/02/2007	41,417
9	Miguel	Shuck	Complaints	39	05/11/2005	33,758
10	Beverly	Blair	IT	39	28/02/2014	28,096
11	Andrew	Thompson	Marketing	43	11/12/2018	24,421
12	Glennie	Butters	IT	34	04/02/2018	36,361
13						

Figure 2-56. *Employees table that we want to filter*

With the CHOOSE function, we can specify the columns that we want, and FILTER can return them.

Note   This technique is useful, though returning the columns using separate FILTER formulas would give you more flexibility if you needed to chart this data or run more formulas off it.

In this formula, CHOOSE uses an array of constants for its index numbers and then returns all the values in its list, which are the table columns.

The FILTER function returns only the employees with a salary of greater than or equal to 35,000 (Figure 2-57).

```
=FILTER(
    CHOOSE({1,2,3,4},Employees[First Name],Employees[Last Name],
    Employees[Age],Employees[Salary]),
    Employees[Salary]>=35000,
    ""
)
```

H	I	J	K
First Name	**Last Name**	**Age**	**Salary**
June	Foster	47	41,936
Jerri	Ebron	28	41,813
Eliza	Fekete	47	41,820
Jean	Shagall	37	41,417
Glennie	Butters	34	36,361

Figure 2-57. CHOOSE picking specific columns for FILTER

XLOOKUP

Availability: Excel for Microsoft 365 only

File   xlookup.xlsx

The XLOOKUP function was introduced as a blend of the best elements of VLOOKUP and the INDEX and MATCH combination all in one function. It also has a few extra advantages.

These are some of the strengths of XLOOKUP:

- It can return values and ranges (VLOOKUP cannot return a range).

- It defaults to an exact match. It's the most used lookup type.

- It can perform robust range lookups that do not depend on the order.

- It has a built-in if not found argument. No need for IFERROR or IFNA to handle the classic #N/A error.

- It can look up from first to last or last to first.

- It can look up vertically or horizontally.

- It can handle wildcard characters.

It is a beast of a function. This is the syntax of XLOOKUP:

```
=XLOOKUP(lookup_value, lookup_array, return_array, [if_not_found], [match_mode], [search_mode])
```

- **lookup_value:** The value you are looking for.

- **lookup_array:** The range or array to search.

- **return_array:** The range or array to return.

- **[if_not_found]:** Value to return if no match is found.

- **[match_mode]:** How to match the lookup value. 0 for an exact match (default), –1 for exact match or next smaller, 1 for exact match or next larger, and 2 for a wildcard character match.

- **[search_mode]:** Enter 1 to search first to last (default), –1 to search last to first, 2 for a binary search ascending, and –2 for a binary search descending.

Quick XLOOKUP Example

Let us begin with a classic XLOOKUP example before we show off its special features.

In this formula, XLOOKUP is being used for an exact match to look for the staff ID and return the member of staff's name (Figure 2-58). Only three arguments are needed because XLOOKUP defaults to the exact match.

`=XLOOKUP(A2,Staff[ID],Staff[Name])`

With XLOOKUP, a range or array is used for the lookup array and return array. In this example, references to the column of a table named *Staff* are used.

	A	B	C	D	E	F
			fx	=XLOOKUP(A2,Staff[ID],Staff[Name])		
1	ID	Name		Name	ID	Department
2	TA302	Helen Bennett		Yoshi Latimer	TA528	Sales
3	TA402	Annette Roulet		Patricia McKenna	TA201	Sales
4	TA600	Renate Messner		Helen Bennett	TA302	IT
5	TA201	Patricia McKenna		Philip Cramer	TA105	Accounting
6				Daniel Tonini	TA537	Sales
7				Annette Roulet	TA402	IT
8				Renate Messner	TA600	Payroll
9						

Figure 2-58. XLOOKUP for an exact match to return staff details

Robust Range Lookup

The XLOOKUP function has a robust range lookup that is not broken when the values of the lookup array are not in order.

Although performing an exact match is more common, range lookups are very useful. In an example like this, they are much more efficient than a multiple condition logical function such as IFS, SWITCH, or CHOOSE.

In this formula, XLOOKUP is used to return the discount dependent upon the total spent (Figure 2-59):

```
=XLOOKUP(B2,discounts[Spent],discounts[Discount],,-1)
```

The *Spent* column of the *Discounts* table is not in order. You can see 200 between 750 and 1000, yet the XLOOKUP formula continues to work perfectly.

The if not found argument has been ignored, and an exact match or next smaller item has been specified by entering –1.

| C2 | ▼ | ⋮ | ✕ | ✓ | *fx* | =XLOOKUP(B2,discounts[Spent],discounts[Discount],,-1) |

	A	B	C	D	E	F	G
1	ID	Total	Discount		Spent	Discount	
2	10011	1106	12%		0	0%	
3	10012	188	2%		100	2%	
4	10013	722	5%		500	5%	
5	10014	782	10%		750	10%	
6	10015	449	3%		200	3%	
7	10016	64	0%		1000	12%	
8	10017	460	3%				
9	10018	879	10%				
10	10019	524	5%				
11	10020	150	2%				

Figure 2-59. *Using XLOOKUP for a robust range lookup*

Multiple Column Lookup

Often users need to match the value from more than one column to find an exact match. XLOOKUP makes this multiple column lookup scenario easy.

In this example, we have a table named *Employees,* and we want to return the employees' salary in cell C2 (Figure 2-60). We need to match their first name and last name so we will need to match two columns.

```
=XLOOKUP(A2&B2,Employees[First Name]&Employees[Last
Name],Employees[Salary])
```

The ampersand (&) is used to join the contents of A2 and B2 together in the lookup value and join the contents of the *First Name* and *Last Name* columns together in the lookup array.

| C2 | ▼ : × ✓ *fx* | =XLOOKUP(A2&B2,Employees[First Name]&Employees[Last Name],Employees[Salary]) |

	A	B	C	D	E	F	G	H	I
1	First Name	Last Name	Salary		First Name	Last Name	Department	Salary	
2	Miguel	Shuck	33,758		June	Foster	Sales	41,936	
3					Brett	Jones	IT	23,669	
4					Maurine	Krieger	IT	30,978	
5					Jerri	Ebron	Admin	41,813	
6					Li	Xi	Sales	23,559	
7					Eliza	Fekete	Admin	41,820	
8					Jean	Shagall	Admin	41,417	
9					Miguel	Shuck	Complaints	33,758	
10					Beverly	Blair	IT	28,096	
11					Andrew	Thompson	Marketing	24,421	
12					Glennie	Butters	IT	36,361	
13									

Figure 2-60. *Multiple column lookup made easy with XLOOKUP*

Return the Last Match

XLOOKUP has the option to search from last to first instead of the classic first to last. This can help to return the last match from a list.

Note   The XMATCH function also has this functionality and can be combined with the INDEX function for powerful lookups.

In this example, we have a table named *Monthly_Sales,* and we want to return the last sales total for a specific salesperson. The table is ordered by month, so we want to return the value for the last instance of the selected salesperson (E2).

The salesperson is identified by two letters at the beginning of the reference. We will use wildcard characters to ignore everything in the salesperson reference except the first two letters.

This is the formula used in cell F2 (Figure 2-61):

```
=XLOOKUP(E2&"*",Monthly_Sales[Sales Person Ref],Monthly_Sales[Total],,2,-1)
```

The asterisk (*) wildcard character is combined with the value from cell E2 for the lookup value. Number 2 is used for the match mode to specify the use of wildcards and –1 for the search mode to specify a last to first lookup.

| F2 | ▼ | : | ✕ | ✓ | *fx* | =XLOOKUP(E2&"*",Monthly_Sales[Sales Person Ref],Monthly_Sales[Total],,2,-1) |

▲	A	B	C	D	E	F	G
1	**Sales Person Ref**	**Month**	**Total**		**Sales Person**	**Last Months Sales**	
2	DH657	Jan	1,328		LK	1,624	
3	LK362	Jan	395				
4	AF800	Jan	790				
5	LK301	Feb	1,872				
6	AF461	Feb	1,728				
7	DH045	Feb	1,207				
8	LK030	Mar	1,109				
9	DH946	Mar	1,244				
10	AF846	Mar	1,176				
11	AF635	Apr	459				
12	DH811	Apr	1,086				
13	LK714	Apr	802				
14	DH119	May	610				
15	LK372	May	1,624				
16	AF643	May	1,213				
17							

Figure 2-61. *Searching last to first and using wildcards with XLOOKUP*

Two-Way Lookup

There is only one thing better than an XLOOKUP. Two XLOOKUPs! And that is what we need to create a two-way lookup.

Earlier in this chapter, we created a two-way lookup with INDEX and two MATCH functions – one to look down a column and another to look along a row. This is much easier with XLOOKUP.

In this example, we want to return the sales value for the product selected in cell A2 and the store location selected in cell B1 (Figure 2-62).

| B2 | ▾ | : | × | ✓ | *fx* | =XLOOKUP(A2,Store_Sales[Product], XLOOKUP(B1,Store_Sales[#Headers],Store_Sales[#Data])) |

	A	B	C	D	E	F	G	H
1	Product	Plymouth		Product	Manchester	Leeds	Plymouth	Lincoln
2	Fruit	453		Cake	592	392	537	306
3				Coffee	111	329	536	412
4				Fruit	342	413	453	398
5				Juice	457	264	402	138
6				Tea	393	106	110	289
7								

Figure 2-62. *Two-way lookup with two XLOOKUP functions*

This formula uses a second XLOOKUP for the return array of the first XLOOKUP. It searches for the store location (B1) along the table headers and returns the location values for the outer XLOOKUP to return the value for the selected product.

```
=XLOOKUP(A2,Store_Sales[Product],
    XLOOKUP(B1,Store_Sales[#Headers],Store_Sales
)
```

We can see a breakdown of this formula more clearly by selecting only the second XLOOKUP in the formula bar and pressing the **F9** key to calculate it. You must be careful to select the second XLOOKUP function completely and precisely.

We can now see the array of values being returned for the selected store location (Plymouth in this example). The outer XLOOKUP then grabs the value for the selected product (453 for Fruit in this example).

```
=XLOOKUP(A2,Store_Sales[Product],
    {537;536;453;402;110}
)
```

Press **Esc** when finished so that the array of values is not kept.

Note   The **F9** key calculates the formulas. This can also be done by clicking **Formulas ➤ Calculate Now**.

Dynamic SUMIFS Columns

The great fun with these formulas is how we can use them together. XLOOKUP is fabulous for using with other formulas to return ranges or values dependent upon user selections.

In this example, we want to sum the values for the product selected in cell A2 and the store location selected in cell B1 (Figure 2-63).

This formula uses XLOOKUP for the sum range of SUMIFS. It returns the range of values for the location selected in B1 for SUMIFS to then do the rest.

```
=SUMIFS(XLOOKUP(B1,Sales[#Headers],Sales),Sales[Product],A2)
```

Using tables makes referencing the different parts of a range such as the headers, columns, and data area so much easier.

| B2 | ▼ | : | × | ✓ | fx | =SUMIFS(XLOOKUP(B1,Sales[#Headers],Sales),Sales[Product],A2) |

◢	A	B	C	D	E	F	G	H	I
1	Product	Leeds		Product	Month	Manchester	Leeds	Plymouth	Lincoln
2	Fruit	1,521		Cake	January	592	392	537	306
3				Coffee	January	111	329	536	412
4				Fruit	January	342	413	453	398
5				Juice	January	457	264	402	138
6				Tea	January	393	106	110	289
7				Cake	February	340	701	592	560
8				Coffee	February	556	238	287	624
9				Fruit	February	244	448	580	432
10				Juice	February	164	527	642	353
11				Tea	February	707	444	362	511
12				Cake	March	373	484	636	450
13				Coffee	March	555	721	570	344
14				Fruit	March	416	660	562	167
15				Juice	March	275	796	451	197
16				Tea	March	503	647	590	584
17									

Figure 2-63. XLOOKUP with SUMIFS for a dynamic sum range

INDIRECT

Availability: All versions

File   indirect.xlsx

The INDIRECT function enables us to create dynamic references to sheets, ranges, tables, and defined names instead of entering them directly into the formula.

A reference in a formula could then be altered without directly changing the formula itself.

This is the syntax for the INDIRECT function:

```
=INDIRECT(ref_text, [a1])
```

- **ref_text:** A reference supplied as text.

- **[a1]:** A logical value that specifies what type of reference was used in the ref text argument. Enter True or ignore the argument for an A1-style reference, or enter False for an R1C1 reference.

Return Table Based on Drop-Down Selection

This book has focused on the use of tables as the base for your formulas. It makes referencing data easier and more meaningful and makes your formulas dynamic.

If you are going to create dynamic references using INDIRECT, you will need to know how to refer to the different parts of a table.

To get familiar with the parts of a table, type = into a cell, followed by the table name and a square bracket ([), to see a list of the table elements (Figure 2-64).

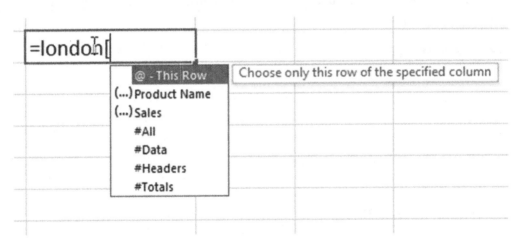

Figure 2-64. *List of the different elements of a table*

In this example, we have three tables named *London, Auckland,* and *Dublin* (Figure 2-65). We have a drop-down list in cell B2 where a user can select a table to return.

London		Auckland		Dublin	
Product Name	**Sales**	**Product Name**	**Sales**	**Product Name**	**Sales**
Product A	313	Product A	87	Product A	425
Product B	94	Product B	177	Product B	136
Product C	161	Product C	231	Product C	109
Product D	435	Product D	299	Product D	92
Product E	429	Product E	320	Product E	310

Figure 2-65. *Three sales tables to return using INDIRECT*

We will bring the table to a range on a worksheet, but it could be fed to another formula such as XLOOKUP or COUNTIFS.

In cell B4, the following formula can be used to return everything including the headers (Figure 2-66):

```
=INDIRECT(B2&"[#All]")
```

=INDIRECT(B2&"[#All]")

B	C	D
Dublin		
Product Name	**Sales**	
Product A	425	
Product B	136	
Product C	109	
Product D	92	
Product E	310	

Figure 2-66. *INDIRECT function to return all of the table*

The INDIRECT function combines the value in cell B2 with the text in the double quotes and returns it as a reference.

This technique uses the dynamic array engine and spills the entire table across the empty cells surrounding it.

This is great! It makes it so simple to return an entire table based on a list selection.

This is returned all in one spill range. It can be beneficial to return table elements separately, so that you can refer to the individual spill ranges in other formulas, charts, or Data Validation lists. For example, you may want to sum the sales values.

This formula uses the INDIRECT function to only return the table headers (Figure 2-67):

```
=INDIRECT(B2&"[#Headers]")
```

Figure 2-67. *INDIRECT function to return table headers only*

Now, we can use a formula to return only the *Product Name* column (Figure 2-68).

```
=INDIRECT(B2&"[Product Name]")
```

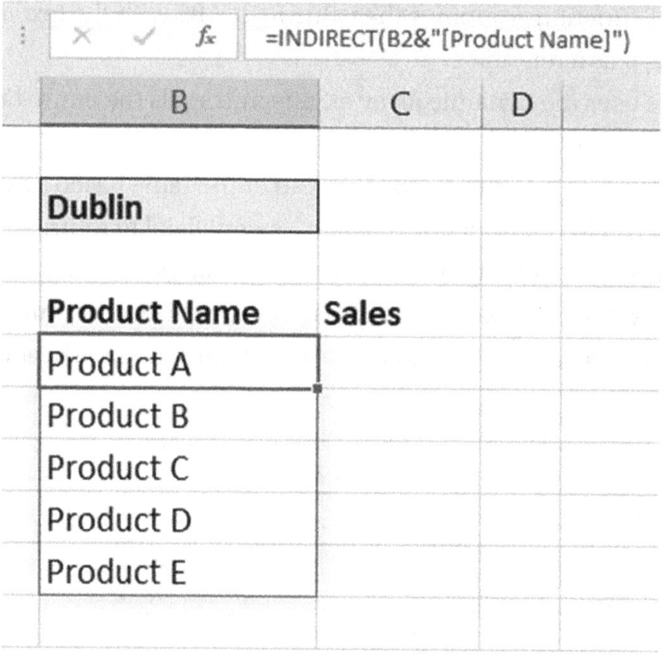

Figure 2-68. *INDIRECT to return a table column only*

And then return the *Sales* column (Figure 2-69).

```
=INDIRECT(B2&"[Sales]")
```

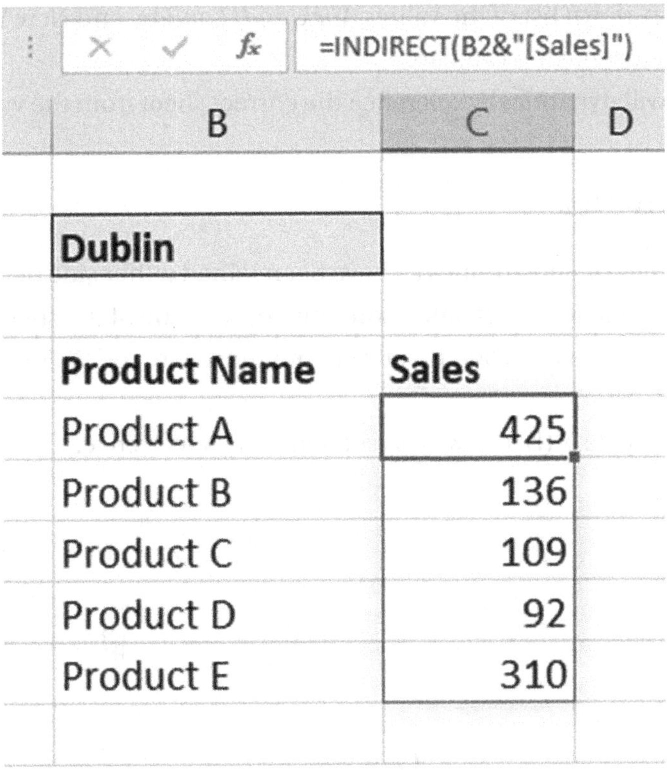

	B	C	D
		=INDIRECT(B2&"[Sales]")	
	Dublin		
	Product Name	**Sales**	
	Product A	425	
	Product B	136	
	Product C	109	
	Product D	92	
	Product E	310	

Figure 2-69. *Separate spill ranges for individual referencing*

They are now separate spill ranges and can be referenced individually. For example, the following formula would sum the sales values:

```
=SUM(C5#)
```

Of course, if we wanted the total sales of the selected table without the table being returned to the worksheet, we could have used this formula:

```
=SUM(INDIRECT(B2&"[Sales]"))
```

Reference Other Sheets with INDIRECT

In addition to referencing elements of a table, you can also reference other sheets from a cell content with INDIRECT.

In this example, we have three sheets named *Auckland, London,* and *New York*. On each sheet, cell C10 contains a total value which we want to return.

We have a drop-down list of the values *Auckland, London,* and New York in cell B3 of the sheet we are returning the value to.

This formula will dynamically reference the correct sheet from the value in cell B3 (Figure 2-70):

```
=INDIRECT("'"&B3&"'!C10")
```

The single quotes or apostrophes (') have been joined either side of the sheet name, as they need to be there if a sheet name contains spaces. One of the sheets is named *New York,* so this is important. It is good practice to put those into the INDIRECT reference just in case.

The exclamation mark (!) follows a sheet name in its reference.

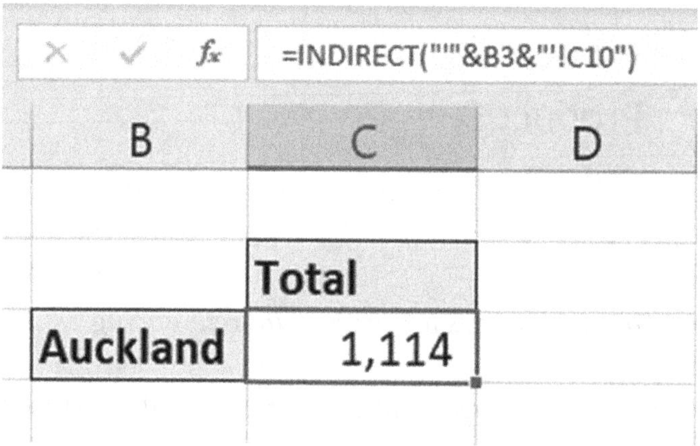

Figure 2-70. Using INDIRECT for dynamic sheet references

SWITCH

Availability: Excel 2019, Excel for Microsoft 365

File   switch.xlsx

The SWITCH function evaluates a value (expression) against a list of values and returns the result for the first matching value.

This is an awesome function that simplifies the testing of multiple values compared to nested IFs.

This is the syntax of the SWITCH function:

```
=SWITCH(expression, value1, result1, [default or value2, result2])
```

- **expression:** The expression to be compared against value1, value2, and so on.

- **value1:** The value to be compared against the expression.

- **result1:** The result to return if the expression and value match. This can be a value, range, or formula.

- **[default or value2, result2]:** Provide more values to compare and their result if true or a provide a default value. Default is the value to return if there are no matches.

Testing Text Values

The SWITCH function is concise and simple to understand, especially when compared to writing nested IFs. You state the expression once and then test a list of values against it. With IF functions, you need to repeat the expression each time.

In this example, we have a table named *Memberships* with three membership grades: *Platinum, Gold,* and *Silver* (Figure 2-71). We want to assign the correct fee for each membership grade. *Platinum* is 90, *Gold* is 65, and *Silver* is 50.

The following formula has been entered into the table in cell B2:

```
=SWITCH([@Grade],"Platinum",90,"Gold",65,"Silver",50)
```

The expression is the grade. This is stated once, and then it is tested against the three values.

| B2 | ▼ | : | × | ✓ | fx | =SWITCH([@Grade],"Platinum",90,"Gold",65,"Silver",50) |

	A	B	C	D	E
1	Grade	Fee			
2	Platinum	90			
3	Gold	65			
4	Silver	50			
5	Gold	65			
6	Silver	50			
7	Gold	65			
8	Platinum	90			
9	Platinum	90			

Figure 2-71. *Testing a list of text values with SWITCH*

We could have added a default value to the SWITCH function on the end. This is the value returned if it finds no matches. This formula displays the text "No match":

```
=SWITCH([@Grade],"Platinum",90,"Gold",65,"Silver",50,"No match")
```

I do not think this is necessary in this instance. If a default value is not used, then the #N/A error is shown.

The SWITCH function is cleaner and more concise than a nested IF equivalent. This formula has been broken over multiple lines to make it easier to read. You can see the multiple references to [@Grade]. With the SWITCH function, [@Grade] is only referenced once.

```
=IF([@Grade]="Platinum",90,
    IF([@Grade]="Gold",65,
        IF([@Grade]="Silver",50,"No match")
    )
)
```

Even an IFS function alternative is not as clean. This function removes the need to write IF and use multiple brackets. However, it still requires constant referencing of [@Grade].

```
=IFS([@Grade]="Platinum",90,[@Grade]="Gold",65,[@Grade]="Silver",50)
```

Note Creating a lookup table and using a lookup formula such as XLOOKUP to find and return the fees would be even better.

Using Logical Operators

To use logical operators such as >, <, and = in the SWITCH function, there is a little trick. You need to set the expression to True.

In this example, we use a SWITCH function to assign a discount dependent upon the years value (Figure 2-72). Years of 8 or more earns a 15% discount, 4 or more is a 10% discount, and anything else is 0%.

```
=SWITCH(TRUE,[@Years]>=8,15%,[@Years]>=4,10%,0%)
```

The order of the values is very important as the SWITCH function tests from first to last. 9 is larger than both 8 and 4 so we need to ensure that 8 is tested first.

Using the word TRUE in the expression allows us to write values such as [@Years]>=8.

	A	B
1	**Years**	**Discount**
2	1	0%
3	8	15%
4	5	10%
5	10	15%
6	3	0%
7	9	15%
8	4	10%
9	6	10%
10		

Figure 2-72. SWITCH function to apply a discount dependent on years

SWITCH and Other Functions

Formulas can also be used for the expression and for the values to return. This opens more potential.

In this example, we have a table named *Work_Pay* with a column of dates and another column of hours worked. The rate that is paid is different on a Saturday and Sunday than other days of the week.

In the following formula (Figure 2-73), the WEEKDAY function has been used to return the day of the week of the date. It is returned as an index number. The 2 in the WEEKDAY function tells it to start the week on a Monday. This means that Saturday is number 6 and Sunday is number 7.

```
=SWITCH(
    WEEKDAY([@Date],2),
    6,[@Hours]*20.5,7,[@Hours]*18.5,[@Hours]*16.5
)
```

The SWITCH function then tests this result against number 6 (Saturday) first and calculates the pay, then tests against number 7 (Sunday), and then uses the default argument to calculate the pay for any other day of the week.

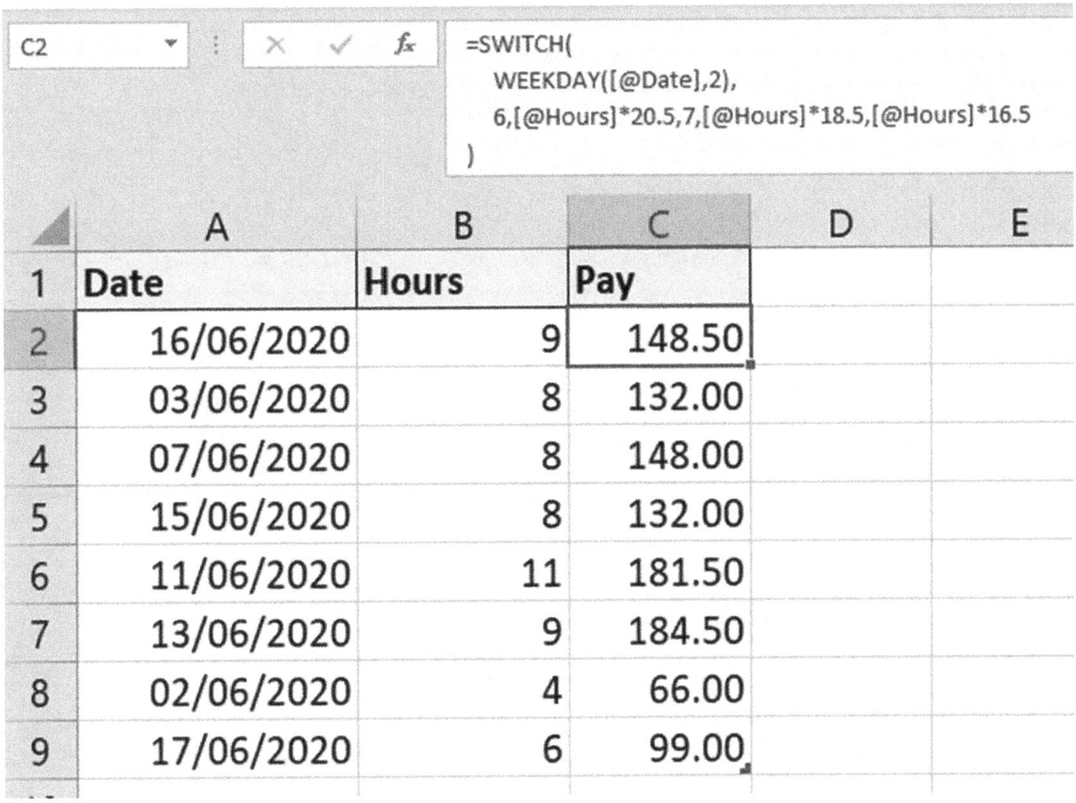

C2			✕	✓	*fx*	=SWITCH(

WEEKDAY([@Date],2),
6,[@Hours]*20.5,7,[@Hours]*18.5,[@Hours]*16.5
)

	A	B	C	D	E
1	Date	Hours	Pay		
2	16/06/2020	9	148.50		
3	03/06/2020	8	132.00		
4	07/06/2020	8	148.00		
5	15/06/2020	8	132.00		
6	11/06/2020	11	181.50		
7	13/06/2020	9	184.50		
8	02/06/2020	4	66.00		
9	17/06/2020	6	99.00		

Figure 2-73. Using formulas in SWITCH for the expression and return values

CHAPTER 3

Advanced Formatting Techniques

You start formatting cells the first day you use an Excel spreadsheet, and then you never stop developing your formatting skills. With some advanced formatting skills, you can give your spreadsheets greater clarity and meaning.

For those involved in creating reports and have a need to track performance to a goal or against a KPI, need to track dates, compare values, or look for trends. Formatting will make what is important "pop" from the screen.

This chapter will explore some advanced Conditional Formatting techniques and then move on to the secret brilliance of custom number formatting.

Conditional Formatting

File   conditional-formatting.xlsx

Conditional Formatting is one of the most used features in Excel. It can do so much, especially when formulas are used within your rules.

In this chapter, we will look at examples of advanced Conditional Formatting techniques and see how they can be applied.

Apply a Rule to an Entire Row

A common question when users first start creating Conditional Formatting rules, is if the rule can be applied to multiple columns or to the entire row.

© Alan Murray 2021
A. Murray, *Advanced Excel Success*, https://doi.org/10.1007/978-1-4842-6467-6_3

Typically, Conditional Formatting rules are applied to single cells, but if you have a table with many columns, this information is not always visible on screen.

In this example, we have a table of members and information such as the date they joined and their membership type (Figure 3-1). We want to format the entire row (columns A:D) for those members with a *Gold* membership.

	A	B	C	D
1	ID	Date Joined	Membership	Price
2	1265	18/03/2012	Bronze	55
3	1542	12/04/2018	Silver	65
4	2734	29/12/2016	Gold	80
5	2145	27/10/2011	Silver	65
6	1460	15/05/2010	Gold	80
7	1298	23/01/2011	Bronze	55
8	1498	20/10/2016	Bronze	55
9	1859	11/03/2010	Bronze	55
10				

Figure 3-1. *Table of members with membership type*

Following on from The Ten Power Functions of Excel chapter, we will continue to use tables where possible to keep our data dynamic and update automatically when additional rows are added.

1. Select all four columns of the table. Ensure that you are selecting the table and not the sheet columns. The arrows are similar, so it is easy to select the wrong area. Figure 3-2 shows the table column selection stops at row 9 (bottom of the table), while selecting the sheet column continues for all 1,048,576 rows.

	A	B	N
1	ID	Date Joined	
2	1265	18/03/2012	B
3	1542	12/04/2018	S
4	2734	29/12/2016	C
5	2145	27/10/2011	S
6	1460	15/05/2010	C
7	1298	23/01/2011	B
8	1498	20/10/2016	B
9	1859	11/03/2010	B

	A ↓	B	Me
1	ID	Date Joined	
2	1265	18/03/2012	Brc
3	1542	12/04/2018	Silv
4	2734	29/12/2016	Go
5	2145	27/10/2011	Silv
6	1460	15/05/2010	Go
7	1298	23/01/2011	Brc
8	1498	20/10/2016	Brc
9	1859	11/03/2010	Brc
10			

Figure 3-2. Selecting a table vs. a sheet column

2. Click **Home ➤ Conditional Formatting ➤ New Rule ➤ Use a formula to determine which cells to format**.

3. Enter the following formula (Figure 3-3). Column C contains the membership type to test, and row 2 is the first row of our selection. The dollar sign before column C keeps this fixed on that column, while the row number will move down to each row of the table to test and format each member.

    `=$C2="Gold"`

Note   Press **F2** to enable "Edit" mode and the ability to move through the formula with the cursor arrows of your keyboard. Otherwise, when you press an arrow key, the formula will point to the active cell. This can be very frustrating, so adopt the habit of pressing F2 as soon as you click the formula box.

You cannot use table references such as [@Membership] in Conditional Formatting rules like we did with the formulas in the previous chapter. Even though we are not referencing the table, the Conditional Formatting will update to new rows that are added.

4. Click **Format** to specify the formatting to apply. Click **OK** when done to close each window.

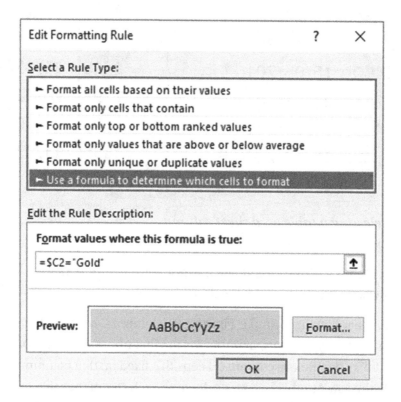

Figure 3-3. *Rule to format the entire row for Gold members*

The Conditional Formatting rule is applied (Figure 3-4). More rules can be added if required.

Note   Formatting is only applied if the formula evaluates to True. Any number other than 0 is True.

	A	B	C	D
1	ID	Date Joined	Membership	Price
2	1265	18/03/2012	Bronze	55
3	1542	12/04/2018	Silver	65
4	2734	29/12/2016	Gold	80
5	2145	27/10/2011	Silver	65
6	1460	15/05/2010	Gold	80
7	1298	23/01/2011	Bronze	55
8	1498	20/10/2016	Bronze	55
9	1859	11/03/2010	Bronze	55
10				

Figure 3-4. Members with a Gold membership formatted in the table

Conditional Formatting with Multiple Columns

Once you know how to reference another cell from a Conditional Formatting rule, testing multiple columns is simple.

In this example, we have a table with member details like the previous example. We want to format the rows where the membership is gold and the years is greater than or equal to 5.

1. Select the four columns of the table.

2. Click **Home ➤ Conditional Formatting ➤ New Rule ➤ Use a formula to determine which cells to format**.

3. Use the following formula. This uses the AND function. With this function, both conditions must be True for the result to be True.

   =AND($B2="Gold",$C2>=5)

4. Click Format and choose the formatting you want to apply.

Only the first two gold memberships are also members for 5 years or more (Figure 3-5).

	A	B	C	D
1	ID	Membership	Years	Price
2	1265	Bronze	5	55
3	1542	Silver	2	65
4	2734	Gold	7	80
5	2145	Silver	4	65
6	1460	Gold	9	80
7	1298	Bronze	3	55
8	1498	Bronze	3	55
9	1859	Gold	4	55
10				

Figure 3-5. *Rule that formats memberships that are gold and >= 5 years*

Let us take this further and format the memberships that are gold or silver and have been members for 5 years or more.

Click **Home ➤ Conditional Formatting ➤ Manage Rules ➤ Edit Rule**.

The following formula can be used as the rule in this example. It uses the OR function to test if the membership is gold or silver and then tests the year condition.

```
=AND(OR($B2="Gold",$B2="Silver"),$C2>=5)
```

No other rows will be formatted as no other membership meets the criteria.

You can of course use any formula you want. We covered many incredible functions in The Ten Power Functions of Excel. The AND and OR functions are brilliant for testing multiple values easily.

Play around to see what is possible. Try some of the other formulas covered in the book. You are on the path to advanced Excel success.

Format Dates That Are Due Soon

Tracking dates such as deadlines and expiry dates are a common requirement of Conditional Formatting.

In this example, we have a table of names and expiry dates for some type of contract (Figure 3-6). We want to apply two Conditional Formatting rules to format:

- Expired dates

- Dates due within the next 21 days

	A	B	C
1	ID	Name	Expiry Date
2	1310	Yoshi Latimer	01/08/2020
3	1333	Patricia McKenna	08/08/2020
4	1265	Helen Bennett	17/09/2020
5	1454	Philip Cramer	04/08/2020
6	1223	Daniel Tonini	08/08/2020
7	1339	Annette Roulet	20/08/2020
8	1368	Renate Messner	30/08/2020
9			

Figure 3-6. *Table of names and expiry dates*

Note   The dates in the screenshot will be different to those on the example file provided. The dates are generated by a formula so that they automatically update, and you can follow along with the examples.

1. Select the *Expired Date* column of the table.

2. Click **Home ➤ Conditional Formatting ➤ Highlight Cells Rules ➤ Less Than.**

3. Enter the following formula into the box (Figure 3-7). The TODAY function returns today's date.

    =TODAY()

4. Select the formatting you want to use from the list.

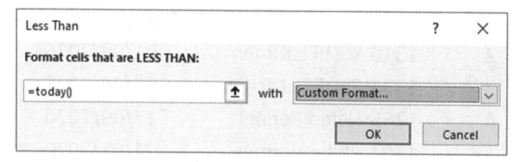

Figure 3-7. *Format cells where the date is less than today's date*

The rule formats the one expired date for Yoshi Latimer (Figure 3-8).

	A	B	C
1	ID	Name	Expiry Date
2	1310	Yoshi Latimer	01/08/2020
3	1333	Patricia McKenna	08/08/2020
4	1265	Helen Bennett	17/09/2020
5	1454	Philip Cramer	04/08/2020
6	1223	Daniel Tonini	08/08/2020
7	1339	Annette Roulet	20/08/2020
8	1368	Renate Messner	30/08/2020
9			

Figure 3-8. Identifying dates that have expired in a table

Let us now format those dates that are due within the next 21 days.

1. Select the *Expired Date* column of the table.

2. Click **Home ➤ Conditional Formatting ➤ Highlight Cells Rules ➤ Between.**

3. In the first box, enter =TODAY( ), and in the second box, enter =TODAY( )+21 (Figure 3-9). This will format a date if it is between today's date and the date in 21 days' time.

4. Specify the formatting you want to use.

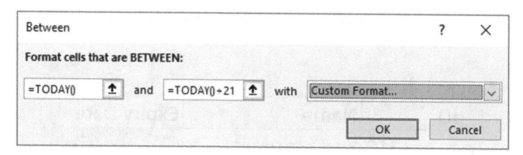

Figure 3-9. *Format dates that occur within the next 21 days*

Four dates are formatted as they occur within the next 21 days of the current date (Figure 3-10).

	A	B	C
1	ID	Name	Expiry Date
2	1310	Yoshi Latimer	04/08/2020
3	1333	Patricia McKenna	11/08/2020
4	1265	Helen Bennett	20/09/2020
5	1454	Philip Cramer	07/08/2020
6	1223	Daniel Tonini	11/08/2020
7	1339	Annette Roulet	23/08/2020
8	1368	Renate Messner	02/09/2020
9			

Figure 3-10. *Conditional Formatting rules identifying expired and due dates*

Format Weekends and Other Important Dates

Often users want to format dates of some significance in a table. Weekend dates are typical, as generally transactions are either lower or higher depending on the nature of your business.

There may be other dates of significance such as holidays, project milestones, office closures, financial deadlines, and so on.

In this example, we have a table of product sales (Figure 3-11) and a table of important dates. We will format the weekend dates in one color and the dates of significance in another color.

▲	A	B	C	D	E	F
1	ID	Pizza	Hot Dogs	Biscuits		Dates
2	06/08/2020	435	422	358		14/08/2020
3	07/08/2020	723	768	382		18/08/2020
4	08/08/2020	421	766	866		25/08/2020
5	09/08/2020	724	885	429		26/08/2020
6	10/08/2020	312	253	702		
7	11/08/2020	700	829	691		
8	12/08/2020	852	792	703		
9	13/08/2020	744	512	437		
10	14/08/2020	666	311	443		
11	15/08/2020	841	297	618		
12	16/08/2020	437	386	873		
13	17/08/2020	363	392	597		
14	18/08/2020	859	882	663		
15	19/08/2020	875	598	791		
16	20/08/2020	311	754	601		
17	21/08/2020	457	335	450		
18	22/08/2020	881	852	680		
19	23/08/2020	482	492	586		
20	24/08/2020	454	369	851		

Figure 3-11. *Product sales table and a table of important dates*

Let us start by creating a rule to format the weekend dates.

1. We will format the entire row, so select all the columns of the table.

2. Click **Home ➤ Conditional Formatting ➤ New Rule ➤ Use a formula to determine which cells to format.**

3. Enter the following formula (Figure 3-12). It uses the WEEKDAY function to return the date's day of the week as an index number. Number 2 specifies that the week starts on a Monday, so any number greater than 5 is therefore Saturday and Sunday.

    `=WEEKDAY($A2,2)>5`

4. Click **Format** to specify the format to apply.

Figure 3-12. Format the weekend dates in a table

Now to format the dates of significance:

1. Select all the columns of the table and start a new rule that uses a formula for the criteria.

2. Enter the following formula (Figure 3-13). It uses the COUNTIFS function to count the occurrences of the dates in the dates table. Any number other than 0 is True, so if the date is in the dates table, then the result is True.

```
=COUNTIFS($F$2:$F$5,$A2)
```

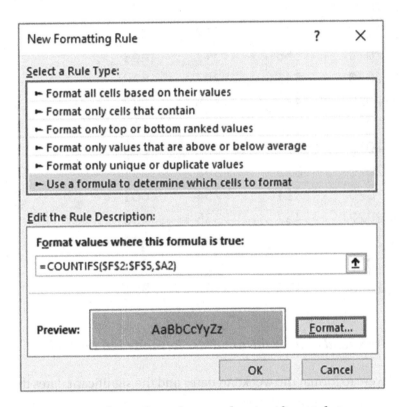

Figure 3-13. *COUNTIFS formula to format the significant dates*

Once again, range references are used, but because the data is formatted as a table, it will update when new dates are added.

The product sales table shows both rules being applied (Figure 3-14).

	A	B	C	D	E	F
1	ID	Pizza	Hot Dogs	Biscuits		Dates
2	06/08/2020	435	422	358		14/08/2020
3	07/08/2020	723	768	382		18/08/2020
4	08/08/2020	421	766	866		25/08/2020
5	09/08/2020	724	885	429		26/08/2020
6	10/08/2020	312	253	702		
7	11/08/2020	700	829	691		
8	12/08/2020	852	792	703		
9	13/08/2020	744	512	437		
10	14/08/2020	666	311	443		
11	15/08/2020	841	297	618		
12	16/08/2020	437	386	873		
13	17/08/2020	363	392	597		
14	18/08/2020	859	882	663		
15	19/08/2020	875	598	791		
16	20/08/2020	311	754	601		
17	21/08/2020	457	335	450		
18	22/08/2020	881	852	680		
19	23/08/2020	482	492	586		
20	24/08/2020	454	369	851		
21						

Figure 3-14. Weekend and significant dates formatted in the table

If the goal were to format the weekend dates and the significant dates the same, we could have used one rule with this formula:

```
=OR(WEEKDAY($A2,2)>5,COUNTIFS($F$2:$F$5,$A2))
```

The OR function ensures that if either condition were True, the rows would be formatted.

Compare Two Lists

Conditional Formatting is an awesome way to visualize the differences between two lists. Which items are in both lists? Or which items are in one list and not the other?

In this example, we have two tables of attendees. The first table is named *Attendees1* and the second named *Attendees2*. We would like to identify the names in *Attendees1* that also appear in *Attendees2* (Figure 3-15).

	A	B	C	D	E	F
1	ID	Name			ID	Name
2	1517	Alejandra Camino			1454	Philip Cramer
3	1310	Yoshi Latimer			1310	Yoshi Latimer
4	1333	Patricia McKenna			1368	Renate Messner
5	1265	Helen Bennett			1265	Helen Bennett
6	1149	Jonas Bergulfsen			1223	Daniel Tonini
7	1454	Philip Cramer			1339	Annette Roulet
8	1223	Daniel Tonini			1333	Patricia McKenna
9	1339	Annette Roulet				
10	2018	Anabela Domingues				
11	1368	Renate Messner				

Figure 3-15. *Two lists of attendees to compare the differences*

1. Select the two columns of *Attendees1*.

2. Click **Home ➤ Conditional Formatting ➤ New Rule ➤ Use a formula to determine which cells to format**.

3. Enter the following formula in the box provided and specify the format to apply:

   ```
   =COUNTIFS($E$2:$E$8,$A2)
   ```

The names in *Attendees1* that also appear in *Attendees2* are formatted (Figure 3-16).

This formula works because it counts the occurrences of the names in the second list using the unique ID. Any number other than 0 is True, so if they appear in the second list, then the formula evaluates to True.

Note   You cannot use table references in a Conditional Formatting rule. However, despite the reference to range $E$2:$E$8, the rule will update if rows are added or removed from the second table.

▲	A	B	C	D	E	F
1	ID	Name			ID	Name
2	1517	Alejandra Camino			1454	Philip Cramer
3	1310	Yoshi Latimer			1310	Yoshi Latimer
4	1333	Patricia McKenna			1368	Renate Messner
5	1265	Helen Bennett			1265	Helen Bennett
6	1149	Jonas Bergulfsen			1223	Daniel Tonini
7	1454	Philip Cramer			1339	Annette Roulet
8	1223	Daniel Tonini			1333	Patricia McKenna
9	1339	Annette Roulet				
10	2018	Anabela Domingues				
11	1368	Renate Messner				
12						

Figure 3-16. *Formatting the names that appear in both lists*

If we wanted to format the names that do not appear in the second list, we can simply add =0 to the end of the formula:

```
=COUNTIFS($E$2:$E$8,$A2)=0
```

The three names that appear in *Attendees1* and not *Attendees2* are formatted (Figure 3-17).

	A	B	C	D	E	F
1	ID	Name			ID	Name
2	1517	Alejandra Camino			1454	Philip Cramer
3	1310	Yoshi Latimer			1310	Yoshi Latimer
4	1333	Patricia McKenna			1368	Renate Messner
5	1265	Helen Bennett			1265	Helen Bennett
6	1149	Jonas Bergulfsen			1223	Daniel Tonini
7	1454	Philip Cramer			1339	Annette Roulet
8	1223	Daniel Tonini			1333	Patricia McKenna
9	1339	Annette Roulet				
10	2018	Anabela Domingues				
11	1368	Renate Messner				
12						

Figure 3-17. *Names that appear in the first list but not the second*

Icon Sets to Show Change

The icon sets in Conditional Formatting are great. With icon sets, we can use arrows, flags, traffic lights, and other icons as a quick visual representation of met targets and number variance.

In this example, we have a table with the sales performance of our sales reps this week and last week (Figure 3-18). A column has been created with the following formula to calculate the percentage increase/decrease this week compared to the previous week:

```
=([@[This Week]]-[@[Last Week]])/[@[Last Week]]
```

	A	B	C	D
1	Name	Last Week	This Week	Variance
2	Kathy	£ 14,000	£ 15,698	12%
3	Sue	£ 5,000	£ 6,424	28%
4	Tom	£ 7,000	£ 14,127	102%
5	Mel	£ 12,000	£ 5,361	-55%
6	Arnold	£ 5,000	£ 8,535	71%
7	Kim	£ 7,000	£ 7,440	6%
8	Craig	£ 7,000	£ 4,875	-30%

Figure 3-18. *Table with last week and this week sales*

We would like to use the green up arrow and red down arrow icons to show the sales value change.

We do not want to show the percentage variance, so this will be hidden. The formula is only used so that we can create the Conditional Formatting rule.

1. Select the *Variance* column of the table.

2. Click **Home ➤ Conditional Formatting ➤ New Rule** (this is quicker than selecting the arrows through the icon sets option and then going back to edit them).

3. Select **Icon Sets** from the *Format Style* list and then the arrow icons from the *Icon Style* list (Figure 3-19).

4. Adjust the *Type* column from percentage to **Number**. Change the logical symbol from >= to > for the green arrow. Ensure both values are set to **0**.

5. Check the box to **Show Icon Only**.

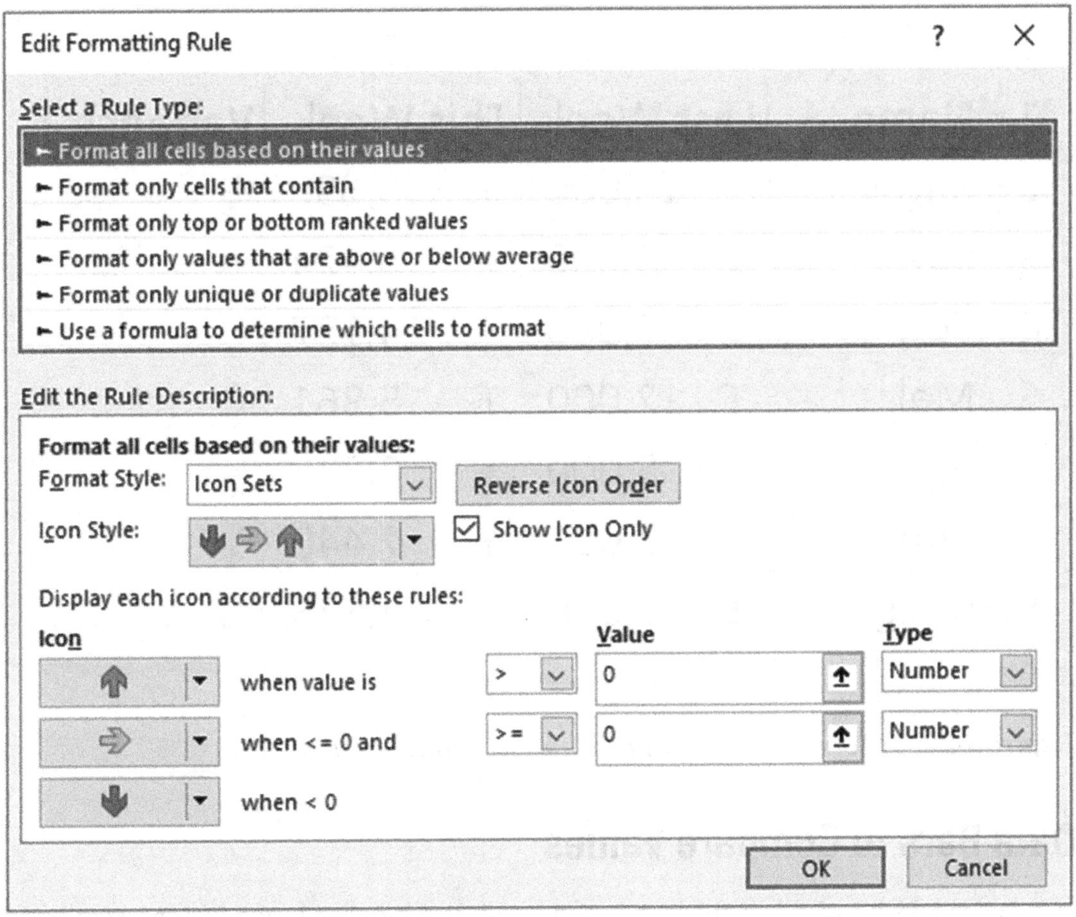

Figure 3-19. *Formatting rule to display arrow icons to visualize variance*

The arrow icons are shown visualizing that the sales value was down for two sales reps (Figure 3-20).

Any formula can be used as the base for your icon sets rule. This gives us great flexibility. We could have applied icon sets instead of formatting the row in the previous "compare two lists" example, by using the COUNTIFS function in a column.

Think about what formulas you could use and how they could benefit your reports.

◢	A	B	C	D
1	**Name**	**Last Week**	**This Week**	**Variance**
2	Kathy	£ 14,000	£ 15,698	⬆
3	Sue	£ 5,000	£ 6,424	⬆
4	Tom	£ 7,000	£ 14,127	⬆
5	Mel	£ 12,000	£ 5,361	⬇
6	Arnold	£ 5,000	£ 8,535	⬆
7	Kim	£ 7,000	£ 7,440	⬆
8	Craig	£ 7,000	£ 4,875	⬇
9				

Figure 3-20. *Arrow icons to compare this week and last week sales*

Data Bars to Compare Values

Data bars make it easy to see the largest and smallest values in a range. This makes them perfect for comparing values.

In this example, we have a table of products and their sales values. We will use data bars to compare each product's performance.

1. Select the column of values.

2. Click **Home ➤ Conditional Formatting ➤ Data bars**. Select the color you want to use (I am a fan of the solid fill option over gradient fill).

The data bars are displayed in the column cells along with the value (Figure 3-21).

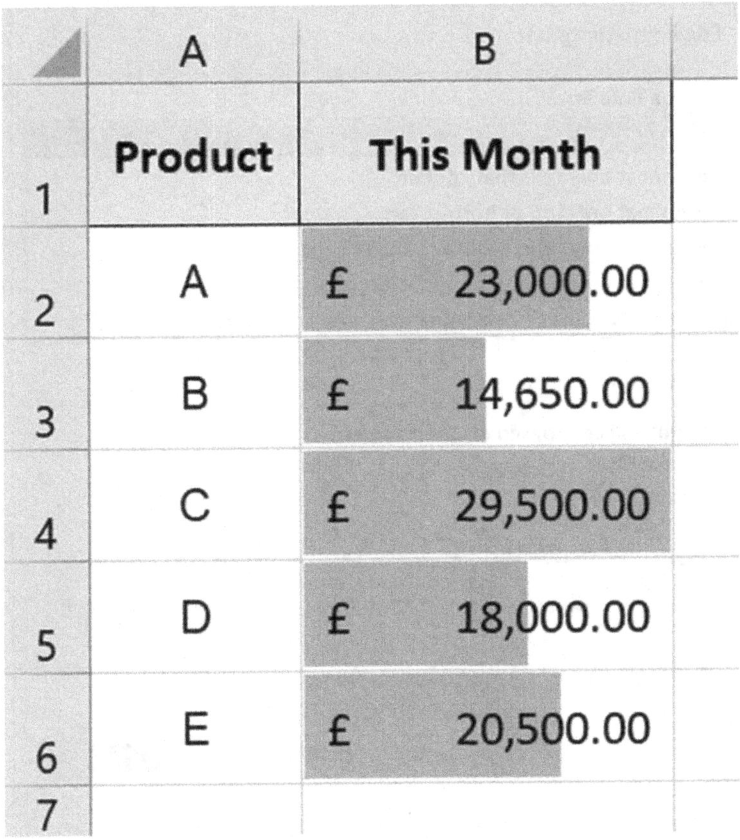

	A	B
1	**Product**	**This Month**
2	A	£ 23,000.00
3	B	£ 14,650.00
4	C	£ 29,500.00
5	D	£ 18,000.00
6	E	£ 20,500.00
7		

Figure 3-21. *Data bars showing sales performance of products*

By default, the data bars will automatically work out the minimum and maximum values for the bars. For the maximum value, the data bar covers the entire cell.

To change this and other aspects of data bars such as color, click **Conditional Formatting ➤ Manage Rules ➤ Edit Rule**.

The *Edit Formatting Rule* dialog window (Figure 3-22) provides a few options for changing your data bars. These include setting your own minimum and maximum values.

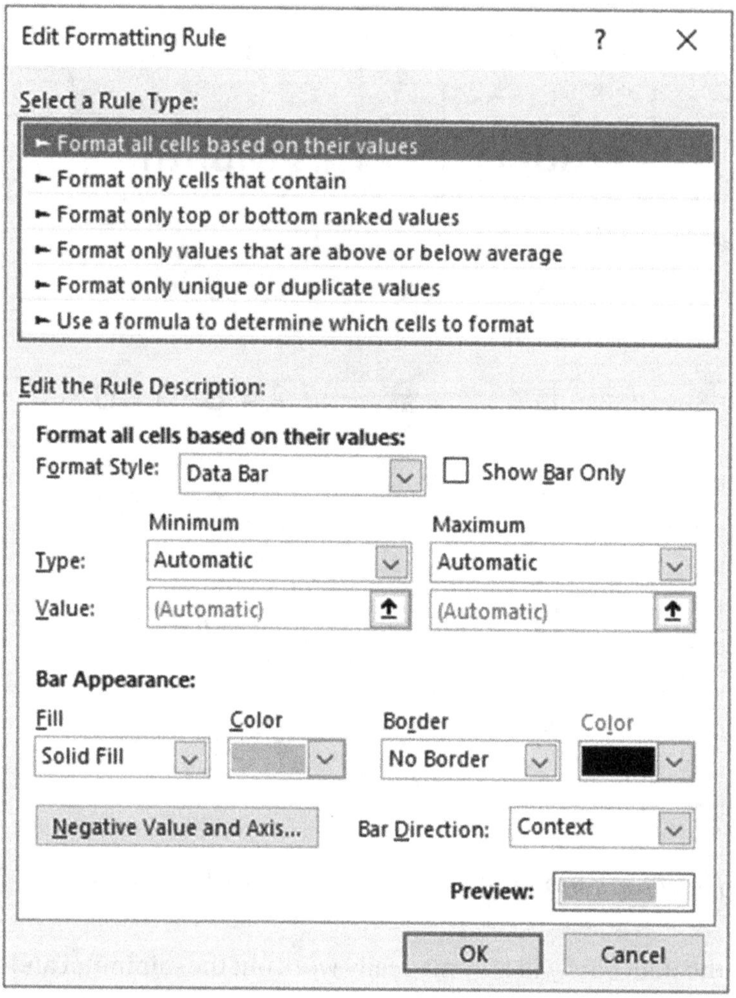

Figure 3-22. *Options to customize your data bars*

Data Bars to Show Progress Toward a Goal

Data bars are also great for showing progress toward a goal. In this example, we have some tasks and their percentage complete (Figure 3-23). We will visualize this progress in a different column using data bars.

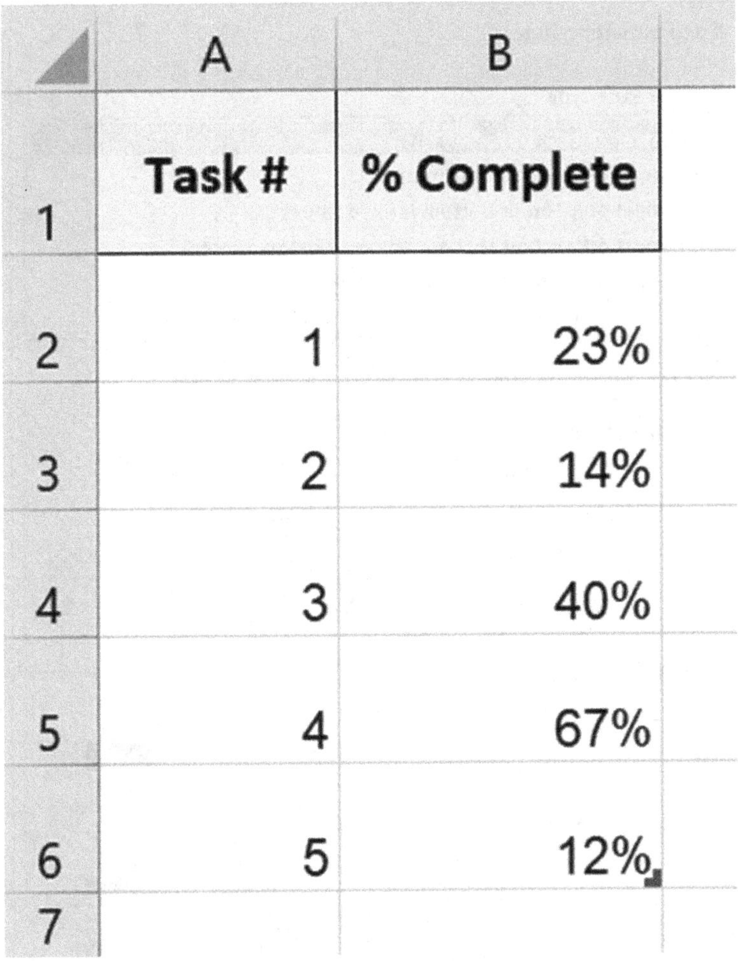

	A	B
1	**Task #**	**% Complete**
2	1	23%
3	2	14%
4	3	40%
5	4	67%
6	5	12%
7		

Figure 3-23. *Task list and their percentage complete*

1. Add a new column to the table and use the formula
   =[@[% Complete]] to link to the percentage complete values.

2. Select the added column and click **Home ➤ Conditional
   Formatting ➤ Data Bars ➤ More Rules**.

3. Check the box to **Show Bar Only** (Figure 3-24).

4. Change the *Type* field for *Minimum* and *Maximum* to **Number**.
   Enter **0** for the minimum value and **1** for the maximum value.

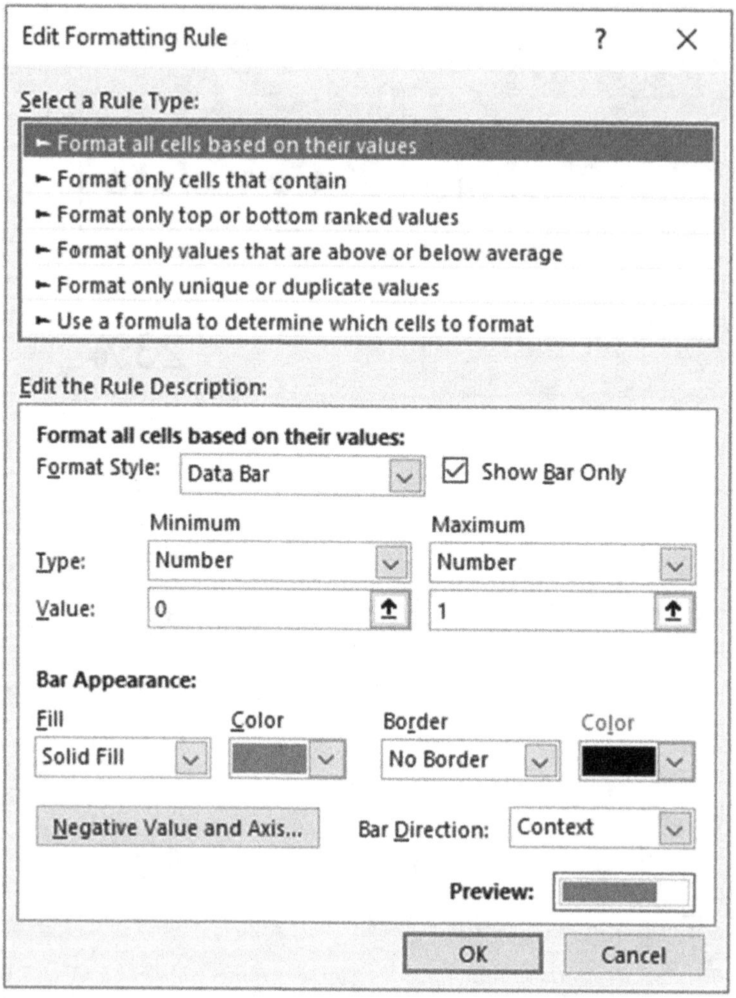

Figure 3-24. *Edit the min and max values of data bars*

The progress bars are shown in their own column next to the percentage complete (Figure 3-25). As this was a progress toward 100%, we set 1 as the maximum value.

You can also refer to another cell for the minimum or maximum value. This is helpful if these values are dependent upon a formula or changed regularly by a user.

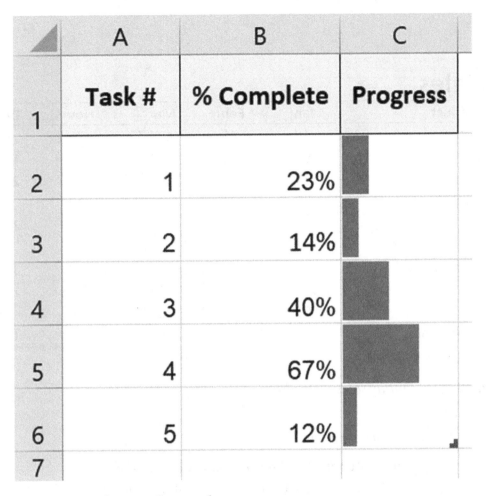

Figure 3-25. *Data bars to show task progress*

Create a Heat Map with Color Scales

Heat maps are used to direct a user's attention to what matters. They are used to show patterns and trends. They focus a user's attention on areas either by location, time, or parts of a surface such as a web page.

In this example, we have a list of ten products and their sales over 12 months (Figure 3-26). We will use the color scales option of Conditional Formatting to visualize the trends and patterns over the year of these product sales.

	A	B	C	D	L	M
1						
2	**Sales**					
3	**Product**	**Jan**	**Feb**	**Mar**	**Nov**	**Dec**
4	Pizza	48	48	134	75	38
5	Hot Dogs	97	113	141	130	127
6	Burgers	249	228	315	304	298
7	Apple Juice	25	21	46	48	33
8	Biscuits	271	227	317	331	276
9	Chicken Wings	49	44	61	62	49
10	Waffles	350	275	356	370	339
11	Coffee	176	135	213	208	183
12	Crisps	63	55	113	68	61
13	Sandwiches	68	74	65	109	105
14						

Figure 3-26. *Monthly sales of products*

1. Select the *Jan* to *Dec* columns.

2. Click *Home* ➤ *Conditional Formatting* ➤ *Color Scales* (Figure 3-27). Select the first option. This applies green to the largest values in the range and red to the smallest values.

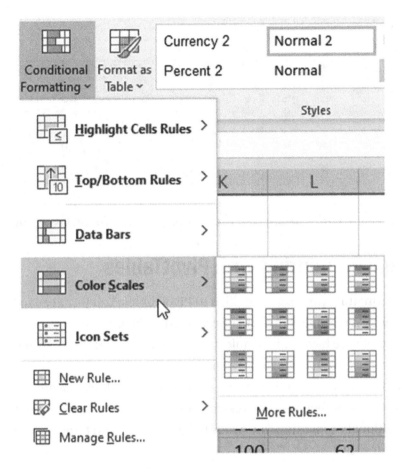

Figure 3-27. *Apply the color scales rule to the sales data*

This now makes it simple to see that the sales of biscuits and waffles were high for all 12 months. Also, the period between July and October was the best for all products (Figure 3-28).

◢	A	B	C	D	E	F	G	H	I	J	K	L	M
1													
2	**Sales**												
3	Product	Jan	Feb	Mar	Apr	May	Jun	Jul	Aug	Sep	Oct	Nov	Dec
4	Pizza	48	48	134	183	269	349	292	242	181	163	75	38
5	Hot Dogs	97	113	141	167	283	306	169	263	291	290	130	127
6	Burgers	249	228	315	339	396	355	402	365	343	253	304	298
7	Apple Juice	25	21	46	54	70	59	94	119	89	67	48	33
8	Biscuits	271	227	317	325	367	374	350	368	331	323	331	276
9	Chicken Wings	49	44	61	50	60	65	127	173	107	100	62	49
10	Waffles	350	275	356	349	447	399	427	435	437	333	370	339
11	Coffee	176	135	213	231	261	253	317	350	280	233	208	183
12	Crisps	63	55	113	133	250	328	268	294	188	150	68	61
13	Sandwiches	68	74	65	52	69	106	170	293	287	208	109	105
14													

Figure 3-28. *Color scales applied to the 12 months' product sales values*

Conditional Formatting with PivotTables

Conditional Formatting can also be applied to PivotTables. You just need to be careful what values the rule is applied to avoid unexpected results.

In this example, we have a PivotTable with sales to customers in Denmark summarized by the product category (Figure 3-29).

We want to use icon sets to show a green circle for the values that are greater than or equal to 2800 and an amber/yellow circle for the values greater than or equal to 1200.

This Conditional Formatting rule needs to ignore the grand totals for the customers and product categories.

◢	A	B		C		D	
1	Country	Denmark	🔽				
2							
3	Total sales		↴				
4	🔽	Simons bistro		Vaffeljernet		Grand Total	
5	Beverages	£	13,175	£	1,735	£	14,910
6	Condiments	£	911	£	3,624	£	4,535
7	Confections	£	994	£	1,896	£	2,890
8	Dairy Products	£	1,276	£	1,586	£	2,861
9	Grains/Cereals			£	100	£	100
10	Meat/Poultry	£	1,080	£	2,512	£	3,592
11	Produce	£	1,193	£	2,762	£	3,955
12	Seafood	£	1,073	£	2,913	£	3,986
13	Grand Total	£	19,702	£	17,127	£	36,829
14							

Figure 3-29. *PivotTable showing sales to customers in Denmark*

1. Click any cell in the PivotTable.

2. Click **Home ➤ Conditional Formatting ➤ New Rule**.

3. Select ***All cells showing "Total sales" values for "Product Category" and "Customer Name"*** from the *Apply rule to* area of the window (Figure 3-30). The options here will change depending on the labels in your PivotTable.

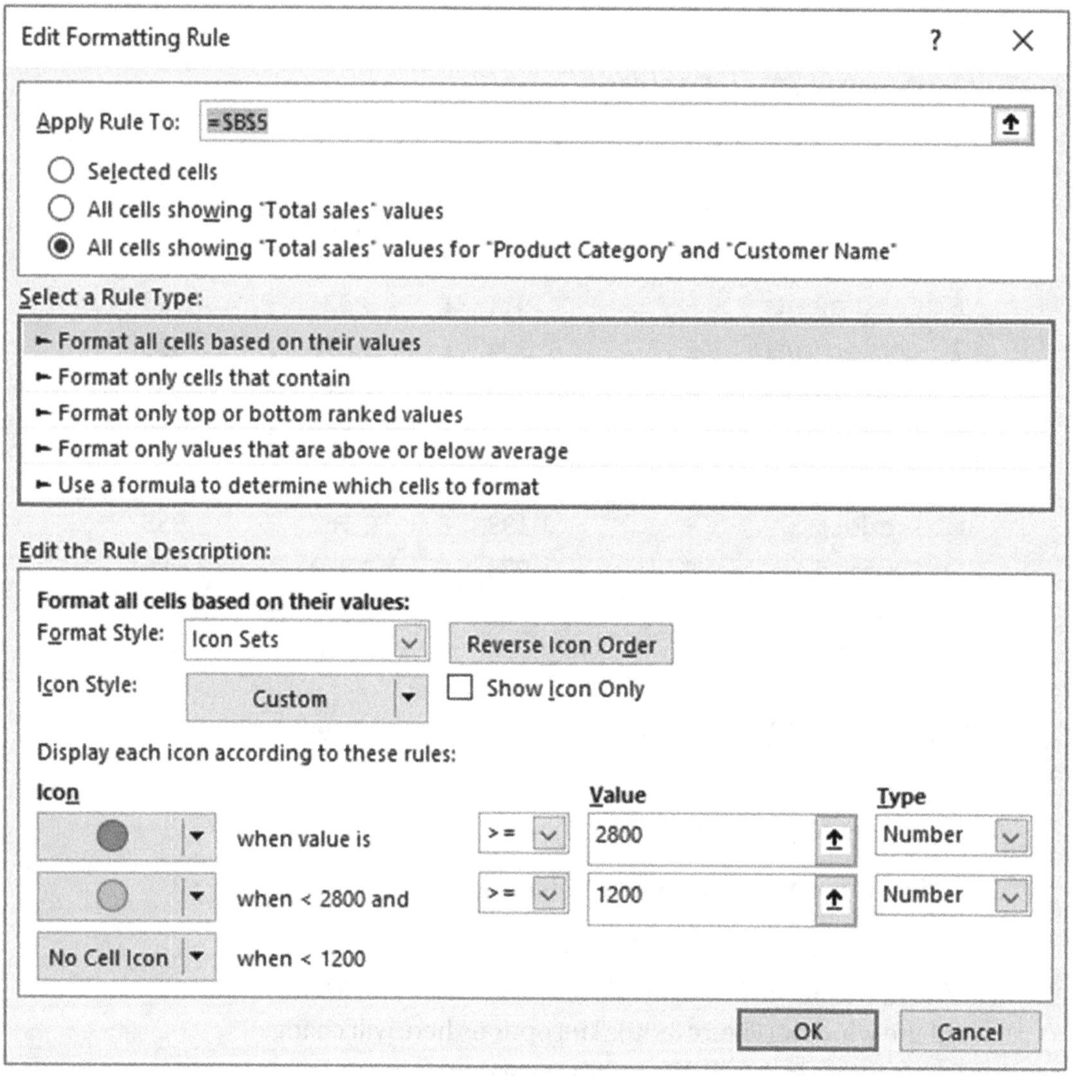

Figure 3-30. *Apply an icon set rule to PivotTable values*

This step ensures that the grand total values will not be formatted.

4. Select **Icon Sets** for the *Format Style* and choose the green, amber, and red circles for the *Icon Style*.

5. Click the arrow next to the red circle icon and select **No Cell Icon** to turn it off.

6. Select **Number** in the *Type* column for both rules. Enter **2800** for the green circle rule and **1200** for the amber/yellow circle rule.

The Conditional Formatting rule is applied only to the values for customers and product category (Figure 3-31).

◢	A	B	C	D
1	Country	Denmark .▼		
2				
3	Total sales	↵		
4	↵	Simons bistro	Vaffeljernet	Grand Total
5	Beverages	● £ 13,175	○ £ 1,735	£ 14,910
6	Condiments	£ 911	● £ 3,624	£ 4,535
7	Confections	£ 994	○ £ 1,896	£ 2,890
8	Dairy Products	○ £ 1,276	○ £ 1,586	£ 2,861
9	Grains/Cereals		£ 100	£ 100
10	Meat/Poultry	£ 1,080	○ £ 2,512	£ 3,592
11	Produce	£ 1,193	◐ £ 2,762	£ 3,955
12	Seafood	£ 1,073	● £ 2,913	£ 3,986
13	Grand Total	£ 19,702	£ 17,127	£ 36,829
14				

Figure 3-31. *Icon sets showing top performing values in a PivotTable*

In-Cell Charts with the REPT Function

File   in-cell-charts.xlsx

There is a fabulous technique to create in-cell charts using the REPT function and some specific formatting. These in-cell charts are a great alternative to using data bars and icon sets.

What makes these a great option is that they are created using a formula, so we have lots of control over how to use them. Also, we can add further Conditional Formatting rules to change their color dependent on conditions (Figure 3-32). You cannot do this with data bars.

	A	B	C
1	**Name**	**Score**	
2	Maurine Krieger	71	71
3	Rosalina Reach	36	36
4	Mikki Rein	55	55
5	Li Xi	87	87
6	Reena Hentz	24	24
7	June Foster	89	89
8	Dan Brown	94	94

Figure 3-32. In-cell charts using the Stencil font and an added conditional rule

We have a range with a column of names and another with score values. In column C, we will create the in-cell charts shown in Figure 3-32.

We will use the REPT function, which repeats a value a specified number of times. The pipe symbol (|) will be repeated the number of times shown in column B using REPT.

Note   The pipe symbol (or vertical bar) is usually found on the same key as the backslash character.

---

1. In cell C2, enter the following formula and copy down:

    ```
    =REPT("|",B2)&" "&B2
    ```

This formula concatenates the score onto the end of the repeated pipe symbol, just like the data labels of a bar chart.

2. This looks terrible at the moment, so let's change the font. Change the font of the cells to *Playbill* or *Stencil*. Both of these work well.

3. Change the font color to something better. I have decided on green (Figure 3-33).

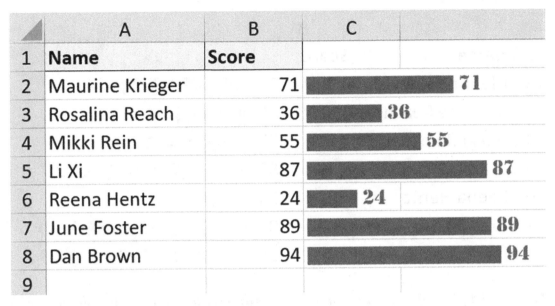

Figure 3-33. In-cell charts using the REPT function and Stencil font

---

Note   If the value being repeated is large, divide it by a value to reduce the number of times the character is repeated.

Because these mini charts are created by using a formula and some font formatting, we are not constrained to a few options like we are with data bars.

Let us add a Conditional Formatting rule to the cells that changes the color of any score less than 60.

4.   Select range C2:C8 and click **Home ➤ Conditional Formatting ➤ New Rule ➤ Use a formula to determine which cells to format**.

5.   Enter the following formula. It refers to the scores in column B and tests if the value is less than 60.

     =B2<60

6.   Click **Format** and choose the formatting you want to use.

We have our completed in-cell charts. They enable us to easily compare the scores and see who met the threshold of 60 (Figure 3-34).

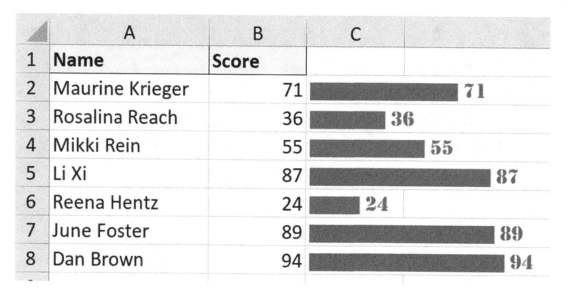

Figure 3-34. *In-cell charts to compare scores and see who met the threshold*

There is much potential with in-cell charts. They are driven using a formula so you can use any criteria needed and add whatever Conditional Formatting rules you might want.

You can also use any symbol Excel will accept. There is a large gallery of symbols in Excel including emojis, thumbs up, currency symbols, and images of objects such as planes.

Custom Number Formatting

File   custom-number-formatting.xlsx

Custom number formatting gives you complete control over how cell content looks. It does not change its value, only its appearance.

You access custom number formatting from the **Custom** category on the **Number** tab of the **Format Cells** dialog window (Figure 3-35).

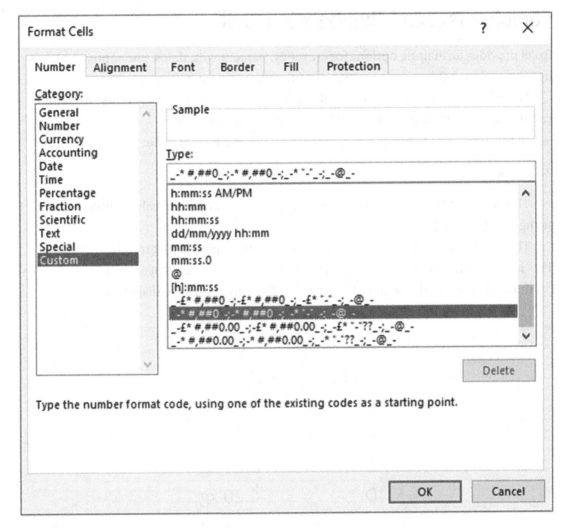

Figure 3-35. *Custom number formatting area of the Format Cells window*

In the *Type* box, you can write or edit a number format. There are many different characters with different roles in formatting.

We will not list the meaning of each character in this book, but instead focus on "real-world" examples of their use.

A number format is split into four sections. Each section controls how a specific type of value is formatted. The sections are separated by semicolons. You do not have to use all four.

```
Positive number; Negative number; Zero value; Text
```

Let us look at some useful examples of custom number formatting.

Combine Text and Numbers in a Cell

Excel provides formatting options for currency, percentages, dates, and more, but it has not covered everything, and you may need to create your own formats.

For example, we have a list of weights which are measured in kilograms. We want to create a format with the unit symbol "kg" after the numeric value.

In the Type box of Format Cells, enter the following format code:

```
0.00 "kg"
```

This formats the values to two decimal places and follows the value with the text string "kg" (Figure 3-36).

The number format character zero (0) forces the display to that number of digits. This is represented well with products C and D. Product C is displayed as 0.86, and product D is displayed as 4.20 rather than 4.2. The zero forces the display to 0.00.

	A	B
1	Product	Weight
2	A	15.13 kg
3	B	10.90 kg
4	C	0.86 kg
5	D	4.20 kg
6	E	12.28 kg
7	F	12.97 kg
8	G	19.47 kg
9	H	4.14 kg
10		

Figure 3-36. *Combine text and numbers in a cell*

The hash or pound sign (#) is the placeholder for optional digits. If the format code #.## "kg" was used, then product C would display as .86 kg and product D as 4.2 kg.

You can also mix the two placeholders. For example, use #.00 "kg" to force the display of two decimal places.

Remember, this does not change the value in the cell. It is just the values' appearance. They are still numeric, and you can perform mathematical operations on them.

Show the Weekday of a Date

Let us now look at a custom number formatting example with dates. Excel offers a limited list of date formats, and displaying the weekday is not in the list.

Enter the following format code into the Type box of Format Cells. This will show the weekday in a shortened form before the date (Figure 3-37).

ddd dd/mm/yyyy

	A	B	C
1	**Date**	**Total**	
2	Thu 26/03/2020	500	
3	Thu 23/04/2020	640	
4	Sun 28/06/2020	186	
5	Thu 18/06/2020	678	
6	Fri 22/05/2020	717	
7	Mon 11/05/2020	172	
8	Sat 15/02/2020	101	
9	Mon 08/06/2020	725	
10	Mon 27/04/2020	161	
11	Sun 24/05/2020	213	
12	Tue 28/01/2020	419	

Figure 3-37. *Display the weekday of a date*

As you can imagine, the number of d's entered will change how the day is represented (Table 3-1).

Table 3-1. *List of day codes and formats*

Code	Format
d	9
dd	09
ddd	Sun
dddd	Sunday

The same works with the month and the use of the letter m in the format code.

We can get inventive with this. In Chapter 2, there was an example of the SUMPRODUCT function summing the values from a specific month. The month number was entered in a cell to specify which month to sum.

It would be better to select a month using a drop-down list of month names rather than enter a month number.

In this example, a list has been created for the first of each month, that is, 01/01/2020, 01/02/2020, and so on. It does not matter what the date is, as long as we have one for each month of the year (Figure 3-38). This list is then formatted with the custom number format code of *mmmm.*

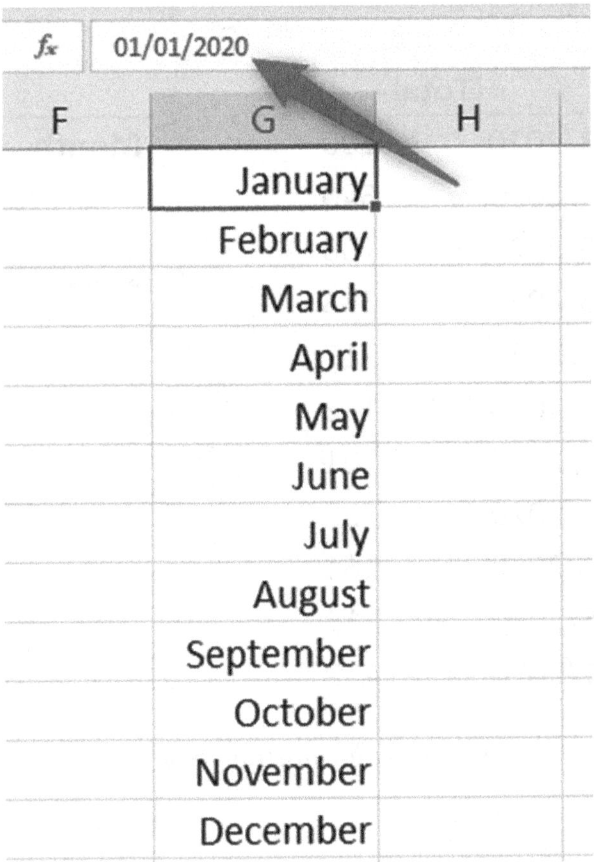

Figure 3-38. *List of dates formatted to show month names*

In cell D3, a Data Validation list is then created from the list of dates/months in range G1:G12.

The following SUMPRODUCT function can then be used in cell E3 (Figure 3-39):

```
=SUMPRODUCT((MONTH(Sales[Date])=MONTH(D3))*Sales[Total])
```

	A	B	C	D	E
1	**Date**	**Total**			
2	Thu 26/03/2020	500		**Month**	**Total Sales**
3	Thu 23/04/2020	640		June	1,589.00
4	Sun 28/06/2020	186	May		
5	Thu 18/06/2020	678	June		
6	Fri 22/05/2020	717	July		
7	Mon 11/05/2020	172	August		
8	Sat 15/02/2020	101	September		
9	Mon 08/06/2020	725	October		
10	Mon 27/04/2020	161	November		
11	Sun 24/05/2020	213	December		
12	Tue 28/01/2020	419			

Figure 3-39. *Using custom number formatting for a nice month name drop-down list*

It tests the month of the *Date* column against the month of the date in cell D3. Remember, although you can see the month name in the list, it is a list of dates.

Keep the Leading Zeroes of a Value

When you enter numbers such as 007 or 051 in Excel, the leading zeroes are removed as they are unnecessary, and Excel is tidying up your formatting.

However, you may need the leading zeroes. The most common approach to dealing with this issue is to format the cells as text. This can be done in the Format Cells window or by typing an apostrophe (') before the number.

This is a useful solution unless you need it to remain a numeric value. Another reason could be that the values need to be a specific number of digits. Using custom number formatting, we can format the cell to add leading zeroes up to a specified number of digits.

If we need the values to be five digits in length, the following format code can be used (Figure 3-40):

00000

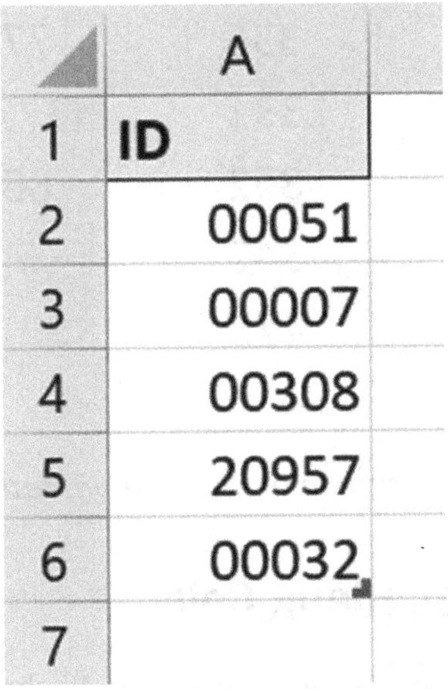

Figure 3-40. *Leading zeroes so all values are five digits in length*

Now when a user enters a number such as 308, two leading zeroes are added to make it five digits, 00308.

Display Negative Values in Red

Format codes are made up of four sections separated by semicolons: positive; negative; zero value; text.

To specify how negative values should be displayed, we need the second section of the format code.

To make things easier, there are built-in custom number formats that we can select and edit. There are already some format codes that display negative values in red. It makes sense to choose one of these.

In this example, I selected one with zero decimal places and added parentheses around the negative number instead of the negative sign (Figure 3-41).

#,##0;[Red](#,##0)

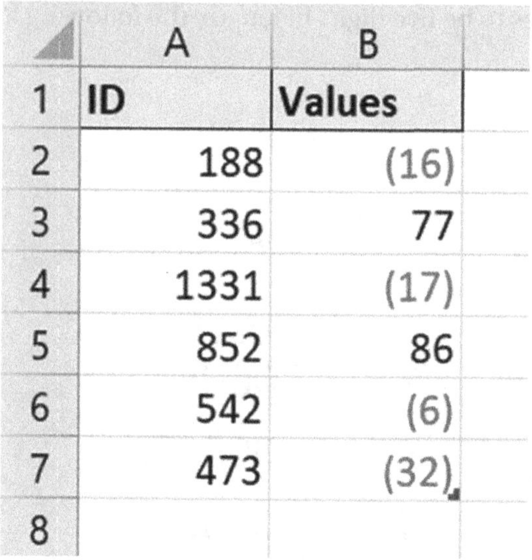

◢	A	B	
1	ID	Values	
2	188	(16)	
3	336	77	
4	1331	(17)	
5	852	86	
6	542	(6)	
7	473	(32)	
8			

Figure 3-41. *Negative values shown in red with parentheses*

Show Zero Values as Blank Cells

The zero value is the third section in the format code. To change how zero values are shown, we enter what we want in this section.

We could display a dash (-) like the accounting format does. Or maybe display the text "zero".

In this example, we want to hide the zero value. We have a table of scores, and the zero is for students who have not taken the test yet. A zero is misleading as it is not their score.

The following format code is used:

```
0;;;
```

This code uses a whole number for the score (positive number) and then ignores negative numbers and zero values. This is done by adding the semicolons and not specifying formatting for that section. A blank cell is shown for the zeroes (Figure 3-42).

	A	B	
1	**Name**	**Scores**	
2	Maurine Krieger	75	
3	Rosalina Reach		
4	Mikki Rein	20	
5	Li Xi	57	
6	Reena Hentz		
7	June Foster	44	
8	Dan Brown	40	
9			

Figure 3-42. *Hide the zero values*

Format Time to Show Duration over 24 Hours

There is a custom number format to display duration over the limit of the standard time unit, for example, 24 hours or 60 minutes. It is to enclose the time unit in square brackets, for example, [h] and [m].

This is useful when calculating duration on timesheets and project trackers.

In this example, we have a table of time spent completing tasks. It is displayed in hours, minutes, and seconds. There is a SUM function in cell D3 to find the total duration (Figure 3-43).

On entering the SUM function, the result is shown as 05:23:02. This is using the default time format of hh:mm:ss. It is only showing the remaining hours after completed days.

To display hours over the 24-hour limit, enclose the hours in square brackets.

[h]:mm

There is a custom number format already provided for this, but it is easier to type this into the Type box. Seconds have been excluded from the result.

The same technique can be used to display minutes or seconds over 60.

⬗	A	B	C	D
1	Task	Duration		
2	1	04:34:20		Total
3	2	10:04:53		29:23
4	3	02:05:35		
5	4	08:42:13		
6	5	03:56:01		
7				

Figure 3-43. *Display duration over 24 hours*

CHAPTER 4

Advanced Chart Tricks

Everybody loves a good chart. However, you find many users stick to the standard chart types provided by Excel and a few tweaks of the standard settings.

You can create some very useful charts that present data effectively with the standard settings. But there is so much more to explore. By combining your charts with the power of tables, formulas, formatting, and Power Query, you can take your charts to the next level.

There are books dedicated to charts in Excel, but we only have this chapter. The rule is to keep it simple but be creative. Let tools such as Power Query and formulas do the heavy lifting and allow charts to focus on effective presentation.

This chapter will cover a variety of advanced charting tricks. These include automatically changing the color of key metrics, dynamically sorting chart data, adding charts that shift with time, and building creative chart labels.

Dynamic Charts

File   dynamic-charts.xlsx

We want to remove as many manual tasks as we can from our day-to-day Excel work. We want to save time and improve accuracy.

There was a focus in Chapter 2 - The Ten Power Functions of Excel with keeping everything dynamic by basing them on tables or dynamic array formulas. It will be more of the same with our Excel charts.

We want our charts to automatically adjust if data is added or removed from its source. This includes expanding to new data, sorting values, and rolling with time.

© Alan Murray 2021
A. Murray, *Advanced Excel Success*, https://doi.org/10.1007/978-1-4842-6467-6_4

Dynamic Chart Range with Tables

The easiest way to ensure that your charts automatically update when new data is added is to use data formatted as a table for its source.

When new rows or columns are added to a table, it automatically expands. If our charts use a table for their source, they will automatically update too.

In this example, we have a table named *Sales_Summary* with the sales of products. We will create a clustered column chart.

1. Select the table data.

2. Click the **Insert** tab and select the **2D Clustered Column Chart**.

That is it! Nothing more to do (Figure 4-1).

If more data is added to the *Sales_Summary* table, the column chart will automatically add the product to the axis and plot the data.

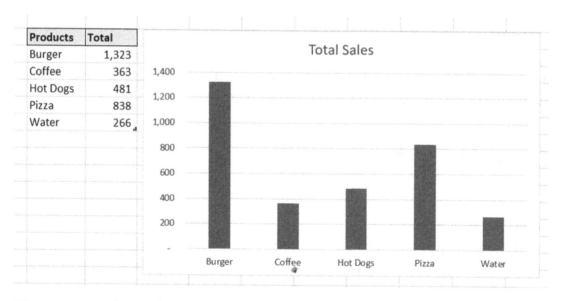

Figure 4-1. *Column chart using data formatted as a table*

If you select the chart and click **Chart Design ➤ Select Data** to view the data source for the chart, you may be surprised to see it references the range 'From Table'!$F$3:$G$7 (Figure 4-2). You may have expected to see the table name *Sales_Summary* like you would in a PivotTable data source or a formula.

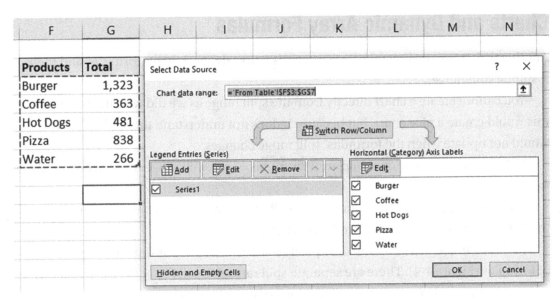

Figure 4-2. Data source for the column chart

Despite the table not being mentioned, rest assured that the chart will react if the table data is changed.

You can check this by resizing the table using the blue handle in its bottom-right corner (Figure 4-3). The chart will adapt to the table range.

Products	Total
Burger	1,323
Coffee	363
Hot Dogs	481
Pizza	838
Water	266

Figure 4-3. The chart will automatically adapt if the table is resized

Charts and Dynamic Array Formulas

Another way to create dynamic chart ranges is to use dynamic array formulas and their resulting spill range.

You cannot create a chart directly from the spill range as we did with the table. Doing this would create a nice chart, but because it does not understand the spill range, it would not update when the formulas' spill range changes.

You also cannot write dynamic array formulas or use spill range references directly in the chart's source.

The way around this is to reference the spill range in a defined name and then use the defined name as the source for the chart elements.

In this example, we have the same product sales data, but this time they are the result of formulas (Figure 4-4). There are separate spill ranges in cell F3 for the distinct list of products and cell G3 for the total sales of each of those products.

F	G	H
Products	**Total**	
Pizza	838	
Coffee	363	
Burger	1,323	
Hot Dogs	481	
Water	266	

Figure 4-4. *Dynamic array formula spill ranges*

Let us begin by creating a defined name for each spill range.

1. Click cell F3 (the location of the spill range).

2. Click **Formulas ➤ Define Name**.

3. Enter a meaningful name. *Product_Labels* has been used here.

4. Type a hash (#) at the end of the F3 reference to refer to the spill range (Figure 4-5). Click **OK**.

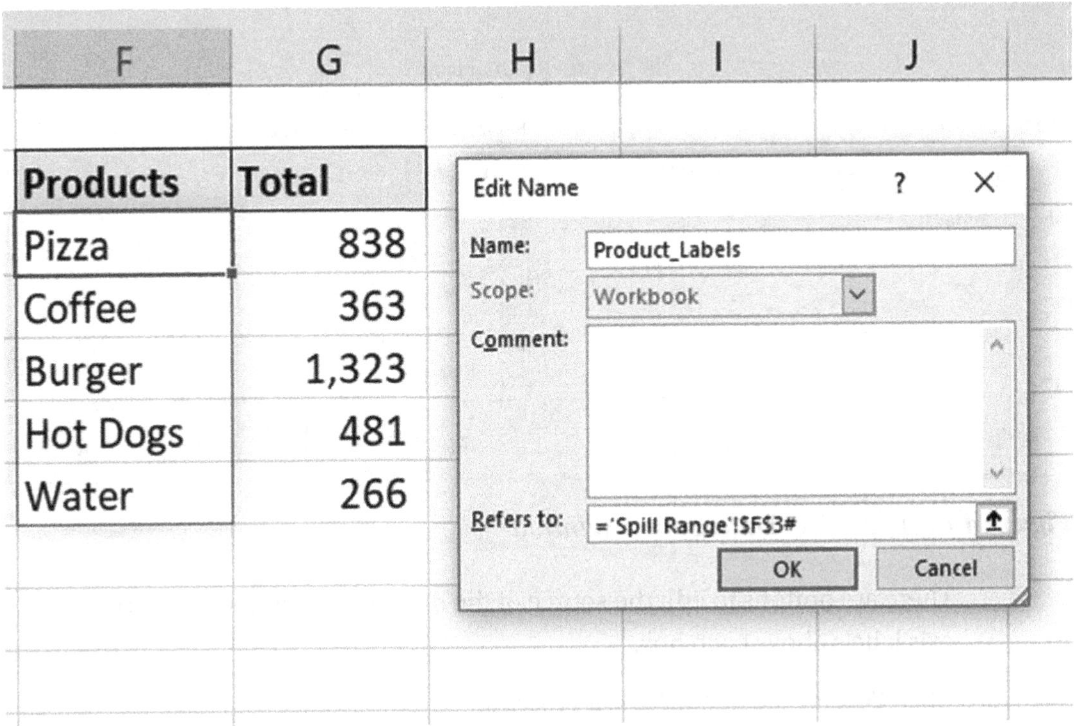

F	G			
Products	**Total**			
Pizza	838			
Coffee	363			
Burger	1,323			
Hot Dogs	481			
Water	266			

Edit Name   ?   ×

Name: Product_Labels

Scope: Workbook

Comment:

Refers to: ='Spill Range'!$F$3#

OK   Cancel

Figure 4-5. Using defined names as a bridge between spill ranges and charts

5. Repeat the steps for the G3 spill range. Name it *Total_Values*.

We will now create the column chart from the range. Then edit the source of the data series and the category axis labels to use the defined names.

1. Select range F3:G7 and click **Insert ➤ Clustered Column Chart**.

2. Click **Chart Design ➤ Select Data** to open the Select Data Source window (Figure 4-6).

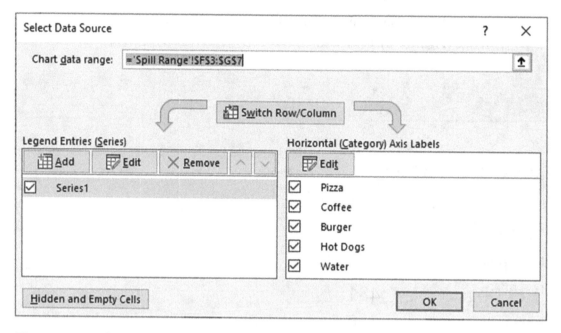

Figure 4-6. *The Select Data Source window*

> There are buttons to edit the source of the data series and the category axis labels above each box.

3.   Click **Edit** for the *Legend Entries (Series)*.

4.   Replace the range with the defined name *Total_Values* (Figure 4-7). Do not delete the sheet name. It is important to keep the sheet name before the defined name.

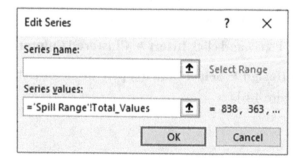

Figure 4-7. *Use the defined name Total_Values for the data series source*

5. Click the **Edit** button for the *Horizontal (Category) Axis Labels*.

6. Replace the range with the defined name *Product_Labels*.

The chart will now automatically update when new data is added to the *Product_ Sales* table and the dynamic array formulas update.

Automatically Sort Chart Values – With Excel 365

It is important that the values in your charts are sorted correctly. And if you have charts hooked up to a dynamic range, the sorting will also need to be dynamic.

You may want to sort the category axis in A–Z order or the values in largest to smallest order. With the SORT and SORTBY functions in Excel 365, this task is simple.

The SORT and SORTBY functions were covered in Chapter 2. And one of the examples was to sort the product sales we have been working with in this chapter in descending order by total sales value.

To recap, this is how it was done.

Beginning with the total sales in cell G3, this formula sums the sales of each distinct product in the table *Product_Sales2* and sorts the values in descending order:

```
=SORT(
    SUMIFS(Product_Sales2[Total],
    Product_Sales2[Product],UNIQUE(Product_Sales2[Product]))
    ,,-1)
```

Then in cell F3, this formula uses SORTBY to sort the distinct products array using the SUMIFS function for the by array argument:

```
=SORTBY(UNIQUE(Product_Sales2[Product]),
    SUMIFS(Product_Sales2[Total],
    Product_Sales2[Product],UNIQUE(Product_Sales2[Product]))
    ,-1)
```

With the formulas written, we then repeat the steps from the previous example. Define names for the two spill ranges, insert the chart, and use the defined names for the data series and category axis (Figure 4-8).

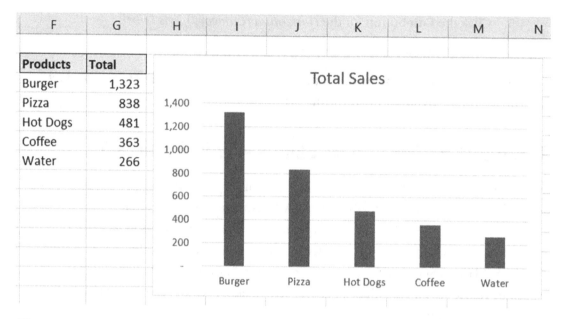

Figure 4-8. *Automatically sort chart values using SORT and SORTBY*

Automatically Sort Chart Values – Without Excel 365

The SORT and SORTBY functions may only be available to Excel 365 users, but there are still ways that we can automatically sort values using formulas.

We will continue with the same example we have been working with in this chapter, the total sales of products. We have a table named *Chart_Prep,* and it uses the SUMIFS function to total the sales of each product.

We will use this table to rank the total sales values. Then order them in another table, which will feed the chart. It follows good practice when creating reports to have separate tables or ranges for the data, the calculations, and then the report.

Note   You can also group, sum, and sort the values for a chart using Power Query or a PivotTable. This chapter is focusing on formulas to prepare your chart source data. The benefits of using formulas include their flexibility and that they automatically update.

To rank the total sales values, the following formula was added to the *Chart_Prep* table (Figure 4-9):

```
=RANK.EQ([@Total],[Total],0)+COUNTIFS($G$3:G3,[@Total])-1
```

Products	Total	Rank
Burger	1,323	1
Coffee	363	4
Hot Dogs	481	3
Pizza	838	2
Water	266	5

Figure 4-9. *Rank the total sales values in the table*

This formula uses the RANK.EQ function to rank each total value in the *Total* column. The *0* specifies descending order, so the largest value is the first and so on.

The COUNTIFS function is used to separate tied values and ensure a unique rank for each total value. It does this by counting the occurrences of each value, the minus is performed, and the result is added to the rank. For example, if a value has occurred twice, the –1 is performed, and then the 1 is added to the rank.

In this example, the values are unique, but in Figure 4-10 the coffee sales are equal to hot dogs. The COUNTIFS function ensures that a unique rank number is applied.

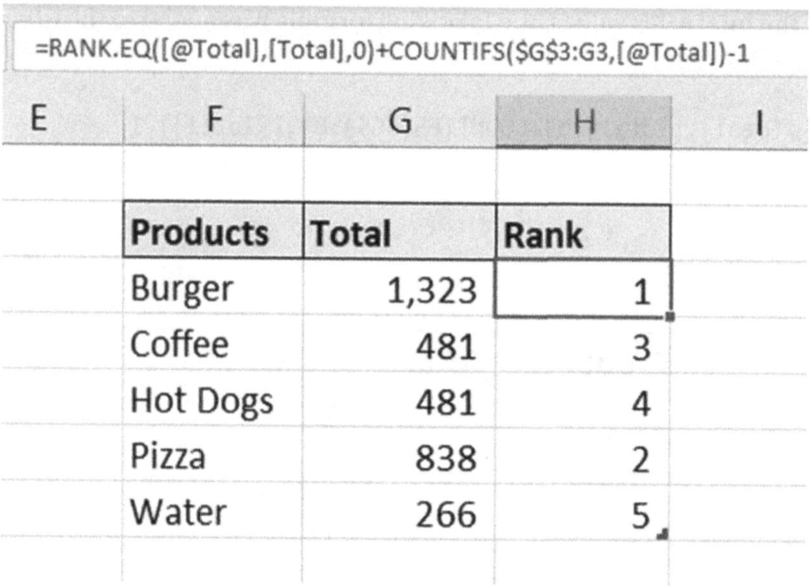

=RANK.EQ([@Total],[Total],0)+COUNTIFS($G$3:G3,[@Total])-1

E	F	G	H	I
	Products	Total	Rank	
	Burger	1,323	1	
	Coffee	481	3	
	Hot Dogs	481	4	
	Pizza	838	2	
	Water	266	5	

Figure 4-10. *Unique ranking for tied values*

We then need to order the product names and totals by their rank. We can do that with lookup formulas. Let us use the INDEX and MATCH combination (Figure 4-11).

This formula has been entered into cell K3 to return the sales value. The same formula has also been used for the product name in cell J3 but with the INDEX array as *Chart_Prep[Products]*.

```
=INDEX(Chart_Prep[Total],MATCH(ROW(I1),Chart_Prep[Rank],0))
```

It uses the ROW function to return the row number from a cell in row 1. Cell I1 has been used for this example. This returns rank number 1, but when the formula is filled down, it returns 2, 3, 4, and so on.

MATCH finds the position of the rank number, and INDEX returns the product name and total.

f_x	=INDEX(Chart_Prep[Total],MATCH(ROW(I1),Chart_Prep[Rank],0))

E	F	G	H	I	J	K
	Products	**Total**	**Rank**		**Products**	**Total**
	Burger	1,323	1		Burger	1323
	Coffee	363	4		Pizza	838
	Hot Dogs	481	3		Hot Dogs	481
	Pizza	838	2		Coffee	363
	Water	266	5		Water	266

Figure 4-11. *Order the ranked values in a table to feed the chart*

The column chart (or any other chart) can then be created from this ordered table (Figure 4-12).

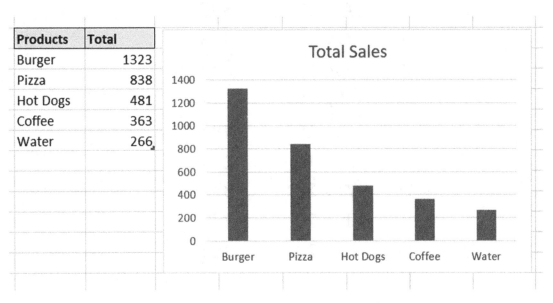

Products	Total
Burger	1323
Pizza	838
Hot Dogs	481
Coffee	363
Water	266

Figure 4-12. *Sorted column chart using a rank table and lookup formulas*

Rolling Excel Chart for Last X Values

It is a common requirement to report on a rolling basis. This could be the last 12 months, 6 weeks, or 14 days.

You do not want to be editing chart source data routinely to chart the correct values. Creating a rolling chart is therefore a valuable technique. The chart will automatically update as new data is added.

As always, we will use formulas to give the chart this power. There are a few functions that can be used for this task. INDEX, OFFSET, and XLOOKUP are all great. We will focus on INDEX. It is the most versatile and accessible function for this task.

In this example, we have a table named *Rolling_Chart* with monthly sales (Figure 4-13). It currently has 16 months of data (Apr-19 to Jul-20), and we want the last 12 months.

	A Period	B Total	C
1	Period	Total	
2	Apr-19	306	
3	May-19	456	
4	Jun-19	484	
5	Jul-19	211	
6	Aug-19	486	
7	Sep-19	276	
15	May-20	372	
16	Jun-20	279	
17	Jul-20	295	
18			

Figure 4-13. *Table with the sales each month for 16 months*

Additional rows will be added to this table, so we will use a formula to ensure we always chart the last 12 months only. We need a formula for the *Period* labels and another for the *Total* values. The formulas will be used in defined names like previous examples.

This formula has been used in the defined name *Period*. It uses two INDEX functions either side of the range operator (:).

```
=INDEX(Rolling_Chart[Period],ROWS(Rolling_Chart[Period])-11,1)
    :
    INDEX(Rolling_Chart[Period],ROWS(Rolling_Chart[Period]),1)
```

The first INDEX function returns the reference at the start of the range. The ROWS function returns the number of rows in the table, and minus 11 brings us to the first month of the last 12.

The second INDEX function then returns the reference for the last row in the *Period* column.

This formula was then used for the defined name *Chart_Values*. It is the same formula except that the INDEX array is the *Total* column.

```
=INDEX(Rolling_Chart[Total],ROWS(Rolling_Chart[Period])-11,1)
    :
    INDEX(Rolling_Chart[Total],ROWS(Rolling_Chart[Period]),1)
```

Create an Excel chart as usual and then edit the chart series and axis labels to use the defined names. Figure 4-14 shows the axis labels being edited to use the defined name *Period*. Remember not to remove the sheet reference.

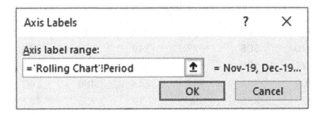

***Figure 4-14.** Defined name used for the chart axis labels to make it dynamic*

Note   When writing complex formulas such as this, it is good practice to write them onto the spreadsheet, check they work, and then copy them into the defined name.

A line chart has been used for this example (Figure 4-15).

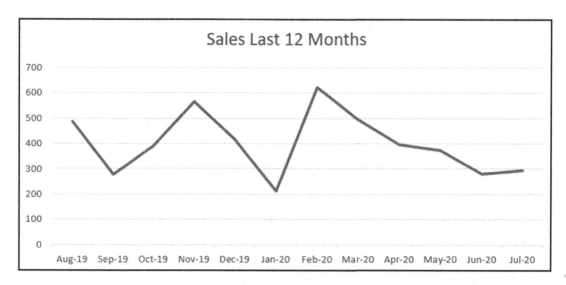

Figure 4-15. *Line chart for sales of the last 12 months*

This same technique can also be used to return the last x number of columns. The COLUMNS function would be used to return the number of columns in a table.

In this example, we have a table named *Period_Sales* (Figure 4-16), and we want to chart the product sales for the last period only.

	A	B	C	D	E	F	G	H	I
1	Product	P1	P 2	P3	P4	P5	P6	P7	P8
2	Pizza	384	203	533	353	416	525	664	455
3	Cookies	370	508	673	249	509	330	695	549
4	Pineapple	271	223	429	400	734	728	222	286
5	Hot Dog	709	724	430	243	486	240	225	288
6	Apple Juice	273	698	696	617	755	482	455	615
7	Crisps	419	658	661	296	314	358	682	231
8									

Figure 4-16. *Product sales for each period*

The axis labels do not need to be dynamic as the product names do not change. The following formula can be used to fetch the values for the last period:

```
=INDEX(Period_Sales,1,COLUMNS(Period_Sales))
   :
   INDEX(Period_Sales,6,COLUMNS(Period_Sales))
```

Note   The ROWS function could have been used instead of 6 in the second INDEX to make the range height dynamic. Without it, if new products are added, the chart ignores them.

This formula is used in a defined name and then used for the data series of the chart (Figure 4-17).

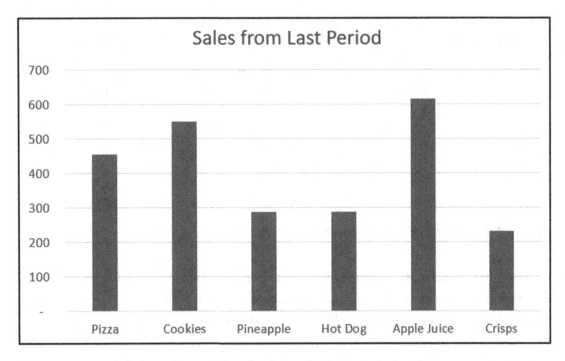

Figure 4-17. *Column chart with sales from the last period only*

Interactive Charts

File   interactive-charts.xlsx

Adding interactivity to your Excel charts will take them to another level. Using features such as drop-down lists and check boxes, we can provide the user with the control to select the elements of a chart that they want to see.

Adding Interactivity with a Data Validation List

In this example, I want to revisit the *Period_Sales* table from the previous example that shows product sales over periods of time.

However, this time we have provided a drop-down list for the user to specify which product to chart and a cell to enter the number of periods to chart for (Figure 4-18).

◢	A	B	C	D	E	F	G	H	I
1									
2	**Product**	Cookies		**Periods**	5				
3									
4	**Product**	**P1**	**P 2**	**P3**	**P4**	**P5**	**P6**	**P7**	**P8**
5	Pizza	384	203	533	353	416	525	664	455
6	Cookies	370	508	673	249	509	330	695	549
7	Pineapple	271	223	429	400	734	728	222	286
8	Hot Dog	709	724	430	243	486	240	225	288
9	Apple Juice	273	698	696	617	755	482	455	615
10	Crisps	419	658	661	296	314	358	682	231
11									

Figure 4-18. *Product sales by period with cells for interaction*

We will use formulas in defined names and use those for the chart source.

We will need a formula for the period names, to be used in the chart axis labels, and another for the values associated with the selected product.

This formula returns the period names for the specified number of periods. It is used to define the name *Period_Names* (Figure 4-19).

```
=INDEX(Period_Sales[#Headers],,COLUMNS(Period_Sales)- 'Data
Validation'!$E$2+1)
    :
    INDEX(Period_Sales[#Headers],,COLUMNS(Period_Sales))
```

It uses the INDEX function to return from the headers area of the table. No row is specified as the headers area is only one row, and cell E2 is used to find the starting reference.

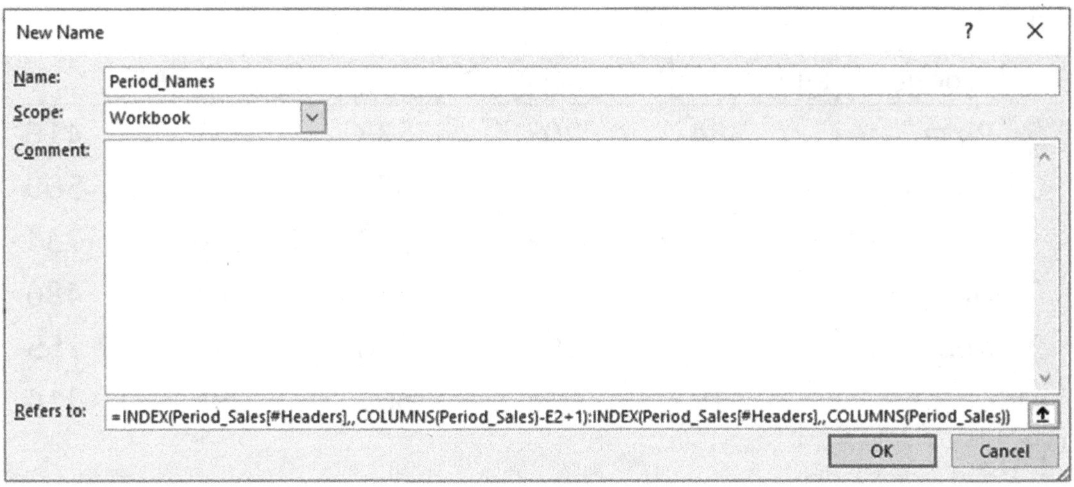

New Name		?	×
Name:	Period_Names		
Scope:	Workbook ⌄		
Comment:			⌃
			⌄
Refers to:	=INDEX(Period_Sales[#Headers],,COLUMNS(Period_Sales)-E2+1):INDEX(Period_Sales[#Headers],,COLUMNS(Period_Sales))	⬆	
		OK	Cancel

Figure 4-19. *Defined name for the chart label axis*

The following formula is used to create the defined name *Product_Values*. It returns the values for the selected product and the specified number of periods.

```
=INDEX(Period_Sales,
    MATCH('Data Validation'!$B$2,Period_Sales[Product],0),COLUMNS
    (Period_Sales)- 'Data Validation'!$E$2+1)
    :
    INDEX(Period_Sales,
MATCH('Data Validation'!$B$2,Period_Sales[Product],0),COLUMNS
(Period_Sales))
```

The MATCH function is used to return the row number of the selected product.

1. Create a chart from a selected range of period labels and a range of product values (Figure 4-20). Does not matter which, as we will edit them to the defined names shortly.

	Product	P1	P 2	P3	P4	P5
3						
4	**Product**	**P1**	**P 2**	**P3**	**P4**	**P5**
5	Pizza	384	203	533	353	416
6	Cookies	370	508	673	249	509
7	Pineapple	271	223	429	400	734
8	Hot Dog	709	724	430	243	486
9	Apple Juic	273	698	696	617	755
10	Crisps	419	658	661	296	314
11						
12						

Figure 4-20. *Periods 1 to 4 and the associated Pineapple values selected*

2. Click **Chart Design ➤ Switch Row/Column** to put the period names on the category label axis.

3. Use *Period_Names* for the axis labels source and *Product_Values* for the data series, as shown in previous examples.

Figure 4-21 shows a line chart based on these defined names. When a different product is selected from the list, or a different number of periods is entered, the chart updates.

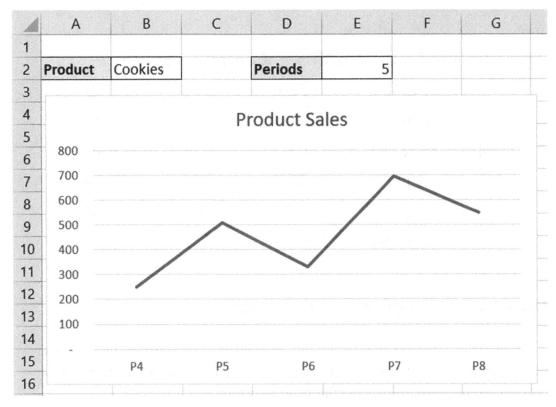

Figure 4-21. *Interactive line chart with a drop-down list and a cell for entry*

Check Boxes to Select Data Series

There are a variety of form controls available for use in Excel, and they are fantastic for adding interactivity. There are option buttons, list boxes, check boxes, and more.

In this example, we have monthly sales for three different regions (Figure 4-22). We want a line chart showing the sales, but only for selected regions. The user will make these selections using check boxes.

◢	A	B	C	D
1	**Product**	**North**	**Central**	**South**
2	Mar-20	767	673	599
3	Apr-20	469	715	697
4	May-20	410	632	436
5	Jun-20	371	273	769
6	Jul-20	639	462	868
7	Aug-20	847	747	389
8				

Figure 4-22. *Product sales for three different regions*

We will use a preparation range for this example. This is an area on the worksheet where formulas will test which check boxes are selected and only show the values for those selections. The chart will use this data for its source.

Let us insert the check boxes first.

1. Click **Developer ➤ Insert ➤ Check Box** from the Form Controls group (Figure 4-23). Insert one for each region.

Note   If you do not have the Developer tab, right-click the Ribbon and click **Customize the Ribbon**. Check the box for **Developer** in the list on the right.

Figure 4-23. *Insert a check box from the Developer tab*

2. Right-click and select **Edit Text** to name them appropriately.

3. Right-click on the first check box and select **Format Control**. On
    the Control tab, click the **Cell link** box and then click a cell on the
    worksheet to link the check box to. Cell B9 has been used in this
    example (Figure 4-24).

4. Repeat the previous step for the other two check boxes.

In this example, the preparation range is underneath the data. The check boxes have
been linked to cells above their column, so that it is clear which value relates to what
check box.

In Figure 4-25, you can see the *North* and *South* check boxes are currently selected.

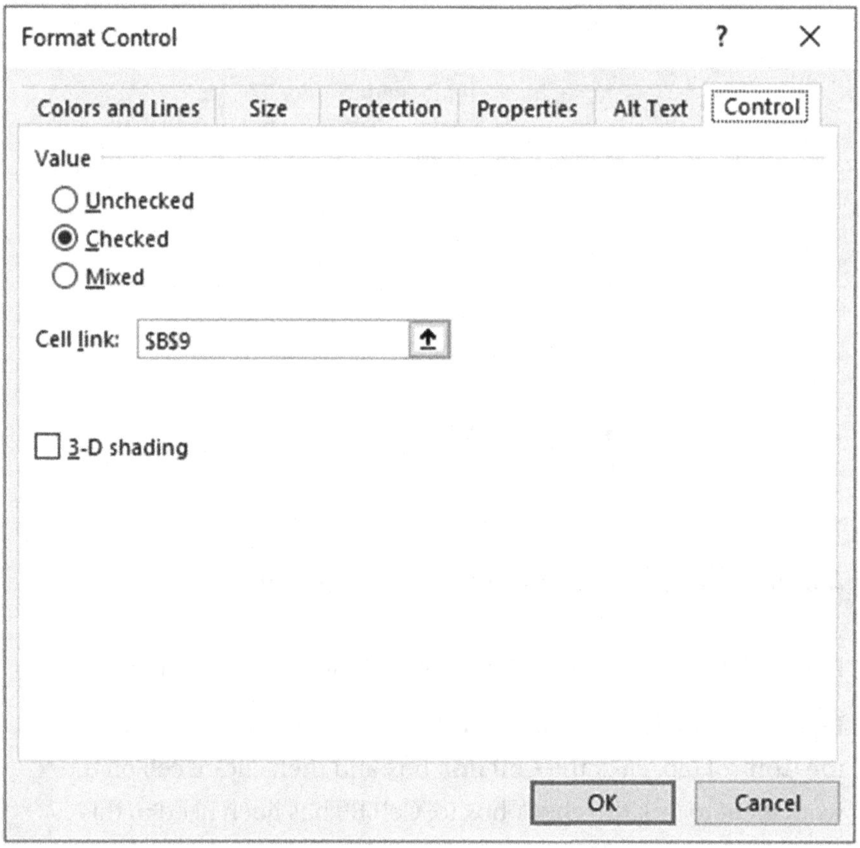

Figure 4-24. *Link the check boxes to a cell on a worksheet*

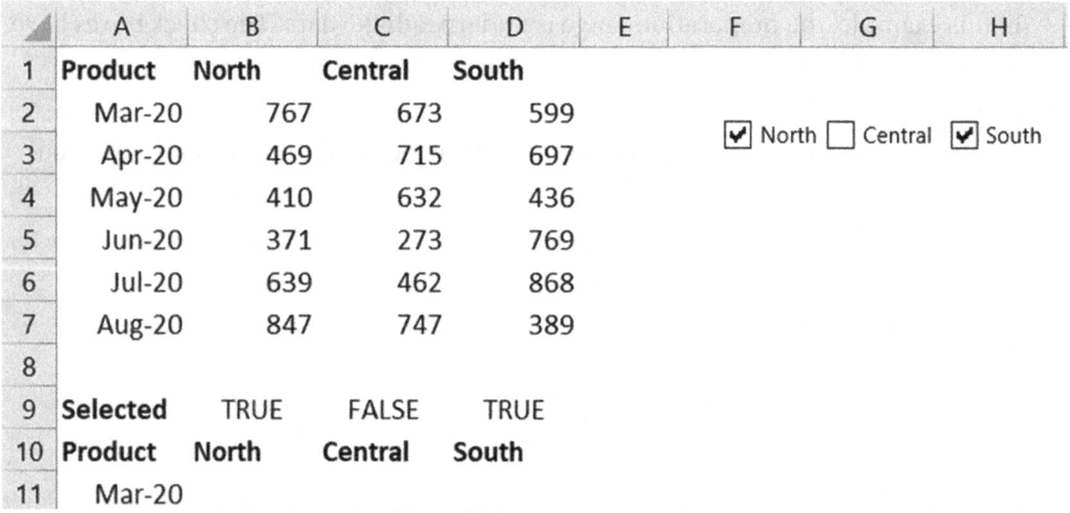

	A	B	C	D	E	F	G	H
1	**Product**	**North**	**Central**	**South**				
2	Mar-20	767	673	599				
3	Apr-20	469	715	697		☑ North ☐ Central ☑ South		
4	May-20	410	632	436				
5	Jun-20	371	273	769				
6	Jul-20	639	462	868				
7	Aug-20	847	747	389				
8								
9	**Selected**	TRUE	FALSE	TRUE				
10	**Product**	**North**	**Central**	**South**				
11	Mar-20							

Figure 4-25. *Check boxes linked to cells in row 9*

The following formula is used in cell B11 and filled across and down for all regions and all months (Figure 4-26):

```
=SWITCH(B$9,TRUE,B2,NA())
```

It tests if the cell in row 9 contains TRUE, indicating that the check box is selected. If it is, then the value is shown; otherwise, the #N/A error is shown. The NA() function is used for this. The #N/A error is used because it is not displayed by the chart.

Users of Excel versions outside of 2019 and 365 will not have the SWITCH function. However, the following formula works just as well using the IF function:

```
=IF(B$9=TRUE,B2,NA())
```

8				
9	**Selected**	TRUE	FALSE	TRUE
10	**Product**	**North**	**Central**	**South**
11	Mar-20	767	#N/A	599
12	Apr-20	469	#N/A	697
13	May-20	410	#N/A	436
14	Jun-20	371	#N/A	769
15	Jul-20	639	#N/A	868
16	Aug-20	847	#N/A	389
17				

Figure 4-26. *SWITCH function to show the value if checked and NA if not*

Now we can insert the line chart. Select range A10:D16 and insert the line chart.

Position the check boxes where you want them. I have positioned them in the top-left corner of the chart (Figure 4-27).

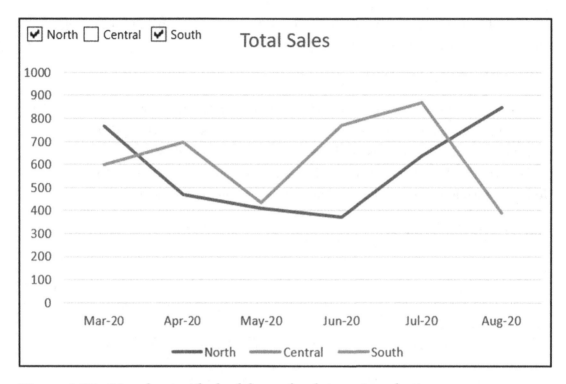

Figure 4-27. *Line chart with check boxes for data series selection*

To position them on the chart like this, you may need to select the check boxes and bring them forward using the shape arrange controls on the **Shape Format** tab (Figure 4-28).

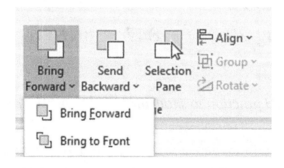

Figure 4-28. *Bring forward shapes to layer them in the correct order*

You can set up some great interactivity for your charts and your reports. Be creative. How can you improve the usability and effectiveness of your charts by adding some interactive elements?

Creative Chart Labels

File   chart-labels.xlsx

Chart labels are a fantastic opportunity to convey more information and insights into your data. It is an opportunity missed by many Excel users.

All chart labels can be linked to cell values. This opens untold potential for your labels. Most importantly, using formulas to feed the labels of a chart keeps everything dynamic.

Let us look at a few examples of how we can take the different labels of a chart further.

Dynamic Chart Title

The chart title is possibly the most well-known label of a chart, and its prominent position above the chart makes it great for summarizing the chart data.

You do not want to update the title every time the data in the chart changes, so let us link it to a cell.

We will revisit the example of product sales over periods of time. There is a *Period_ Sales* table on another worksheet, and two interactive cells where a user can specify a product and the number of periods to chart.

This feeds a line chart using defined names, which currently has a standard chart title (Figure 4-29). Let us link the title to the selected values in cells B2 and E2.

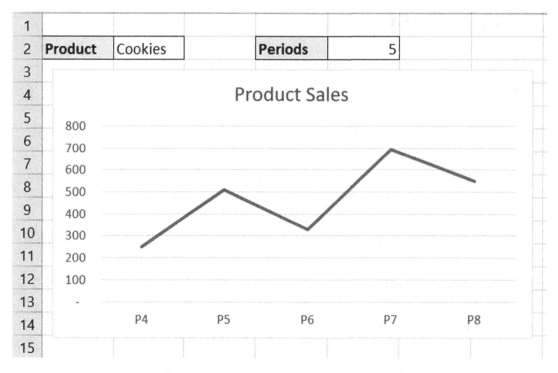

Figure 4-29. *Line chart with a standard title*

Enter the following formula in any cell. In this example, I have used cell G2, but this is normally on another sheet hidden from the user.

```
=B2&" sales for the last "&E2&" periods"
```

It uses the ampersand to join the content of the cells with some written text. Now we need to link the chart title to the cell.

1. Click the chart title.

2. Click the Formula Bar and type =.

3. Click the cell containing the formula and press Enter.

We now have a dynamic chart title that will change when the data changes (Figure 4-30). This is just a small example of what is possible. On a more detailed report, it may not be clear which controls a chart is connected to. Therefore, efficient labeling is essential.

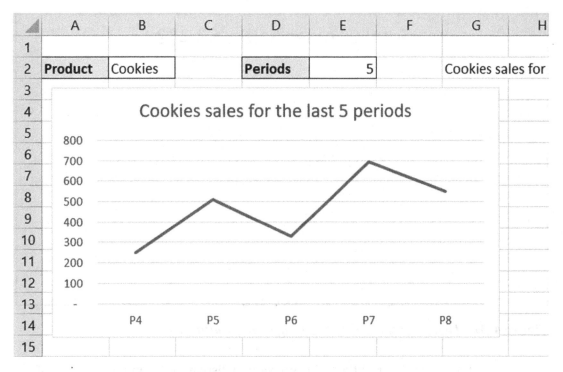

Figure 4-30. *Dynamic chart title showing selected cell values*

In this example, the cell values are directly above the chart. So maybe this title is not necessary. We will use a chart title more effectively by displaying other more useful information.

We will show the total sales value for the selected product and number of periods instead.

The following formula has been used in cell G2:

```
="Total "&B2&" Sales: "&TEXT(G1,"$#,#")
```

Cell G1 contains a formula that sums the selected values (the formula from the *Product_Values* defined name with a SUM wrapped around it).

The TEXT function is fantastic. It formats text in a specified number format. It enables us to use the dollar currency format in a text label (Figure 4-31). Without TEXT, it would lose all number formatting.

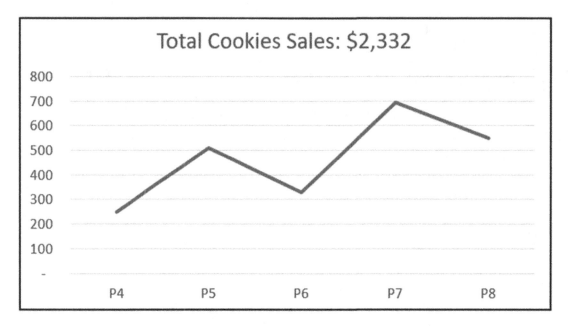

Figure 4-31. *Dynamic chart title showing total product sales*

You may have more information that you want to display, for example, the rank of the product sales value or the percentage difference between the last period and the period before.

In addition to the chart title, text boxes or shapes can be inserted and linked to cell values in the same way.

It is a delicate balance between presenting useful information and cluttering the chart too much.

Advanced Data Labels

Data labels are another great option for displaying extra information that is not charted.

In this example, we have a table with product sales this month and last month (Figure 4-32). The following formula has been used in the *Variance* column to calculate the percentage variance and display the appropriate symbol:

```
=SWITCH(TRUE,
    [@[This Month]]>[@[Last Month]],
    "▲ "&TEXT((([@[This Month]]-[@[Last Month]])/[@[Last Month]],"0%"),
    [@[This Month]]<[@[Last Month]],
```

```
"▼ "&TEXT((([@[This Month]]-[@[Last Month]])/[@[Last Month]],"0%"),
"► "&TEXT(0,"0%"))
```

◢	A	B	C	D
1	**Product**	**Last Month**	**This Month**	**Variance**
2	Pizza	743	838	▲ 13%
3	Cookies	701	669	▼ -5%
4	Pineapple	438	630	▲ 44%
5	Hot Dog	324	401	▲ 24%
6	Apple Juice	792	501	▼ -37%
7	Crisps	432	596	▲ 38%

Figure 4-32. *Product sales with variance data for use in data labels*

Note   The IFS function can be used instead of SWITCH if it is not available on your Excel version.

The SWITCH function is used to handle the multiple conditions of whether sales have increased, decreased, or are equal.

The symbols have been inserted from the Arial font directory. They were inserted into the worksheet first and then copied and pasted into the formula after it had been written.

To insert symbols:

1. Click **Insert ➤ Symbol.**

2. Select **Arial** from the *Font* list.

3. Locate the symbol you want to use, select it, and click **Insert** (Figure 4-33).

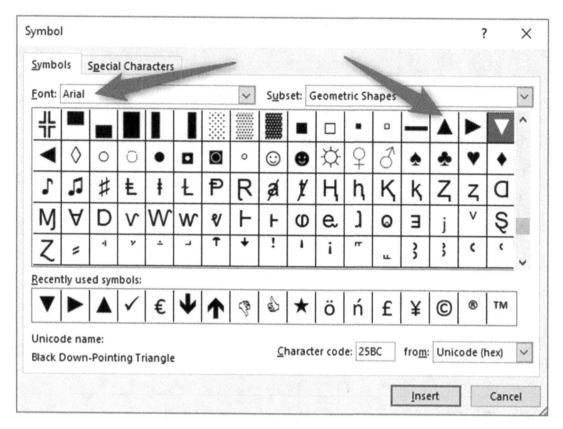

Figure 4-33. *Insert triangle symbols to present variance clearly*

A column chart has been created to show only this month's sales for each product. We would like to add the information from the Variance column as data labels.

1. Select the chart.

2. Click **Chart Elements ➤ Data Labels** arrow ➤ **More Options** (Figure 4-34).

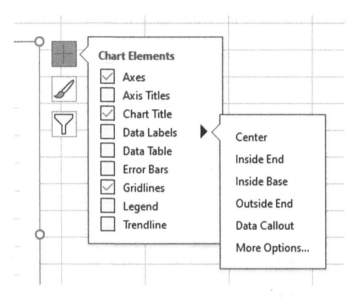

Figure 4-34. *Adding data labels to a chart*

3. From the *Format Data Labels* pane, select the **Label Options** category, click **Value From Cells,** and select the *Variance* column (Figure 4-35).

4. Uncheck the **Value** data labels box.

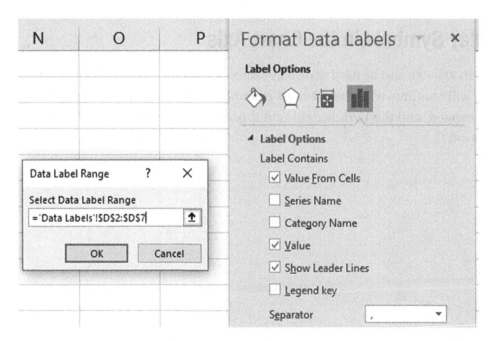

Figure 4-35. *Using values from cells for chart data labels*

The Variance column is added to the data labels of the column chart (Figure 4-36).

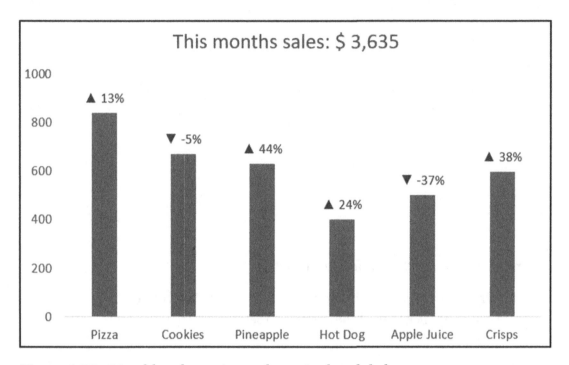

Figure 4-36. *Monthly sales variance shown in data labels*

Display Symbols in the Chart Axis

The chart axis can also be used to display symbols and other useful information.

We will continue with the previous example, but now the table layout has been changed, and the *Variance* column is positioned before the *Product* column (Figure 4-37).

◢	A	B	C	D
1	**Variance**	**Product**	**Last Month**	**This Month**
2	▲ 13%	Pizza	743	838
3	▼ -5%	Cookies	701	669
4	▲ 44%	Pineapple	438	630
5	▲ 24%	Hot Dog	324	401
6	▼ -37%	Apple Juice	792	501
7	▲ 38%	Crisps	432	596

Figure 4-37. *Table with the Variance column positioned before the Product*

1. Select range **A1:B7** (axis labels), hold **Ctrl,** and select range **D1:D7** (data series).

2. Insert a column chart.

3. Link the chart title to cell G2.

The variance information is shown in the category axis labels as an alternative to the use of data labels (Figure 4-38).

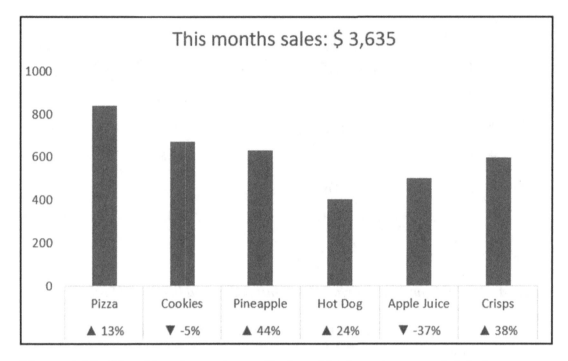

Figure 4-38. *Monthly sales variance displayed in the category axis labels*

Advanced Formatting with Charts

File   advanced-formatting.xlsx

In this section, we look at some examples of advanced formatting tricks to make your charts "pop" a little more.

Conditional Formatting on Charts

Although Excel does not have a Conditional Formatting feature for charts as it does for ranges, it is easy to set up.

We will write formulas to prepare conditional ranges and then feed these to the chart as additional data series. We will then overlap the data series so that they appear as one that changes color.

For the first example, we have a column chart displaying product sales, and we would like to conditionally format the minimum and maximum values.

We will use the following SWITCH function in an additional column to show the value if it is the maximum or show the #N/A error if not:

=SWITCH(TRUE,[@Total]=MAX([Total]),[@Total],NA())

We will then add another column with the following conditional formula for the minimum value:

=SWITCH(TRUE,[@Total]=MIN([Total]),[@Total],NA())

We currently have the column chart in Figure 4-39 using all the columns from the table. You can see that apple juice (maximum value) and hot dog (minimum value) have an extra column in the chart.

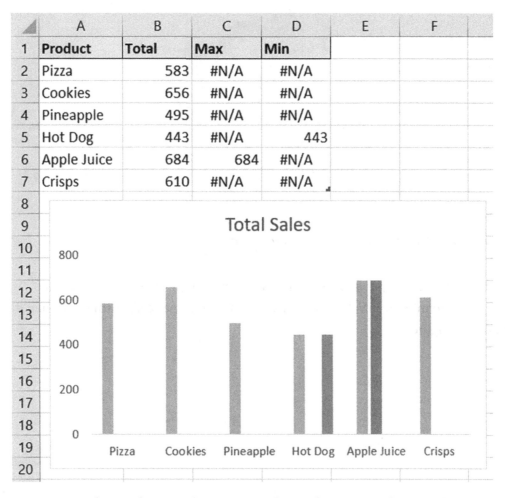

	A	B	C	D	E	F
1	**Product**	**Total**	**Max**	**Min**		
2	Pizza	583	#N/A	#N/A		
3	Cookies	656	#N/A	#N/A		
4	Pineapple	495	#N/A	#N/A		
5	Hot Dog	443	#N/A	443		
6	Apple Juice	684	684	#N/A		
7	Crisps	610	#N/A	#N/A		

Figure 4-39. Column chart with an extra column for max and min values

Change the color of the maximum and minimum data series (columns) to what you want. I am using green for the maximum and red for the minimum.

Now we will overlap the columns so that they appear as one.

1. Right-click a column and click **Format Data Series**.

2. Select the **Series Options** category and set the **Series Overlap** to **100%** (Figure 4-40).

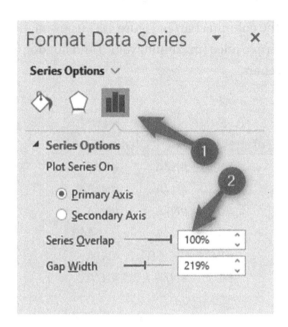

Figure 4-40. *Overlap the data series to appear as one*

That is it! With the power of formulas and some simple chart formatting, the maximum and minimum values of the chart will be automatically formatted when data is updated (Figure 4-41).

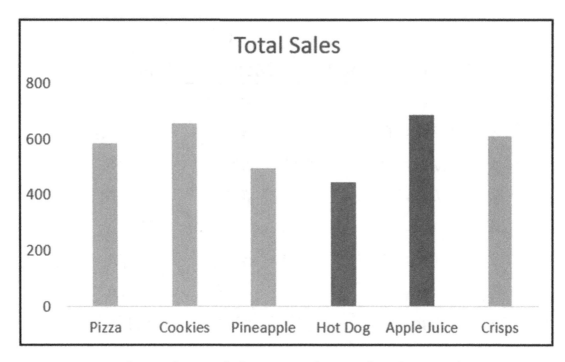

Figure 4-41. *Column chart with the max and min values formatted*

In this example, we formatted the min and max values, but you can set any conditions you need with your formulas. You may want to format the items that are selected from a list or those that reach a specific target value.

Conditionally Format Markers on a Line Chart

The same technique can be used to conditionally format markers on a line chart. Let us use the example of formatting the max and min values again.

The SWITCH function is used to add Max and Min columns to the table as before, showing the #N/A error to hide a marker (Figure 4-42).

	A	B	C	D
1	**Period**	**Total**	**Max**	**Min**
2	Jan-20	563	#N/A	#N/A
3	Feb-20	263	#N/A	263
4	Mar-20	421	#N/A	#N/A
5	Apr-20	734	#N/A	#N/A
6	May-20	796	796	#N/A
7	Jun-20	489	#N/A	#N/A
8	Jul-20	455	#N/A	#N/A
9	Aug-20	523	#N/A	#N/A

Figure 4-42. *SWITCH function to identify the max and min values*

Select the range and insert a line chart with markers. You will not need to overlap the data series with a line chart.

When formatting the max and min markers:

- Set the line to no line. If there are tied min or max values, this prevents the line from being shown.

- Set the marker color and a width of 2.5 points to make it clearly visible.

- Add the data label for each marker.

Figure 4-43 shows the line chart with formatted min and max markers.

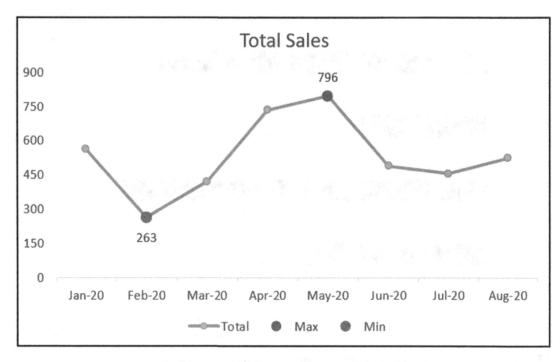

Figure 4-43. *Format the max and min markers on a line chart*

Bar in Bar Chart to Compare Actual Against Target

A bar in bar chart is a great way to compare values such as actual against target or this period against the previous period (Figure 4-44).

To create one, we will overlap the data series like we did with the max and min column chart. And then add a little extra formatting.

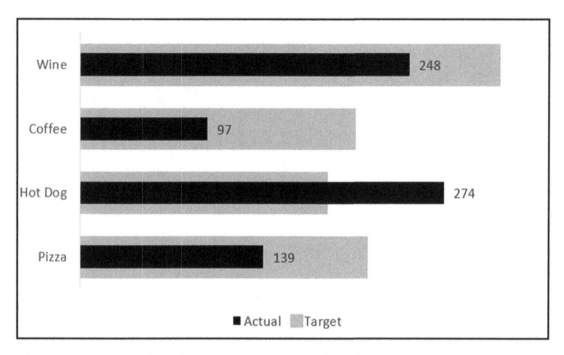

Figure 4-44. *Bar in bar chart to compare actual and target*

In this example, we have the product sales table with actual and target values (Figure 4-45).

	A	B	C
1	**Product**	**Target**	**Actual**
2	Pizza	210	139
3	Hot Dog	180	274
4	Coffee	201	97
5	Wine	309	248
6			

Figure 4-45. *Product sales with target and actual values*

1. Select the table and insert a 2D clustered bar chart.

2. Right-click a data series and click **Format Data Series**.

3. Select the **Series Options** category and set the **Series Overlap** to **100%**.

4. Select the *Target* data series. Click the **Fill & Line** category and set a fill color. I have used green.

5. Expand the **Border** section, and set the same color you used for the fill (green), the **Width** to **12** points, and the **Join type** to **Miter** (Figure 4-46).

6. Select the *Actual* data series and set the fill color. I have used black. Then add data labels.

7. Make any other necessary changes such as removing the chart title, axis, and gridlines.

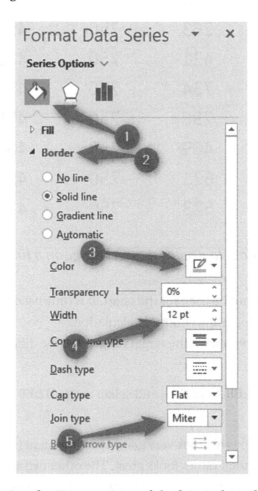

Figure 4-46. *Formatting the Target series of the bar in bar chart*

Add a Target Range to a Line Chart

Adding a target range to a column or line chart makes it easy to see if values are within range or are too low or too high.

Let us use a line chart for this example and the sales data shown in Figure 4-47. The *Period* and *Total* columns will be used as data for the line graph. The other columns are for the target range.

	A	B	C	D	E
1	Period	Total	Top	Bottom	Difference
2	Jan-20	563	750	450	300
3	Feb-20	263	750	450	300
4	Mar-20	421	750	450	300
5	Apr-20	734	750	450	300
6	May-20	796	750	450	300
7	Jun-20	489	750	450	300
8	Jul-20	621	750	450	300
9	Aug-20	523	750	450	300

Figure 4-47. Table of data to display a target range on a line chart

The *Top* column will not be used for the chart. It is only used to calculate the difference with a simple top minus bottom calculation.

The bottom value is the start of the target range, and the difference is the height of the target range.

1. Select range **A2:B9**, hold **Ctrl,** and select range **D2:E9** also. Insert a line chart.

   The line chart does not look very good at the moment (Figure 4-48). The line for the total values looks great. The other two are the target range, but they need fixing. We will now format the target range.

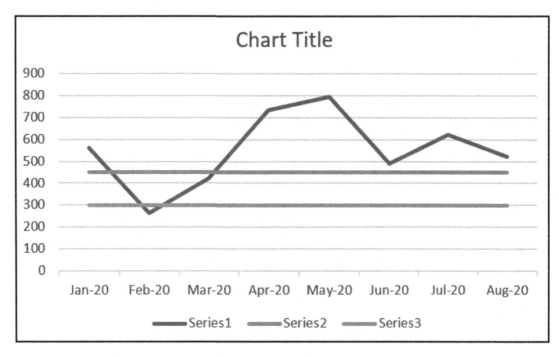

Figure 4-48.   *The line chart looks bad initially*

2.   Right-click one of the straight lines representing the target range
     and click **Change Series Chart Type**. Change the chart type for
     series 2 and 3 to a stacked column (Figure 4-49).

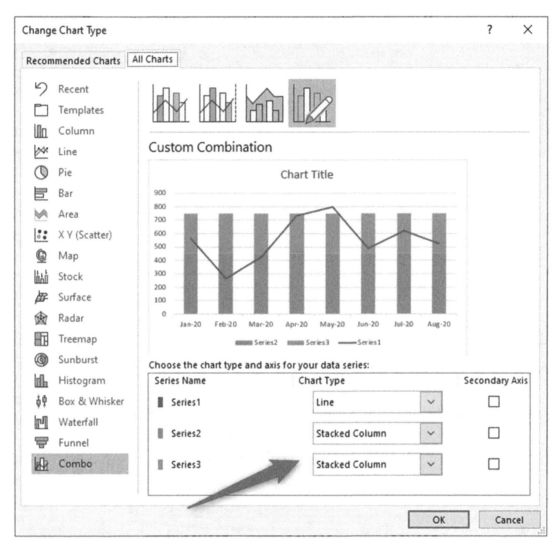

Figure 4-49. *Change chart type for series 2 and 3 to a stacked column*

3. Right-click the stacked column on the chart and click **Format Data Series**. Select the **Series Options** category and change the **Gap Width** to **0%**.

4. Select the bottom of the stacked column (series 2). Click the **Line & Fill** category and select **No Fill**.

5. Make some final adjustments such as removing the legend and gridlines and editing the chart title.

It is easy to add a target range to a chart and yet very effective (Figure 4-50).

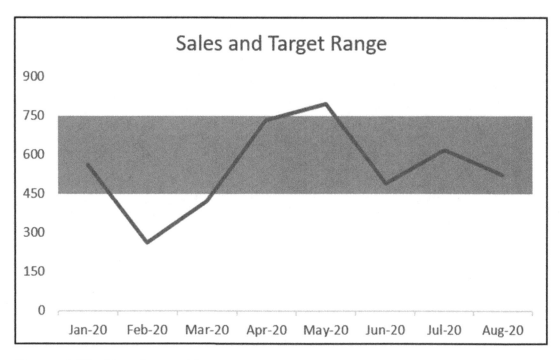

Figure 4-50. *Line chart with target range*

This chapter showed just a few examples of how you can take your Excel charts to the next level. There is much more that you can do, and there are many resources available online to learn from.

CHAPTER 5

Power Query – You Will Never Work the Same Way Again

Power Query is one of the most important updates in the history of Excel. What once seemed impossible or would require VBA is now very simple. Understanding the role of Power Query will change the way you work with data.

This chapter will walk through several examples of how you can use Power Query to streamline tasks and prepare data for analysis. Be ready! You will never work the same way again.

Introduction to Power Query

Power Query first appeared as an add-in in Excel 2013, named Power Query. And in versions after that is now native to Excel and found on the Data tab, under the name Get & Transform (Figure 5-1).

Microsoft is regularly making improvements and releasing updates to Power Query, so Microsoft 365 users will always have the latest features available.

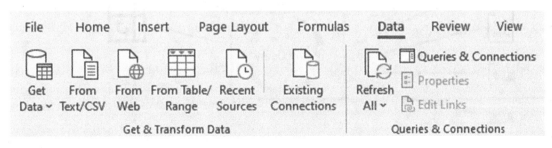

Figure 5-1. *Get & Transform on the Data tab*

© Alan Murray 2021
A. Murray, *Advanced Excel Success*, https://doi.org/10.1007/978-1-4842-6467-6_5

The role of Power Query is to import, clean, and prepare data for analysis.

Excel in the past was limited in how we got external data into Excel. We relied on the external software or website having good export to Excel functionality.

Once in Excel, we then used formulas and features such as Text to Columns, Filter, Remove Duplicates, and Find and Replace to transform it. This was frustrating and took time.

Power Query fills in this gap. And better yet, it has a nice easy-to-use interface with buttons that many Excel users will recognize. Most operations can be performed without knowing advanced formulas or any code.

Power Query is an ETL tool. This stands for extract, transform, and load. Let us look at the three different aspects of the Power Query role (Figure 5-2):

- **Connect:** Easily connect to and extract data from a variety of external sources such as CSV, a folder of files, PDF, web page, SharePoint, and more. Once this connection is established, it is refreshed with the click of a button. You do not need to find the file or specify the URL every time you import.

- **Transform:** The stage that is the most fun. Remove, sort, filter, split, replace, and load more transformation steps to shape and clean the data into something usable.

- **Load:** Load the data ready for use. This could be directly to a PivotTable, to a table on the worksheet, into the data model for Power Pivot, or as connection only for other queries to use.

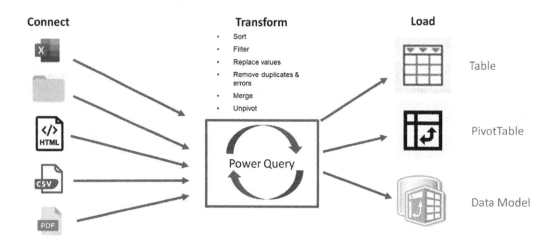

Figure 5-2. *Connect, transform, and load data with Power Query*

As users perform commands to transform the data in the Power Query Editor, each action is recorded in the *Applied Steps* pane (Figure 5-3). The entire process can be run again by simply clicking **Refresh** in Excel. And these steps can also be deleted or edited later if things change.

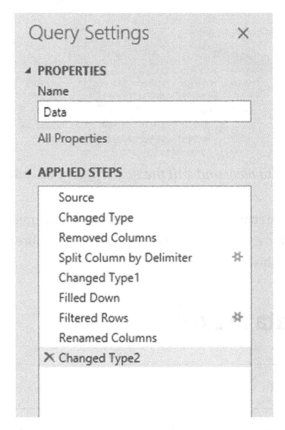

Figure 5-3. *Each action in Power Query is recorded in Applied Steps*

Note   There is no Undo button in Power Query. You undo an action by deleting the applied step using the black X by the step name.

For each command, behind the scenes, M code was created. This is the language of Power Query. It can be complicated to learn, and fortunately you can do incredible things in Power Query without knowing any of it.

In fact, by default, Power Query hides the M code, so that it does not scare you. However, you can view and edit it (Figure 5-4) by showing the Formula Bar (click **View** ➤ **Formula Bar**) or by opening the Advanced Editor (click **Home** ➤ **Advanced Editor**). Learning M code will make you a Power Query Jedi.

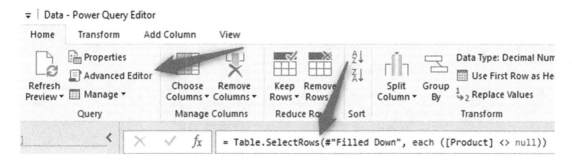

Figure 5-4. *Methods to view and edit the Power Query M code*

The examples in the chapter have been chosen to demonstrate as many features of Power Query as possible and barely any M code. There is far more to Power Query for you to explore beyond this chapter.

Transform Data in Excel

File   excel-data.xlsx

Let us look at our first example of using Power Query to clean and prepare data. This first example will be data already in Excel. However, this data has many problems and is not currently in a tabular structure for us to analyze with formulas, PivotTable, or other Excel features.

Figure 5-5 shows the data we have received. It contains total rows, empty columns, blank cells, and even a cell with the name and ID number combined.

This is a typical example of data we can receive from software outputs or from other Excel users.

▲	A	B	C	D	E	F	G
1							
2							
3		**Name**		**Region**	**Product**	**Amount**	
4		Janine Labrune, 2819		**North West**			
5					Product C	5,941.61	
6					Product D	10,011.81	
7		**Total**				15,953.42	
8		Carine Schmitt, 0819		**South**			
9					Product C	7,529.59	
10		**Total**				7,529.59	
11		Elizabeth Lincoln, 19278		**South**			
12					Product A	1,433.45	
13					Product D	9,717.00	
14		Total				11,150.45	
24		Annette Roulet, 221		North West			
25					Product A	5,832.79	
26					Product B	7,585.01	
27					Product C	5,732.02	
28					Product D	1,030.08	
29		**Total**				20,179.90	
30		**TOTAL**				87,735.87	
31							

Figure 5-5. *Unstructured data in Excel to transform*

Let us go through the steps of loading the data into Power Query, transforming it, and loading it back as a table on the worksheet.

1. Select the range B3:F30 and click **Data ➤ From Table/Range**.

2. You will be prompted to format the range as a table. Check the **My table has headers** box.

3. The table is loaded into the Power Query Editor. This is where all the magic happens. We should name the query first. Expand the *Queries* pane on the left, right-click the query, click **Rename**, and name it *Data* (Figure 5-6).

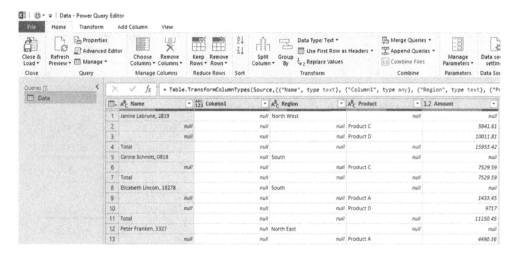

Figure 5-6. *Data table loaded into the Power Query Editor*

We will now walk through the transformation steps.

4. Right-click the second column (named *Column 1*) and click
    Remove to delete this empty column.

5. Select the *Name* column. Click **Home ➤ Split Column ➤ By
    Delimiter**. Select **Custom** from the list and enter a comma
    followed by a space (,) as the delimiter (Figure 5-7).

    This step splits the name and the ID into separate columns.

×

Split Column by Delimiter

Specify the delimiter used to split the text column.

Select or enter delimiter

| --Custom-- ▼ |

| , |

Split at

○ Left-most delimiter
○ Right-most delimiter
◉ Each occurrence of the delimiter

▷ Advanced options

| OK | | Cancel |

Figure 5-7. *Split the column using the comma and space as the delimiter*

232

6. Select the *Name.1, Name.2,* and *Region* columns and click
    Transform ➤ Fill ➤ Down.

This replaces the empty cells with the value from the cell above (Figure 5-8). We can
now remove the *null* values from the *Product* column. This will remove the Total rows.

	A^B_C Name.1	1²₃ Name.2	A^B_C Region	A^B_C Product	1.2 Amount
1	Janine Labrune	2819	North West	null	null
2	Janine Labrune	2819	North West	Product C	5941.61
3	Janine Labrune	2819	North West	Product D	10011.81
4	Total	2819	North West	null	15953.42
5	Carine Schmitt	819	South	null	null
6	Carine Schmitt	819	South	Product C	7529.59
7	Total	819	South	null	7529.59
8	Elizabeth Lincoln	19278	South	null	null
9	Elizabeth Lincoln	19278	South	Product A	1433.45
10	Elizabeth Lincoln	19278	South	Product D	9717
11	Total	19278	South	null	11150.45
12	Peter Franken	5327	North East	null	null
13	Peter Franken	5327	North East	Product A	4490.36
14	Peter Franken	5327	North East	Product B	6746.34
15	Peter Franken	5327	North East	Product D	3036.16
16	Total	5327	North East	null	14272.86

Figure 5-8. *Data table with the empty cells from columns 1–3 populated*

7. Click the filter arrow in the *Product* column and uncheck the
    (null) box.

8. Click and drag the *Name.2* column to the first position so that the
    ID column is before the name column.

9. Double-click the *Name.2* header and rename it **ID**. Repeat for the
    Name.2 column and rename it **Name**.

10. Click the data type button (Figure 5-9) in the *Amount* column
    header and change the data type to **Currency**.

A^BC Product ▼	$ Amount ▼
Product C	5,941.61
Product D	10,011.81
Product C	7,529.59
Product A	1,433.45
Product D	9,717.00
Product A	4,490.36
Product B	6,746.34

Figure 5-9. *Changing the data type to Currency for fixed decimal places*

Note   Do not confuse the data type with formatting. You will still need to format your cell and PivotTable values. Specifying the correct data type is critical to work with the data.

The transformation steps are complete. Each step has been recorded in the Applied Steps box (Figure 5-10).

Multiple Changed Type steps have been produced by Power Query. Only *Changed Type2* was directly actioned by us. This is not a problem, but we could delete *Changed Type* and *Changed Type1* to tidy up the query and specify each column's data type at the end ourselves, especially if the query was more elaborate than this one.

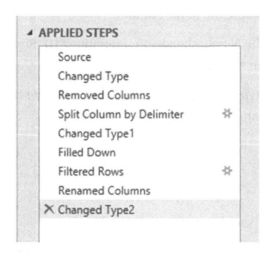

Figure 5-10. *Applied Steps including multiple Changed Type steps*

You will be warned if you delete a Changed Type step, as it could affect the performance of a subsequent step (Figure 5-11). In this example, it does not.

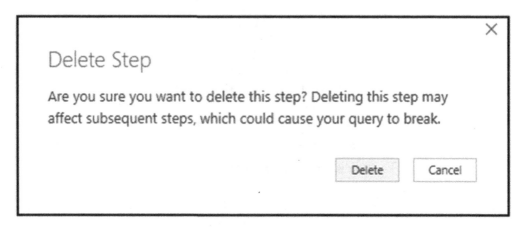

Figure 5-11. *Warning as deleting a step may affect subsequent steps*

Note   You can stop Power Query from automatically adding Changed Type steps. Click **File ➤ Options and settings ➤ Query Options** and specify to never detect column types.

Now, we will load the query as a table on the worksheet.

11.   Click **Home ➤ Close & Load** list ➤ **Close & Load To**. Specify **Table** to an **Existing worksheet** and select a cell to import to (Figure 5-12).

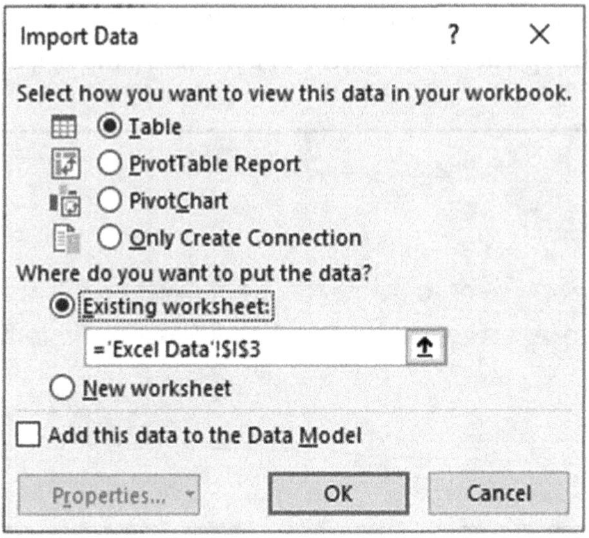

Figure 5-12. *Close and load to a table on the existing worksheet*

The transformed table is loaded to the worksheet for us to perform further Excel tasks (Figure 5-13). The query appears in the Queries & Connections pane.

ID	Name	Region	Product	Amount
Janine Labrune	2819	North West	Product C	5941.61
Janine Labrune	2819	North West	Product D	10011.81
Carine Schmitt	819	South	Product C	7529.59
Elizabeth Lincoln	19278	South	Product A	1433.45
Elizabeth Lincoln	19278	South	Product D	9717
Peter Franken	5327	North East	Product A	4490.36
Peter Franken	5327	North East	Product B	6746.34
Peter Franken	5327	North East	Product D	3036.16
Paolo Accorti	3819	South	Product B	9195.51
Paolo Accorti	3819	South	Product C	9454.14
Annette Roulet	221	North West	Product A	5832.79
Annette Roulet	221	North West	Product B	7585.01
Annette Roulet	221	North West	Product C	5732.02
Annette Roulet	221	North West	Product D	1030.08

Figure 5-13. *The transformed table is now easy to work with*

If you need to edit the query, click the table and click the **Query** tab and then **Edit**, right-click the query in the Queries & Connections pane and **Edit**, or click **Data ➤ Get Data ➤ Launch Power Query Editor** to get access to all the workbook queries.

Combine Multiple Sheets into One

File   combine-tables.xlsx

A very common requirement in Excel is to combine multiple tables into one. The days of copying and pasting or using Macros are gone. Power Query makes this easy.

In this example, we have a workbook with 12 sheet tabs named after the months of the year (January–December). On each sheet, we have data formatted as a table (as it should be), and the tables are also named after the months of the year. The data is for product sales for that month, and each sheet has between 200 and 500 rows.

We want to create a master sheet with all 12 tables combined into one. We can then easily interrogate and analyze this one table of data.

1. Click **Data ➤ Get Data ➤ From Other Sources ➤ Blank Query**.

2. The Power Query Editor opens, and you are taken to the Formula Bar (click **View ➤ Formula Bar** if you do not see one). Type the following formula:

    ```
    =Excel.CurrentWorkbook()
    ```

Note   The M language is case sensitive. So, check your typing and ensure it is exactly the same.

---

3. All the tables from the workbook are shown. We want to combine all of them into one table. Click the double arrow button in the Content column header (Figure 5-14).

Note   If there were tables in the list we wanted to exclude, they could be filtered out at this stage.

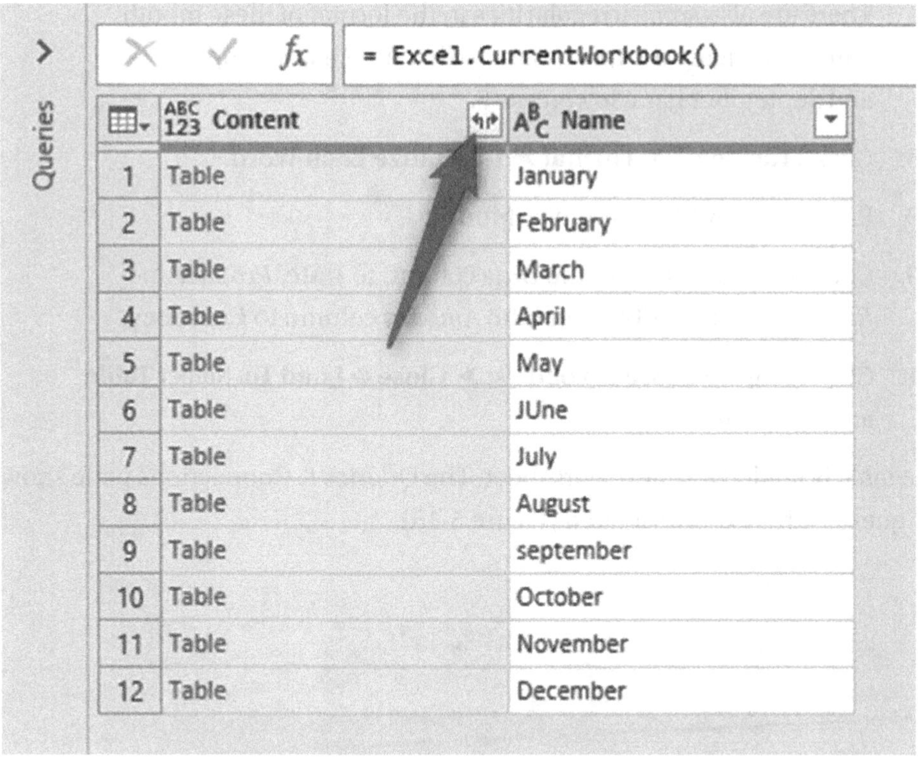

Figure 5-14. *Combine all the tables into one*

4. Ensure all the column boxes are checked to be included in the result. Uncheck the **Use original column name as prefix** box.

    All the tables are expanded and stacked into one table. The table name is displayed in a column called *Name*. We do not really need this column as we have a *Date* column, but we will keep it as a label for our tables and charts.

5. Rename the query *Master*.

6. Move the *Name* column to the second position before the *Product* column.

    We will shorten the month name to only the first three letters as this would work better in the axis of a chart.

7. Select the *Name* column and click **Transform ➤ Extract ➤ First Characters**. Enter 3 as the number of characters.

There are also some irregularities in the format of these month names. In Figure 5-14, you can see that June has an uppercase U and September has a lowercase S.

8. Click **Transform ➤ Format ➤ Capitalize Each Word**.

9. Rename the *Name* column as **Month**.

10. Change the data type of the *Date* column to **Date**, *Product* and *Region* columns to **Text,** and the *Amount* column to **Currency**.

11. Click **Home ➤ Close & Load** list ➤ **Close & Load To**. Select **Table** and **New worksheet**.

The table is loaded to a new worksheet. The Queries & Connections pane shows the *Master* query with 4434 rows loaded (Figure 5-15).

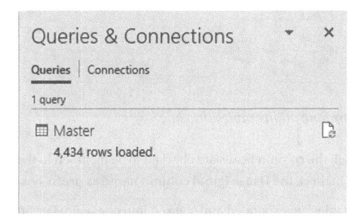

Figure 5-15. *Master query loaded 4434 rows*

Excel.CurrentWorkbook() Problem

When data on any of those worksheets is changed, the query can be refreshed by clicking **Data ➤ Refresh**.

However, at the moment, there is a problem when we do so. When refresh is clicked, the Queries & Connections pane shows 8867 rows loaded (Figure 5-16). And if you click refresh again, more rows are loaded.

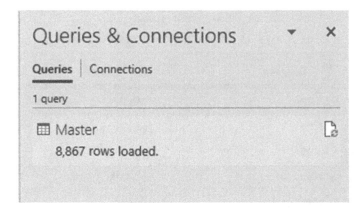

Figure 5-16. *More rows loaded to the Master table on refreshing the query*

This is happening because the *Master* query itself is a table in the workbook and is therefore included in the import.

To fix this, we need to edit the query and add a step to filter out the *Master* table.

1. Right-click the *Master* query in the Queries & Connections pane and click **Edit**.

2. Click the **Source** step in the Applied Steps box.

3. Click **Home ➤ Refresh Preview** to see the *Master* table included in the list of tables (Figure 5-17).

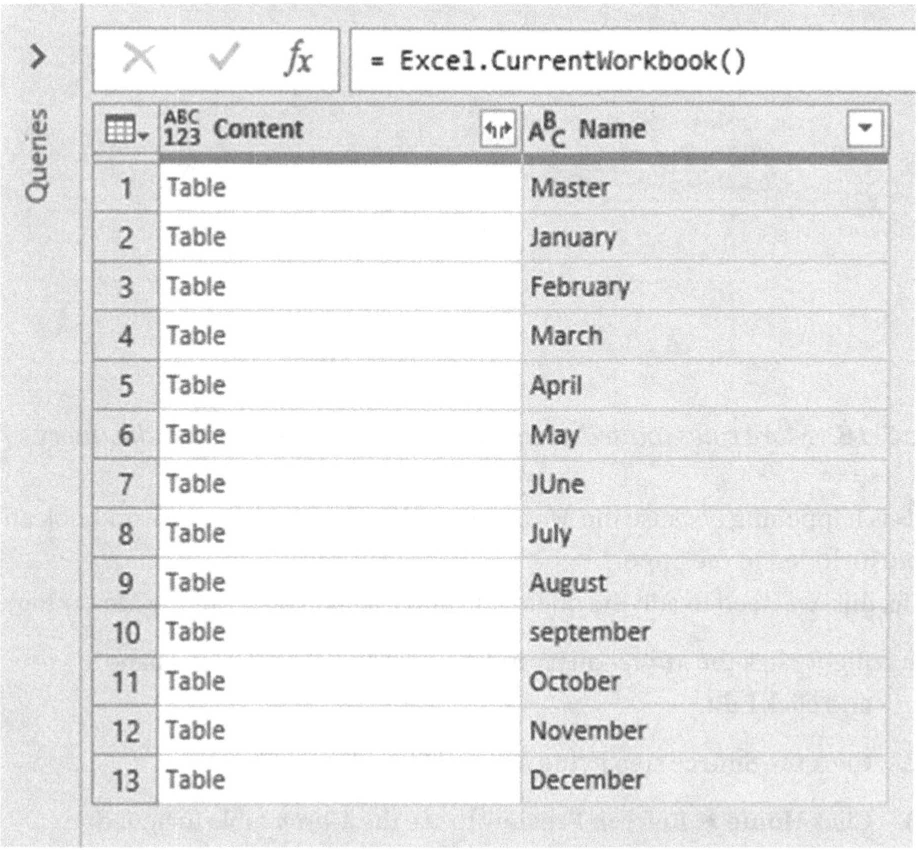

	Content	Name
1	Table	Master
2	Table	January
3	Table	February
4	Table	March
5	Table	April
6	Table	May
7	Table	JUne
8	Table	July
9	Table	August
10	Table	september
11	Table	October
12	Table	November
13	Table	December

Figure 5-17. *Master table included in the list of tables to be appended*

4. Click the filter arrow for the *Name* column and uncheck the **Master** box.

5. Click **Home ➤ Close & Load**.

Connect to Another Excel Workbook

File	another-excel-workbook.xlsx

Power Query also makes it simple to import data from an external Excel workbook. When changes are made to the Excel workbook, the connection can be refreshed to load the updates.

And if the workbook is renamed or has moved location, the query source can be edited easily without re-creating the entire query.

In this example, we have an Excel workbook which contains four worksheets, one table, and a defined name. We wish to import three of the worksheets and append them into one list. We also want to import the table but load that query as a connection only.

1. From a blank Excel workbook, click **Data ➤ Get Data ➤ From File ➤ From Workbook**.

2. Locate and select **another-excel-workbook.xlsx**.

3. The Navigator window opens, listing all the tables, sheets, and defined names in the workbook (Figure 5-18). Check the **Select multiple items** box. Check the boxes for the **Products** table and the **Angel**, **Bloomsbury,** and **Victoria** sheets only.

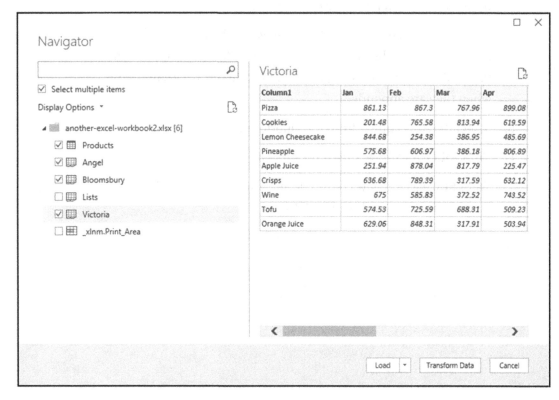

Figure 5-18. *Select only the table and three of the worksheets to import*

The defined name is for a print area that has been set, and the *Lists* sheet is the sheet where the *Products* table resides. We do not need these.

Note   Instead of selecting the desired tables and sheets in this window, we could have filtered out those we do not want in the Power Query Editor. This approach is more dynamic as it will handle changes to the workbook such as additional print areas being created.

---

4. Click **Transform Data**.

   Each workbook item has been loaded as a separate query. The *Products* query is perfect. However, we need to perform some transformation steps on the other three.

   We will append the *Angel, Bloomsbury,* and *Victoria* tables together to one table. But first we need to add a column with the name of the table to distinguish which store the sales came from when they are appended.

5. Select the *Angel* query from the Queries pane on the left.

6. Click **Add Column ➤ Custom Column**.

7. Enter **Store** as the new column name and enter = "Angel" in the formula box provided (Figure 5-19).

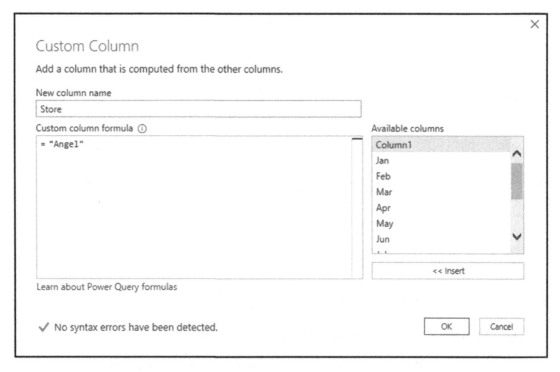

Figure 5-19. *Add a custom column with the table name*

8. Move the *Store* column to the first position in the table.

9. We now need the month names and sales values in columns instead of rows. Select the *Store* and *Column1* (product) columns. Right-click and click **Unpivot Other Columns**.

10. Rename *Column1* to **Product**, *Attribute* to **Month,** and *Values* to **Amount**.

11. Change the data type of the *Store* column to **Text** and the *Amount* column to **Currency**.

The *Angel* query is now completed (Figure 5-20).

⊞▾	A⁸ᶜ Store	▾	A⁸ᶜ Product	▾	A⁸ᶜ Month	▾	$ Amount	▾
1	Angel		Pizza		Jan			690.06
2	Angel		Pizza		Feb			764.08
3	Angel		Pizza		Mar			887.01
4	Angel		Pizza		Apr			811.92
5	Angel		Pizza		May			226.64
6	Angel		Pizza		Jun			887.49
7	Angel		Pizza		Jul			872.99
8	Angel		Pizza		Aug			718.17
9	Angel		Pizza		Sep			642.08
10	Angel		Pizza		Oct			200.31
11	Angel		Pizza		Nov			246.72
12	Angel		Pizza		Dec			674.32
13	Angel		Key Lime Pie		Jan			520.64
14	Angel		Key Lime Pie		Feb			534.82

Figure 5-20. *The completed Angel query*

12. Repeat steps 5–12 for the *Bloomsbury* and *Victoria* queries.

    With the query for each store transformed, we will now append them into one sales table.

Note We could have appended the tables after adding the custom column and then only performed the unpivot, column naming, and data type steps once. I decided to keep the transformations local to the specific queries to make troubleshooting problems easier in the future.

---

13. Select the *Angel* query and click **Home ➤ Append Queries** list ➤ **Append Queries as New**.

14. Select the **Three or more tables** option, select the *Bloomsbury* table, and click **Add** and then repeat for the *Victoria* table (Figure 5-21).

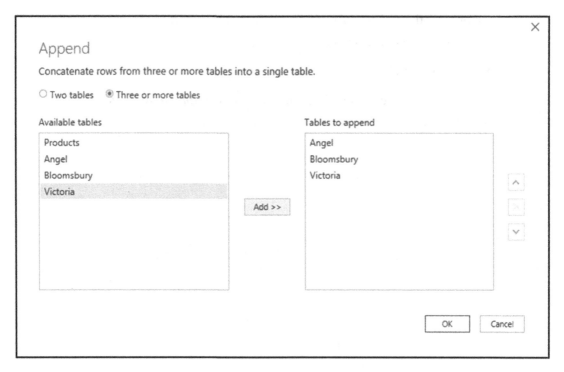

Figure 5-21. *Append query with three or more tables*

15. Name the query **SalesCombined**.

   All three tables are stacked into one table. Perfect for a PivotTable or Excel functions such as SUMIFS to analyze.

   The append query still references the three store queries. So, any changes to the Excel workbook, when refreshed, will update through to the *SalesCombined* query.

16. Click **Home ➤ Close & Load** list ➤ **Close & Load To**. Select **Only Create Connection**.

   All five queries are loaded, but they will not appear on the worksheet as they are connection only.

   The three store queries were staging queries which we then appended. The *Products* query we will use in a Merge query shortly. The *SalesCombined* query is the only one we need to load to a table on the worksheet.

17. Right-click the *SalesCombined* query in the Queries & Connections pane and click **Load To**.

18. Select table and load it to the existing worksheet.

All five queries are loaded, but only the *SalesCombined* query is loaded as a table to the worksheet (Figure 5-22).

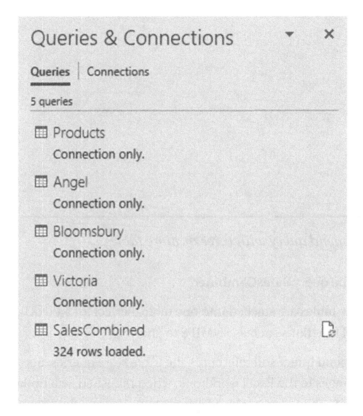

Figure 5-22. *Five loaded queries, only one loaded as a table*

19. Save the workbook as **store-sales.xlsx**.

Merge Queries – A Lookup Alternative

File   store-sales.xlsx

Lookup formulas in Excel such as VLOOKUP, INDEX and MATCH, and XLOOKUP have many needs. They are incredibly versatile, and we saw demonstrations of some of their uses in Chapter 2. A popular use for them is to combine columns from different tables into one.

Merge Queries in Power Query are a fantastic alternative to this specific use of lookup formulas.

In this example, we will continue with the workbook from the previous section named store-sales.xlsx. We have a query named *SalesCombined* which contains data on product sales. And another query named *Products* which contains the category each product belongs to.

We want to merge these two queries and bring the *Category* column into the *SalesCombined* table.

1. Click **Data ➤ Get Data ➤ Launch Power Query Editor**.

2. Select the *SalesCombined* query from the Queries pane.

3. Click **Home ➤ Merge Queries**. This will merge to the currently selected query.

4. Select **Products** from the list of tables to merge *SalesCombined* with.

5. Click the **Product** column in the *SalesCombined* table and then the **Product** column in the *Products* table (Figure 5-23).

    These are the two key fields to uniquely identify and link the products correctly. The message at the bottom of the Merge window confirms a complete match of 324 out of 324 rows.

Note   You can select multiple columns to identify records correctly from two tables. For example, it could be product name and size.

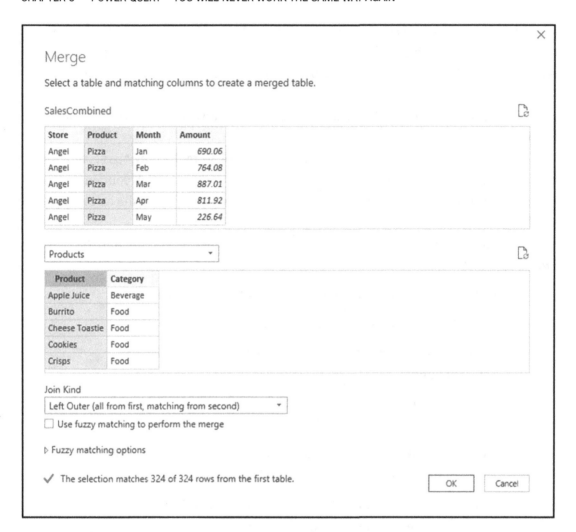

Figure 5-23. *Merge query to add columns from another table*

6. The *Join Kind* is set to **Left Outer**. This is what we need for this example. There are six different join kinds.

7. The *Products* table is added as a column to the *SalesCombined* query. Click the double arrow button in the column header. Uncheck the **Product** column and the **Use original column name as prefix** box (Figure 5-24).

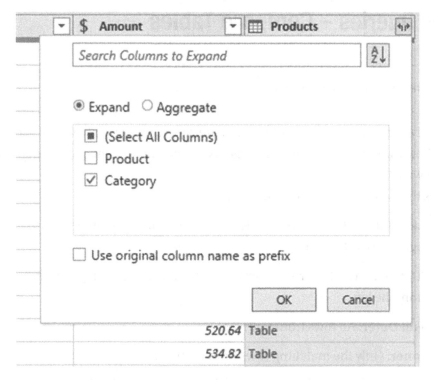

Figure 5-24. *Add the Category column to the SalesCombined table*

8. Move the column to the third position after the *Product* column.

9. Click **Home ➤ Close & Load**.

The category information is loaded to the table on the worksheet (Figure 5-25).

	A	B	C	D	E
1	Store	Product	Category	Month	Amount
2	Angel	Pizza	Food	Jan	690.06
3	Angel	Pizza	Food	Feb	764.08
4	Angel	Pizza	Food	Mar	887.01
5	Angel	Pizza	Food	Apr	811.92
6	Angel	Pizza	Food	May	226.64
7	Angel	Pizza	Food	Jun	887.49
8	Angel	Pizza	Food	Jul	872.99
9	Angel	Pizza	Food	Aug	718.17

Figure 5-25. *Completed SalesCombined table with added category column*

Merge Queries – Compare Tables

File   merge-queries-compare.xlsx

There are five other join kinds in addition to the classic merge we have just seen. The different join kinds will return different results, so the one you choose will depend on the result you want.

This is the description of the six different joins:

- **Left Outer**: All rows from the left table and only the matches from the right (classic lookup)

- **Right Outer**: All the rows from the right table and only the matches from the left

- **Full Outer**: All rows from both tables

- **Inner**: Only the matching rows from both tables

- **Left Anti**: Rows in the left table without a match in the right table

- **Right Anti**: Rows in the right table without a match in the left table

In this example, we have a table named *Event1* and another named *Event2* (Figure 5-26). Both tables have already been loaded as connection only queries.

The tables contain the names of attendees for two events. We would like to compare the two tables to output the names of those who attended both events. And another query with the names of those who attended event 2, but not event 1. These attendees are new visitors.

	A	B	C	D	E	F
1	**Attendees Event 1**				**Attendees Event 2**	
2						
3	Name	Location			Name	Location
4	Anabela Domingues	São Paulo			Felipe Izquierdo	I. de Margarita
5	Lino Rodriguez	Lisboa			Paula Parente	Resende
6	Paolo Accorti	Torino			Diego Roel	Madrid
7	Giovanni Rovelli	Bergamo			Giovanni Rovelli	Bergamo
8	Yvonne Moncada	Buenos Aires			Zbyszek Piestrzeniewicz	Warszawa
9	Annette Roulet	Toulouse			Georg Pipps	Salzburg
10	Marie Bertrand	Paris			Renate Messner	Frankfurt a.M.
11	André Fonseca	Campinas			Martine Rancé	Lille
27	Yang Wang	Bern			René Phillips	Anchorage
28	Janete Limeira	Rio de Janeiro			Maria Larsson	Bräcke
29	Georg Pipps	Salzburg			Guillermo Fernández	México D.F.
30					Ann Devon	London
31					Antonio Moreno	México D.F.
32						

Figure 5-26. *Two tables with event attendees to compare*

1. Click **Data ➤ Get Data ➤ Combine Queries ➤ Merge**.

2. Select *Event1* from the first list of tables and *Event2* from the second list.

3. Click the **Name** column in *Event1* and then again in *Event2*. This is the identifying value in both columns.

4. Select **Inner** from the *Join Kind* list (Figure 5-27).

   This will produce the results of those who attended both events. The preview text at the bottom of the window informs us that there will be eight names returned.

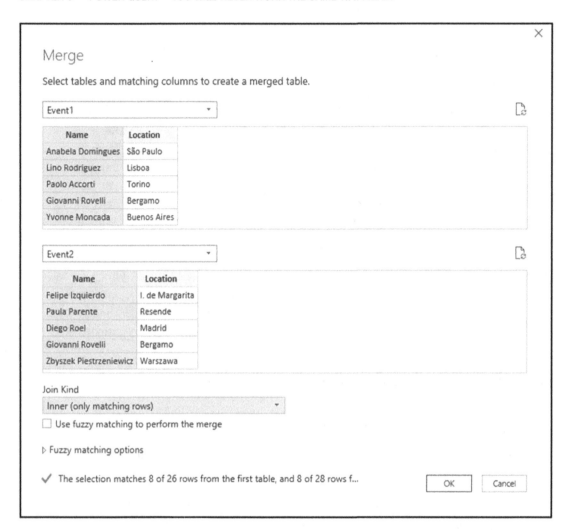

Figure 5-27. Perform an inner join between two tables

The eight names are returned, and we are taken to the Power Query Editor to perform further transformations (Figure 5-28).

The right table is added as a column. We used this in the previous example to add columns to the left table. This time, it is unnecessary as the left and right tables have the same columns.

	A^B_C Name	A^B_C Location	Event2
1	Felipe Izquierdo	I. de Margarita	Table
2	Lino Rodriguez	Lisboa	Table
3	Giovanni Rovelli	Bergamo	Table
4	Georg Pipps	Salzburg	Table
5	André Fonseca	Campinas	Table
6	Martín Sommer	Madrid	Table
7	Paul Henriot	Reims	Table
8	Antonio Moreno	México D.F.	Table

Figure 5-28. *Eight rows appear in both the left and the right tables*

5. Name the query **AttendedBoth**.

6. Close and load the query as a table to the worksheet.

To return the names of those who attended event 2 but not event 1, we would use a right anti join.

1. Start another merge query with the two tables and specify the **Right Anti** from the *Join Kind* list.

2. Name the query **Event2Only**.

Figure 5-29 shows the results of the right anti join. This join returns rows that exist in the right table only. Therefore, the left table returns no rows, and we need to expand the right table to get the results.

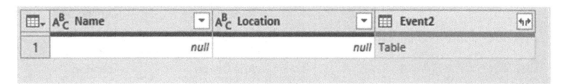

	A^B_C Name	A^B_C Location	Event2
1	*null*	*null*	Table

Figure 5-29. *Right Anti join results*

3. Click the double arrow button in the *Event2* header, keep both columns checked, and uncheck the **Use original column name as prefix** box.

4. Remove the first two columns and rename the *Name.1* column to **Name** and the *Location.1* column to **Location**.

5. Close and load the query as a table to the worksheet.

Figure 5-30 shows the results from both queries.

H	I	J	K	L	M
	Attend Both			**Attended Event 2 Only**	
	Name	Location		Name	Location
	Felipe Izquierdo	I. de Margarita		Paula Parente	Resende
	Lino Rodriguez	Lisboa		Diego Roel	Madrid
	Giovanni Rovelli	Bergamo		Zbyszek Piestrzeniewicz	Warszawa
	Georg Pipps	Salzburg		Renate Messner	Frankfurt a.M.
	André Fonseca	Campinas		Martine Rancé	Lille
	Martín Sommer	Madrid		Pascale Cartrain	Charleroi
	Paul Henriot	Reims		Rita Müller	Stuttgart
	Antonio Moreno	México D.F.		Maurizio Moroni	Reggio Emilia
				Henriette Pfalzheim	Köln
				Michael Holz	Genève
				Frédérique Citeaux	Strasbourg
				Janine Labrune	Nantes
				Aria Cruz	São Paulo
				Lúcia Carvalho	São Paulo
				Patricia McKenna	Cork
				Helen Bennett	Cowes
				Rene Phillips	Anchorage
				Maria Larsson	Bräcke
				Guillermo Fernández	México D.F.
				Ann Devon	London

Figure 5-30. *The results from both merge queries*

The six different joins of merge queries can be very useful. Explore their capabilities and think about scenarios where they could prove useful to you.

Import Files from a Folder

File   sales-data folder

This feature of Power Query is magnificent. The hours of time I have saved many users by demonstrating this functionality are "off the chart."

With Power Query, it is simple to import all or just some of the files from a folder. You choose which files to import by specifying filter criteria on the file attributes such as name, extension, or date modified. Or import them all and filter out the content you do not need.

This connection can then update with the click of a button when files are added, removed, or changed in that folder.

In this example, we have a folder named *sales-data* (Figure 5-31). It contains 12 CSV files that we want to import, one for each month of the year.

It also contains a text document named *exciting* and a PDF file named *new-members*. We have no interest in using these files in this query.

Name	Date modified	Type	Size
April	24/08/2020 10:34	Microsoft Excel Comma Separated Values ...	10 KB
August	24/08/2020 10:37	Microsoft Excel Comma Separated Values ...	18 KB
December	24/08/2020 10:40	Microsoft Excel Comma Separated Values ...	18 KB
exciting	24/08/2020 20:49	Text Document	1 KB
February	23/08/2020 23:10	Microsoft Excel Comma Separated Values ...	11 KB
January	23/08/2020 23:09	Microsoft Excel Comma Separated Values ...	8 KB
July	24/08/2020 10:37	Microsoft Excel Comma Separated Values ...	12 KB
June	24/08/2020 10:36	Microsoft Excel Comma Separated Values ...	14 KB
March	24/08/2020 10:33	Microsoft Excel Comma Separated Values ...	12 KB
May	24/08/2020 10:35	Microsoft Excel Comma Separated Values ...	15 KB
new-members	23/08/2020 19:58	Microsoft Edge PDF Document	136 KB
November	24/08/2020 10:39	Microsoft Excel Comma Separated Values ...	15 KB
October	24/08/2020 10:39	Microsoft Excel Comma Separated Values ...	16 KB
September	24/08/2020 10:38	Microsoft Excel Comma Separated Values ...	13 KB

Path: advanced-excel-tricks-book › Ch05_power_query › sales-data — Search sales-data

Figure 5-31. *The sales-data folder with the CSV files to import*

For this query, we will load it directly into a PivotTable. Most of the previous queries have been loaded as a table to the worksheet. This is great as you can continue using Excel tools with the data.

However, if the goal is to analyze the data with a PivotTable or load it into the data model (covered in Chapter 6) for further analysis, then it is unnecessary to store it on the worksheet. And doing so will add unnecessary bulk and weight to your Excel file.

So, if you are handling large volumes of data, maybe even more than the physical limitations of the spreadsheet (1,048,576 rows), then loading directly into a PivotTable or the data model is even more useful.

1. Start a new workbook and click **Data ➤ Get Data ➤ From File ➤ From Folder**.

2. Click **Browse** and locate the sales-data folder (Figure 5-32).

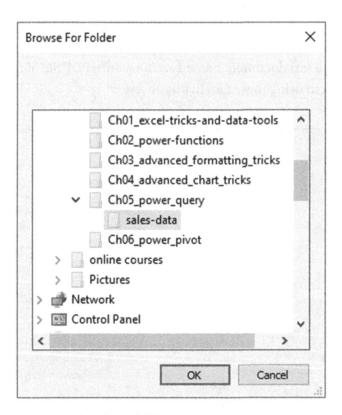

Figure 5-32. *Locate the sales-data folder*

3. A window appears listing all the files found in that folder. Click **Transform Data**.

> **Note**   There are buttons in this window to combine or load the files. It is good practice to click **Transform Data**, even if your intent is to combine or load the files. This gives you the chance to check the quality of your data and make any required transformations.

The Power Query Editor is opened with the list of files (Figure 5-33). The formula bar shows the folder path. This can be edited in the future if the path changes. It can also be edited by clicking the gear icon next to **Source** in the *Applied Steps* box.

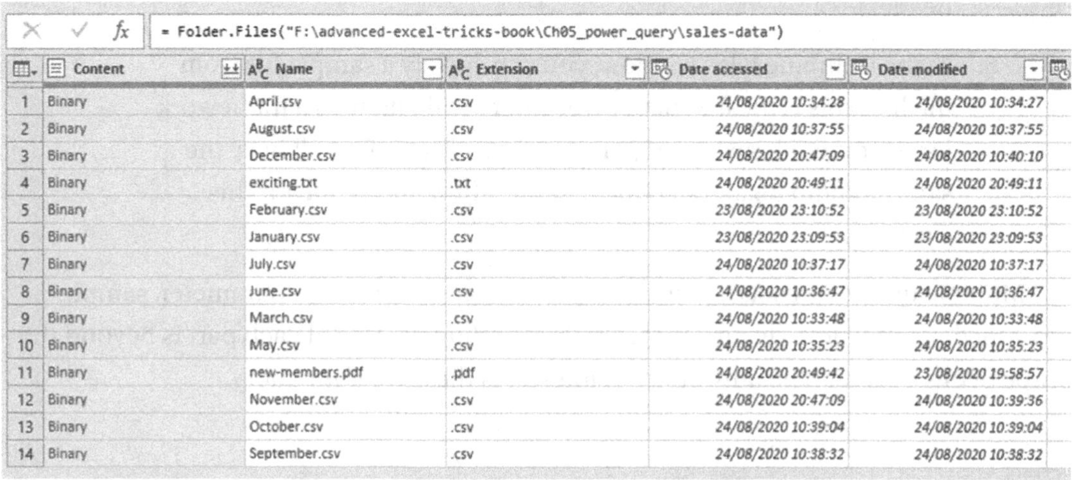

	Content	A^B_C Name	A^B_C Extension	Date accessed	Date modified	
1	Binary	April.csv	.csv	24/08/2020 10:34:28	24/08/2020 10:34:27	
2	Binary	August.csv	.csv	24/08/2020 10:37:55	24/08/2020 10:37:55	
3	Binary	December.csv	.csv	24/08/2020 20:47:09	24/08/2020 10:40:10	
4	Binary	exciting.txt	.txt	24/08/2020 20:49:11	24/08/2020 20:49:11	
5	Binary	February.csv	.csv	23/08/2020 23:10:52	23/08/2020 23:10:52	
6	Binary	January.csv	.csv	23/08/2020 23:09:53	23/08/2020 23:09:53	
7	Binary	July.csv	.csv	24/08/2020 10:37:17	24/08/2020 10:37:17	
8	Binary	June.csv	.csv	24/08/2020 10:36:47	24/08/2020 10:36:47	
9	Binary	March.csv	.csv	24/08/2020 10:33:48	24/08/2020 10:33:48	
10	Binary	May.csv	.csv	24/08/2020 10:35:23	24/08/2020 10:35:23	
11	Binary	new-members.pdf	.pdf	24/08/2020 20:49:42	23/08/2020 19:58:57	
12	Binary	November.csv	.csv	24/08/2020 20:47:09	24/08/2020 10:39:36	
13	Binary	October.csv	.csv	24/08/2020 10:39:04	24/08/2020 10:39:04	
14	Binary	September.csv	.csv	24/08/2020 10:38:32	24/08/2020 10:38:32	

The formula bar shows: `= Folder.Files("F:\advanced-excel-tricks-book\Ch05_power_query\sales-data")`

Figure 5-33. *All content from the folder is loaded into Power Query*

4. Click the filter arrow for the *Extension* column and clear the check boxes for the **.pdf** and **.txt** extensions.

The following M code is produced for the step. It can be worth checking the code, both to learn and understand the code better and to check what step was created.

```
= Table.SelectRows(Source, each ([Extension] = ".csv"))
```

Even though our action was to remove the pdf and txt files, the step created was to include CSV files only. This is what we wanted. So, it is important that it did not record our specific actions.

To explain further, if it had recorded the specific actions of removing pdf and txt files, there would be problems if an avi, png, or pptx file was to appear in that folder in the future.

Note   You could also have filtered the list using the **Text Filters** option in the filter list. These options are great for more flexible filter criteria. For example, to filter for extensions that begin with .xls would also include .xlsx, .xls, .xlsm, and .xlsb files.

---

5.   Click the **Combine Files** button (double arrow in the *Content* header).

6.   In the Combine Files window, you can specify a sample file from the list. This is the file that Power Query will follow as a framework for the other files when appending them. These files all have the same column headers, so the first file (*April.csv*) is fine for this example.

Multiple queries are loaded into the *Queries* pane including a parameter, sample file, function, and more (Figure 5-34). Understanding the role of each part is beyond the scope of this chapter. The only query of interest is the *sales-data* query.

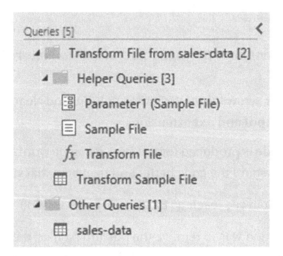

Figure 5-34. *Multiple queries in the Queries pane*

7. With the *Source.Name* column selected, click **Home ➤ Replace Values**. Enter *.csv* as the *Value To Find* and leave the *Replace With* box empty (Figure 5-35).

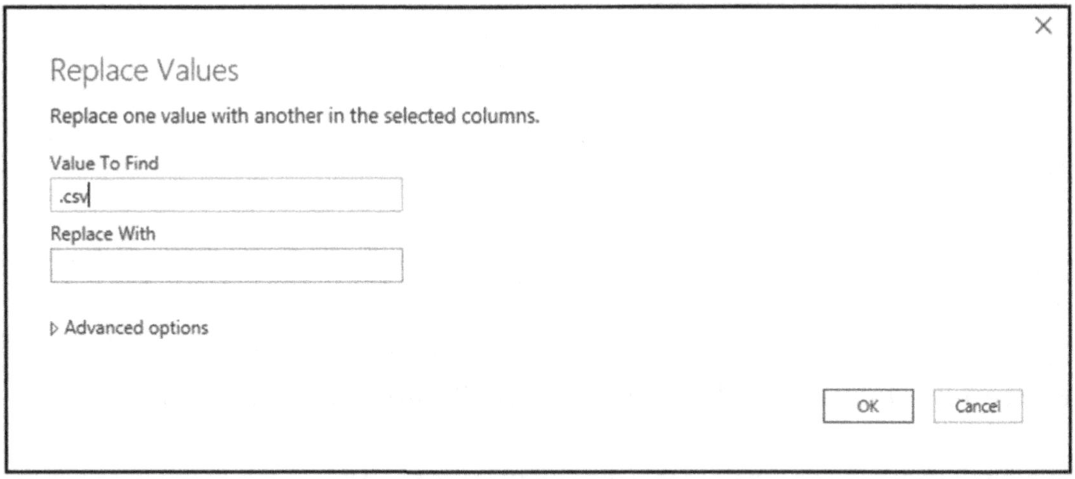

Figure 5-35. *Using Replace Values to remove the CSV file extension*

8. Rename the *Source.Name* column as **Month**.

9. Select the *Date* column and click **Home ➤ Sort Ascending**.

10. Change the data type of the *Amount* column to **Currency**.

11. Rename the query as **AllMonthsSales**.

All the data from the CSV files have been appended into one table and transformed (Figure 5-36). We are now ready to load the query to a PivotTable.

	A^B_C Month		Date	A^B_C Product	A^B_C Region	$ Amount
1	January		01/01/2020	Beef	East	108.87
2	January		01/01/2020	Sandwiches	North	168.15
3	January		01/01/2020	Broccoli	East	32.97
4	January		01/01/2020	Tomatoes	East	262.94
5	January		01/01/2020	Green Tea	East	258.37
6	January		01/01/2020	Beef	Central	273.73
7	January		01/01/2020	Chicken	North	315.10
8	January		01/01/2020	Sandwiches	South	267.89
9	January		01/01/2020	Broccoli	Central	130.96
10	January		01/01/2020	Sandwiches	South West	247.30
11	January		01/01/2020	Cucumber	South	178.24
12	January		01/01/2020	Green Tea	Central	324.98
13	January		01/01/2020	Cucumber	Central	314.37
14	January		02/01/2020	Pizza	Central	191.09
15	January		02/01/2020	Tomatoes	North	11.12
16	January		02/01/2020	Pizza	East	220.17
17	January		02/01/2020	Broccoli	South West	243.46

Figure 5-36. *Imported and transformed CSV files from the sales-data folder*

12.   Click **Home ➤ Close & Load** list **➤ Close & Load To**.

13.   Select **PivotTable Report** and place it on an existing worksheet.

We can then quickly and easily create a PivotTable such as the one in Figure 5-37. We have gone from a folder of files to a report in a matter of minutes and just a few clicks.

	A	B
1	**Product** ↓	**Sales Total**
2	Beef	£ 109,542.45
3	Chicken	£ 105,174.44
4	Green Tea	£ 102,872.22
5	Broccoli	£ 100,136.97
6	Pizza	£ 98,048.90
7	Tomatoes	£ 96,685.27
8	Orange Juice	£ 96,673.48
9	Sandwiches	£ 96,088.37
10	Cucumber	£ 94,006.03
11	**Grand Total**	**£ 899,228.13**

Figure 5-37. *PivotTable showing product sales in descending order by sales total*

The data exists nowhere physically on a worksheet. Power Query connects the folder to the PivotTable. On clicking **Data ➤ Refresh ➤ Refresh All,** it would pull in all the CSV files, perform the transformation steps, and update the PivotTable.

Extract Data from the Web

The Web is full of information that we may be interested in pulling into our Excel spreadsheets. Unfortunately, this is not always as simple as we would wish due to how the web page has been structured. And this is often out of our control.

Power Query provides a friendly interface to import data from the Web, but it does rely on the required data being formatted as a table on the web page.

Note   There are continuous improvements in Excel's ability to extract data from the Web. Hopefully, since the publication of this book, there will be extra features to help extract less structured data from the Web.

In this example, we want to import the table of the top 250 films of all time from the IMDb.com website. Figure 5-38 shows the first few rows of this table.

	Rank & Title	IMDb Rating	Your Rating	
	1. The Shawshank Redemption (1994)	⭐9.2 ☆		+
	2. The Godfather (1972)	⭐9.1 ☆		+
	3. The Godfather: Part II (1974)	⭐9.0 ☆		+
	4. The Dark Knight (2008)	⭐9.0 ☆		+
	5. 12 Angry Men (1957)	⭐8.9 ☆		+
	6. Schindler's List (1993)	⭐8.9 ☆		+

Figure 5-38. *The IMDb top 250 films to be imported*

On importing the data, we will extract the year that the films were released into its own column and create a custom column with the decade of each film's release.

This will be loaded to a table on the worksheet and then a PivotTable produced to summarize the number of films by decade.

1. Click **Data ➤ Get Data ➤ From Other Sources ➤ From Web**.

2. Enter the following URL into the box provided (Figure 5-39):

```
https://www.imdb.com/chart/top/?ref_=nv_mv_250
```

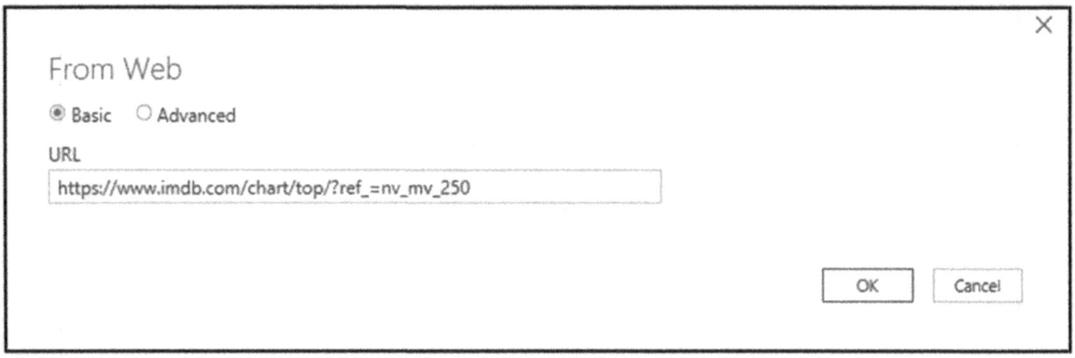

Figure 5-39. *Enter the URL of the page to import into Excel*

Note   This URL may have changed since the publication of this book. Enter "IMDb top 250" into a search engine to grab the most up-to-date URL.

The Navigator window lists the different tables that Power Query has identified on the page. A preview is shown to help you find the table(s) you want to import (Figure 5-40).

3. In this example, only the document itself and one table are returned. Select **Table 0** and click **Transform Data**.

Figure 5-40. *Select the table from the web page to import*

4. In the Power Query Editor, rename the query **TopFilms**.

    Figure 5-41 shows the data loaded into Power Query. There are
    a few transformations to walk through to get the rank, title, year,
    decade, and rating columns that we want.

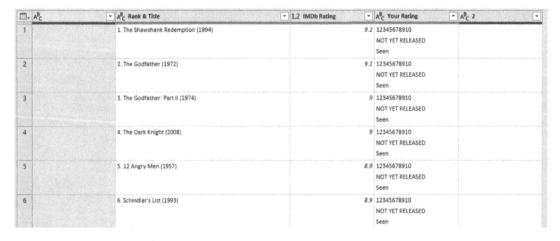

Figure 5-41. *Top 250 film data loaded into Power Query*

5. Select the *Rank & Title* and *IMDb Rating* columns and click **Home**
   ➤ **Remove Columns** list ➤ **Remove Other Columns**.

   Let us split the rank and title into separate columns.

6. With the *Rank & Title* column selected, click **Home** ➤ **Split**
   Column ➤ **By Delimiter**. Use a custom delimiter and enter a
   full stop (period) followed by a space (.) (Figure 5-42). Select
   Left-most delimiter as some of the film titles include full stops in
   their name.

   We will now split the film title and the year into separate columns.

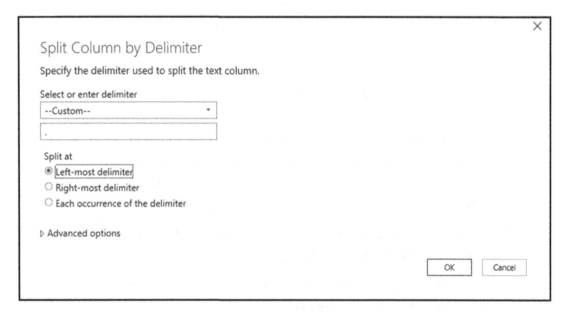

Figure 5-42. *Splitting the rank and film title into separate columns*

7. Select the *Rank & Title.2* column and click **Home** ➤ **Split Column**
   ➤ **By Delimiter**. Use a custom delimiter and enter a space
   followed by an opening parenthesis " (".

8. To remove the closing parenthesis from the year, select the *Rank*
   & Title.2.2 column and click **Home** ➤ **Replace Values**. Enter a
   closing parenthesis ")" for the *Value To Find* and leave the *Replace*
   With box empty.

9. Rename the first column to **Rank**, the second column to **Title,** and the third column to **Year**.

Figure 5-43 shows the progress so far with the *TopFilms* query.

1²₃ Rank	A⁰C Title	A⁰C Year	1.2 IMDb Rating
1	1 The Shawshank Redemption	1994	9.2
2	2 The Godfather	1972	9.1
3	3 The Godfather: Part II	1974	9
4	4 The Dark Knight	2008	9
5	5 12 Angry Men	1957	8.9
6	6 Schindler's List	1993	8.9
7	7 The Lord of the Rings: The Return of the King	2003	8.9
8	8 Pulp Fiction	1994	8.8
9	9 The Good, the Bad and the Ugly	1966	8.8
10	10 The Lord of the Rings: The Fellowship of the Ring	2001	8.8
11	11 Fight Club	1999	8.8
12	12 Forrest Gump	1994	8.8
13	13 Inception	2010	8.7

Figure 5-43. *Transforming the IMDb top 250 films table*

We will now create the decade column using a Power Query feature named *Column From Examples*. We will provide this feature with examples of the data we need, and it will write the conditional formula for us.

10. Select the *Year* column and click **Add Column ➤ Column From Examples** list **➤ From Selection**.

We will now enter example values for the rows, and Power Query will try and work out what we need.

11. Enter **1990-1999** for the first film into the column provided on the right and press **Enter**. This film (your list may be different as it changes over time) was released in 1994 so 1990–1999 is the decade.

Column From Examples' first attempt to understand what we need is incorrect (Figure 5-44).

A^B_C Year	1.2 IMDb Rating	Range
1994	9.2	1990-1999
1972	9.1	1972-1981
1974	9	1972-1981
2008	9	2008-2017
1957	8.9	1954-1963
1993	8.9	1990-1999
2003	8.9	1999-2008
1994	8.8	1990-1999
1966	8.8	1963-1972
2001	8.8	1999-2008
1999	8.8	1999-2008
1994	8.8	1990-1999
2010	8.7	2008-2017

Figure 5-44. *First attempt by Column From Examples*

12.   Enter **1970-1979** for the second film and press **Enter**. Column
      From Examples has now successfully understood what we want
      (Figure 5-45). Click **OK**.

A^B_C Year	1.2 IMDb Rating	Range
1994	9.2	1990-1999
1972	9.1	1970-1979
1974	9	1970-1979
2008	9	2000-2009
1957	8.9	1950-1959
1993	8.9	1990-1999
2003	8.9	2000-2009
1994	8.8	1990-1999
1966	8.8	1960-1969
2001	8.8	2000-2009
1999	8.8	1990-1999
1994	8.8	1990-1999

Figure 5-45. *Column From Examples to create a custom column*

13.   Click and drag the *Range* column to between the *Year* and *IMDb*
      Rating columns.

14. Rename the *Range* column to **Decade**.

15. Change the data type of the *Year* column to **Whole Number**.

    All the transformation steps of the query are complete. However, we could clean up the Applied Steps box.

    Earlier in this chapter, we covered deleting the *Changed Type* steps. We can also rename steps. For example, we have two split column steps. Renaming these will provide more transparency to the query steps.

16. Right-click the *Split Column by Delimiter* step and click **Rename**. Name this step **Split Rank and Title**.

17. Right-click the *Split Column by Delimiter1* step and click **Rename**. Name this step **Split Title and Year**.

    You will be thankful for the time taken to rename steps when you revisit the query in the future. It will be much easier to understand. Figure 5-46 shows the Applied Steps after renaming the two split column steps.

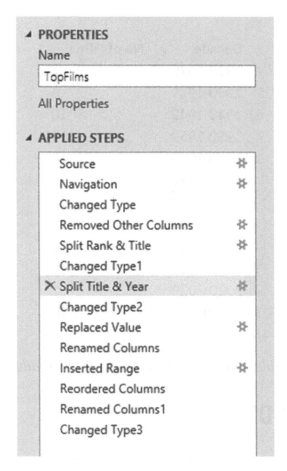

Figure 5-46. *Applied Steps with steps renamed for greater meaning*

Note   The gear icon to the right of the steps can be used to edit the step. If a step does not have a gear icon, it can only be edited with the M code in the Formula Bar or Advanced Editor.

---

18.   Close and load the query as a table to a worksheet.

We can now perform some analysis on this web data import using Excel tools and formulas. For example, the PivotTable in Figure 5-47 uses the custom column we added to return the number of films from each decade.

Decade	No of Films
1920-1929	7
1930-1939	6
1940-1949	10
1950-1959	24
1960-1969	18
1970-1979	18
1980-1989	29
1990-1999	40
2000-2009	49
2010-2019	48
2020-2029	1
Grand Total	**250**

Figure 5-47. PivotTable showing the count of films by decade

Import from PDF

File   new-members.pdf

Power Query also makes it easy to import PDF data into Excel. We can then clean and tidy the data as we need it.

In this example, we have a three-page PDF document with information about new members that we want to analyze in Excel. It contains a table with information about the PDF export and a table with the new member details. We are only interested in the member details.

1. Click **Data ➤ Get Data ➤ From File ➤ From PDF**.

2. Locate the *new-members.pdf* document and click **Import**.

In the Navigator window, Power Query lists all of the tables and pages that it has identified in the document (Figure 5-48). The table with new member data that continues over three pages has been identified as three different tables by Power Query (tables 2, 3, and 4).

The preview area in the window is great to help discern the different tables.

3. Check the **Select multiple items** box and check the boxes for **Table002**, **Table003,** and **Table004**.

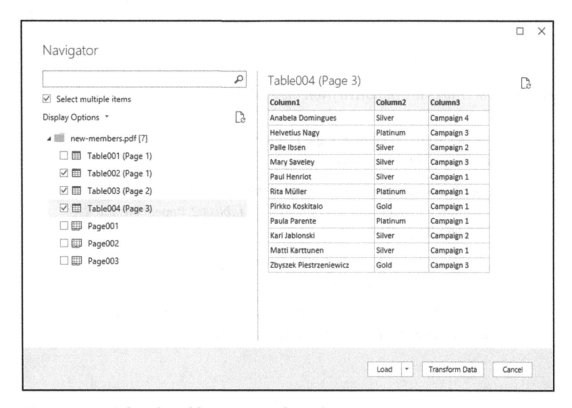

Figure 5-48. *Select the tables to import from the PDF*

4. Click **Transform Data**.

The three tables are imported as separate queries (Figure 5-49). These queries make up the three parts of the new members data table, so we will append them shortly.

Firstly, let us tidy up the table headers. In the first query, the first row of data are the headers.

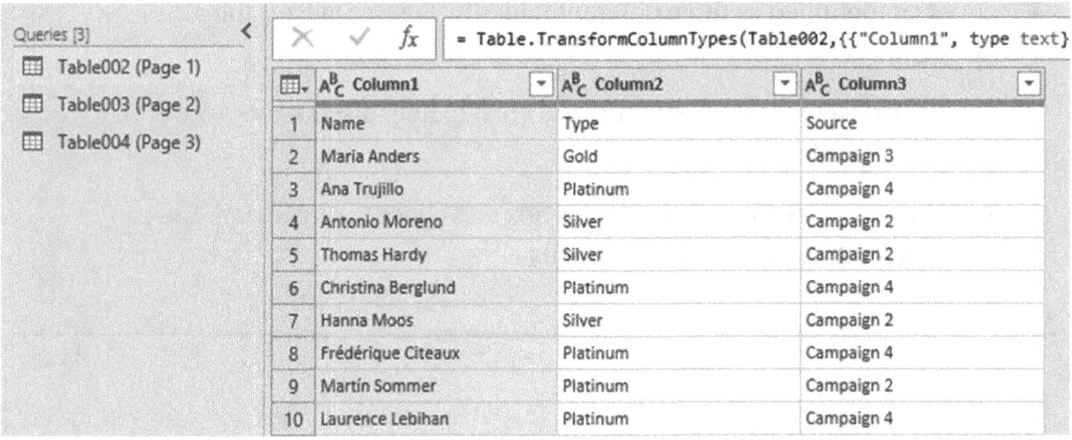

Figure 5-49. *Tables are imported from the PDF as separate queries*

5. Ensure that the **Table002 (Page 1)** query is selected and click **Home ➤ Use first row as headers**.

6. Select **Table003 (Page 2)** and rename the headers **Name**, **Type**, and **Source** to match the headers used in *Table002*. Repeat for **Table003 (Page 3)**.

7. Select *Table002 (Page 1)* and click **Home ➤ Append Queries** list **➤ Append Queries as New**.

8. In the Append window, select **Three or more tables**. Add the two other tables to the *Tables to append* box (Figure 5-50).

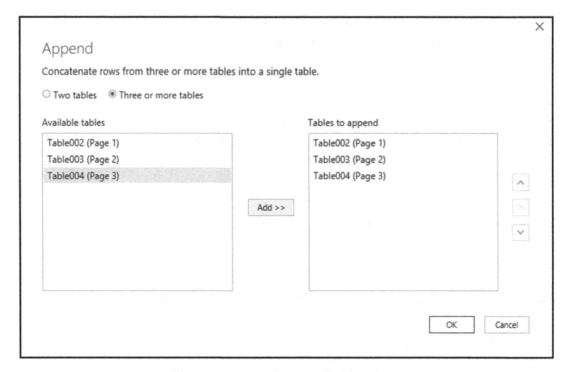

Figure 5-50. Append all three tables imported from the PDF

9. Name the query **NewMembers**.

10. Close and load it as a table to the worksheet.

Group By and Pivot

File   group-by-and-pivot.xlsx

Power Query is typically used to import and prepare data for a PivotTable or Excel formulas to summarize. However, Power Query itself has the functionality to group, summarize, and pivot data.

In this example, we will work with the completed query from the "Combine Multiple Sheets into One" example. This query has been loaded as a table to the worksheet. We want to change this to a connection only query.

1. Right-click the *Master* query in the Queries & Connections pane (click **Data ➤ Queries & Connections** if it is hidden) and click **Load To**.

2. Select **Only Create Connection** and click **OK**.

3. Changing the query back to a connection only query will remove the table on the worksheet (Figure 5-51). Click **OK** to confirm this.

Possible Data Loss   ✕

ⓘ   This query is currently connected to a table in your workbook. Loading the query as a connection will delete the table.
Do you want to continue?

[OK]   [Cancel]

Figure 5-51. *Warning as the connection only query will remove the table*

We will create two reports from this query:

- The first report will show the total sales from the regions for all months of the year (Figure 5-52).

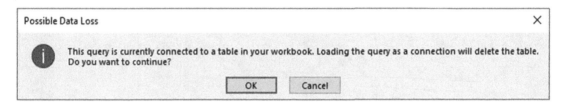

⊞˅	AᴮC Region ˅	$ Jan ˅	$ Feb ˅	$ Mar ˅
1	Central	8,765.02	12,705.98	13,396.14
2	East	10,463.06	13,676.89	15,643.89
3	North	7,814.66	10,290.87	17,359.53
4	South	8,917.22	11,926.18	11,824.50
5	South West	8,432.95	11,661.07	12,845.39

Figure 5-52. *Monthly sales by region report*

- The second report will show the total sales and number of sales for each product. This will be sorted in descending order by total sales (Figure 5-53).

	A^B_C Product	$ Total Sales	1²₃ No of Sales
1	Beef	109,542.45	531
2	Chicken	105,174.44	505
3	Green Tea	102,872.22	515
4	Broccoli	100,136.97	501
5	Pizza	98,048.90	481
6	Tomatoes	96,685.27	487
7	Orange Juice	96,673.48	473
8	Sandwiches	96,088.37	466
9	Cucumber	94,006.03	474

Figure 5-53. *Total and number of sales by product report*

1. Click **Data ➤ Get Data ➤ Launch Power Query Editor**.

2. Right-click the *Master* query and click **Reference**. Repeat this step so that we have two new queries.

3. Rename one of the queries **MonthlySalesByRegion** and the other query **ProductSales**.

This creates two queries that are linked to the Master query. This ensures that the combining of the sheets and the transformation steps is only performed once, and then the two query reports are run. It's better than duplicating a query and unnecessarily repeating the steps.

You can view the dependencies between queries as a diagram in the Query Dependencies window (Figure 5-54). Click **View ➤ Query Dependencies**.

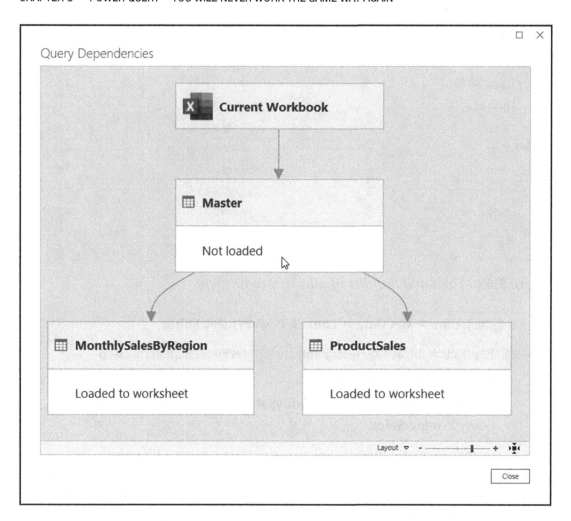

Figure 5-54. *Viewing the dependencies between the queries*

Let us now work on the first report.

4. Select the *MonthlySalesByRegion* query and click **Home ➤ Group By**.

5. Select **Advanced** so that we can group by more than one column. Select **Region** from the list, click **Add grouping,** and then select **Month** from the second list (Figure 5-55).

6. Enter **Total** for the new column name and specify the operation as **Sum** and the column to sum as **Amount**.

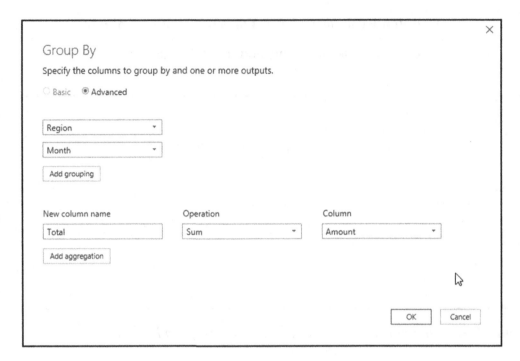

Figure 5-55. *Group by region and month with total sales*

Figure 5-56 shows the results from this grouping. To complete the report, we now need to pivot the *Month* column so that they become column headers.

	Aᴮ꜀ Region	Aᴮ꜀ Month	1.2 Total
1	East	Jan	10463.06
2	Central	Jan	8765.02
3	South	Jan	8917.22
4	South West	Jan	8432.95
5	North	Jan	7814.66
6	North	Feb	10290.87
7	East	Feb	13676.89
8	Central	Feb	12705.98
9	South West	Feb	11661.07
10	South	Feb	11926.18
11	South West	Mar	12845.39

Figure 5-56. *Group by region and month*

7. Select the **Month** column and click **Transform ➤ Pivot Column**.

8. Select **Total** as the Values Column and click **OK** (Figure 5-57).

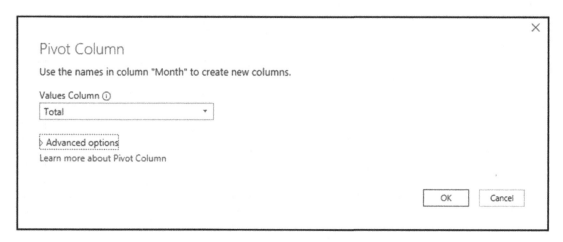

Figure 5-57. *Pivot the month column to become column headers*

9. Select the *Jan* column, press **Shift,** and select the *Dec* column.
    Click **Home ➤ Data Type** list ➤ **Currency**.

    Let us now create the second report.

10. Select the *ProductSales* query and click **Home ➤ Group By**.

11. Select **Advanced** and select the **Product** column to group by.

12. This report has two aggregations. For the first one, enter **Total
    Sales** for the column name and to **Sum** the **Amount** column. For
    the second aggregation, use **No of Sales** for the column name and
    Count Rows for the operation (Figure 5-58).

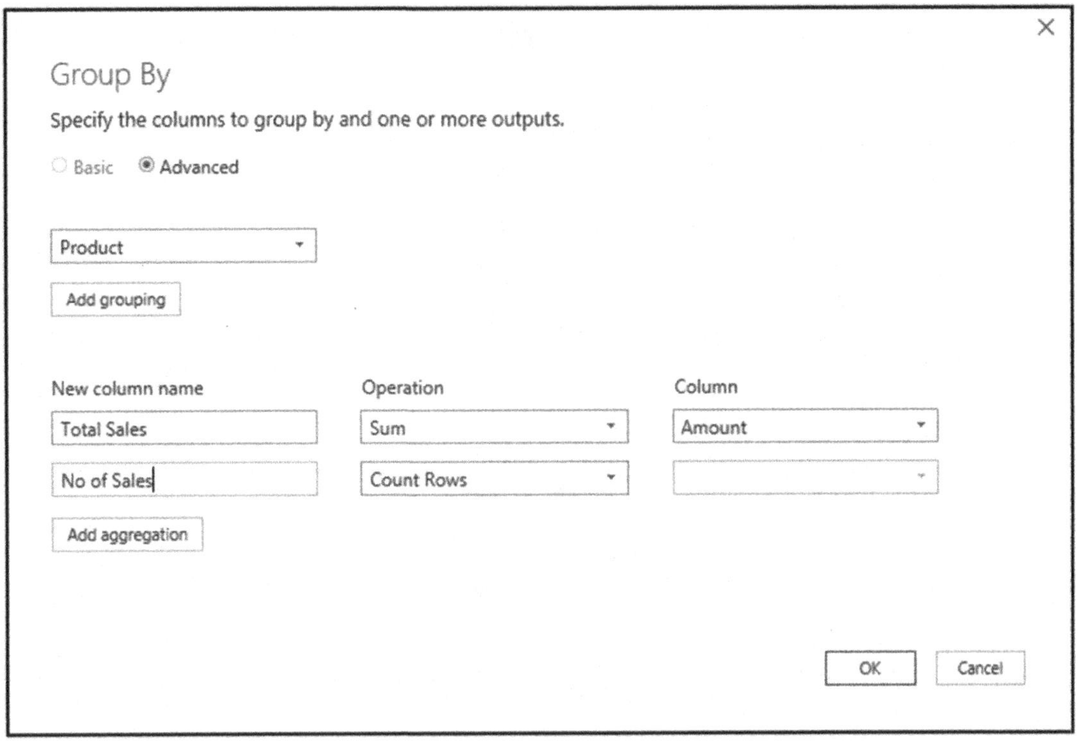

Figure 5-58. *Group by product with sum and count rows aggregations*

13. Change the data type of the *Total Sales* column to **Currency**.

14. Select the *Total Sales* column and click **Home ➤ Sort Descending**.

15. Close and load the queries.

The tables are loaded onto separate sheets, but you can organize these how you want.

These two additional queries do re-create the "Excel.CurrentWorkbook() Problem" discussed earlier. So, let us go back to that query and deal with it.

1. Click **Data ➤ Get Data ➤ Launch Power Query Editor**.

2. Select the *Master* query.

3. Select the **Source** step in the Applied Steps box and click **Home ➤ Refresh Preview**.

     The *ProductSales* and *MonthlySalesByRegion* tables are being picked up when combining all the workbook tables (Figure 5-59).

	ABC 123 Content	A B C Name	
1	Table	ProductSales	
2	Table	MonthlySalesByRegion	
3	Table	January	
4	Table	February	
5	Table	March	
6	Table	April	
7	Table	May	
8	Table	JUne	
9	Table	July	
10	Table	August	
11	Table	september	
12	Table	October	
13	Table	November	
14	Table	December	

Figure 5-59. *The report tables are recognized by Excel.CurrentWorkbook()*

4.   Delete the current **Filtered Rows** step. We will insert a new one.

5.   Select the **Source** step and filter out the **MonthlySalesByRegion**
     and **ProductSales** tables from the *Name* column.

6.   Refresh the queries, and they work perfectly.

Power Query can also be used to create PivotTable-style reports.

CHAPTER 6

Power Pivot – The Internal Data Model of Excel

Power Pivot is a feature that takes us beyond the Excel spreadsheet. We can do things with Power Pivot that are unheard of with traditional Excel techniques.

This chapter will walk through the creation of a Power Pivot model from start to finish. We will produce different reports to showcase the power of this internal data model of Excel.

What Is Power Pivot?

Power Pivot allows us to surpass the limitations of an Excel spreadsheet and perform powerful data analysis.

We can load tables from different sources into Excel memory and create relationships between them using a common column. This is known as the data model. Simply put, Power Pivot is PivotTables created from the data model. However, there is a lot more to it than that description suggests. It is a vast feature with its own formula language and nuances. This chapter is an introduction to its capabilities.

Note   The names of features can be confusing. The terms Power Pivot and data model are interchangeable. It is possible to work with the model without using PivotTables, but it is often still referred to as Power Pivot.

© Alan Murray 2021
A. Murray, *Advanced Excel Success*, https://doi.org/10.1007/978-1-4842-6467-6_6

The advantages to using Power Pivot include

- **Work with large volumes of data:** Using the data model, we are not limited to the 1,048,576 rows of an Excel spreadsheet. We can connect to and analyze millions of rows of data and not experience the same struggle of traditional Excel working with only a few hundred thousand rows.

- **Create relationships between tables:** When working with multiple tables, traditional Excel use involves using lookup functions to add columns so that you have one table with all the data. Figure 6-1 shows a VLOOKUP being used to search for the product in another table and return its price. With Power Pivot, the tables are kept separate, and a relationship is created between them. This is much more efficient, especially when working with many tables and lots of data.

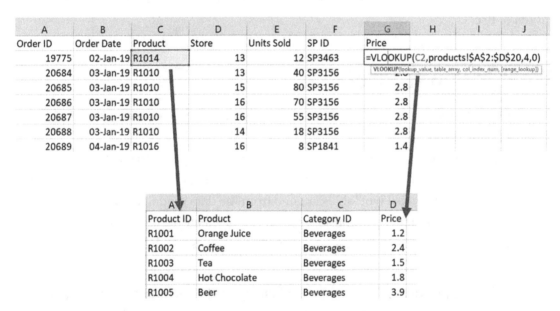

Figure 6-1. *VLOOKUP being used to add columns from other tables*

- **DAX formulas:** Power Pivot has its own formula language known as Data Analysis Expressions or simply as DAX. This rich formula language offers powerful and flexible functions that are far superior to the 11 standard functions available with PivotTables.

You will see all these advantages as we work through the example in this chapter.

Enable the Power Pivot Add-In

Power Pivot is a COM add-in and needs to be enabled before you can start using it. You can open the Power Pivot window and access the data model by clicking **Data ➤ Manage Data Model**, but if the add-in is not enabled, you will see the message in Figure 6-2. Click **Enable** and you have Power Pivot.

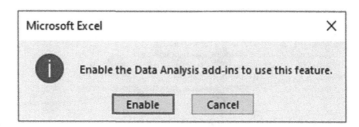

Figure 6-2. *Prompt to enable Power Pivot*

You can also enable Power Pivot by following these steps:

1. Click **File ➤ Options ➤ Add-ins**.

2. Select **COM Add-ins** from the *Manage* list and click **Go** (Figure 6-3).

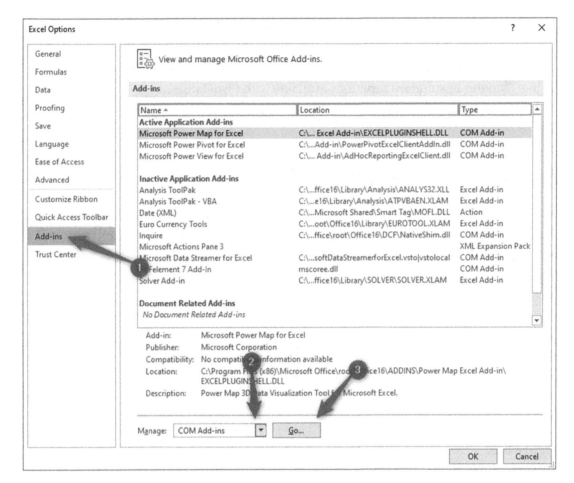

Figure 6-3. *Access COM add-ins through Excel options*

3. Check the **Microsoft Power Pivot for Excel** box and click **OK**
    (Figure 6-4).

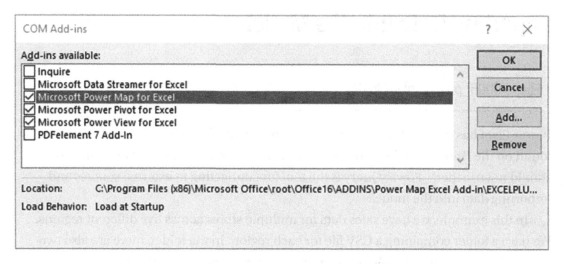

Figure 6-4. *Enable Power Pivot from the COM Add-ins window*

A Power Pivot tab appears on the Ribbon (Figure 6-5). There are only a few buttons on it. This tab will be useful in creating measures later in this chapter without needing to open the Power Pivot window.

Most of our work however will require opening the window to access the data model. This can be done by clicking the **Manage** button on the **Power Pivot** tab or by clicking **Data ➤ Manage Data Model**.

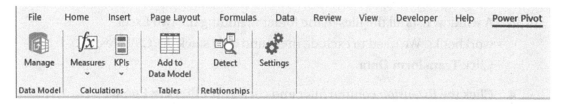

Figure 6-5. *The Power Pivot tab on the Ribbon*

Importing Data into the Model

File   Ch06_power_pivot folder

Power Pivot has the functionality to connect to external data sources. These can be found on the **Home** tab of the Power Pivot window. However, they are limited, and you should not use them. Power Query is the tool for connecting to external sources and importing data into the model.

In this example, we have sales data for multiple stores across five different regions. We have a folder containing a CSV file for each region. In the folder, there are also two Excel workbooks with data about the products, stores, and the sales reps.

So, our model will contain four tables when all the data is imported – sales, products, sales reps, and stores.

Import from Folder

Let us start by importing the CSV files from the *Ch06_power_pivot* folder.

1. Click **Data ➤ Get Data ➤ From File ➤ From Folder**.

2. Click **Browse** and locate the **Ch06_power_pivot** folder. Click **OK**.

3. A window lists all the files in the folder including the two Excel workbooks. We need to exclude these and only stack the CSV files. Click **Transform Data**.

4. Click the *Extension* column filter and click **Text Filters ➤ Equals**. Enter **.csv** for the rows to keep and click **OK** (Figure 6-6).

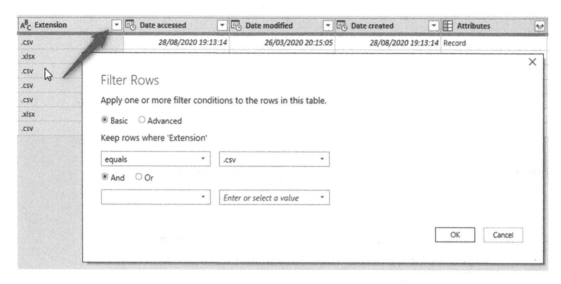

Figure 6-6. *Filter out all file types except CSV*

5. Click the **Combine Files** button in the *Content* column header
    (Figure 6-7). This will stack the files into one table.

🏛▾	☰ Content	↓↓	A⁸c Name	▾
1	Binary		east.csv	
2	Binary		north-east.csv	
3	Binary		north-west.csv	
4	Binary		south.csv	
5	Binary		west.csv	

Figure 6-7. *Combine the files into one table*

6. The Combine Files window offers the first file as the sample file
    and provides the opportunity to change this. This is the file that is
    most reliable, and its column headers will be used. The first file is
    fine in this example, so click **OK**.

The five CSV files are stacked into one list of 9020 rows (Figure 6-8). There are a few
more transformations to perform before we load the table into the data model.

Source.Name	Order ID	Order Date	Product	Store	Units Sold	SP ID
1	east.csv	11000	01/01/2019	R1005	9	30	SP3774
2	east.csv	11001	01/01/2019	R1005	6	20	SP3774
3	east.csv	10940	02/01/2019	R1004	8	12	SP2886
4	east.csv	11339	04/01/2019	R1020	6	8	SP1131
5	east.csv	11340	04/01/2019	R1020	8	14	SP1131
6	east.csv	11341	04/01/2019	R1020	6	5	SP1131
7	east.csv	12134	04/01/2019	R1014	6	8	SP2365
8	east.csv	12135	04/01/2019	R1014	6	40	SP2365
9	east.csv	10967	05/01/2019	R1004	9	5	SP3774
10	east.csv	11184	05/01/2019	R1020	6	15	SP2365
11	east.csv	11185	05/01/2019	R1020	6	50	SP2365
12	east.csv	11186	05/01/2019	R1020	8	70	SP2365

Figure 6-8. *The stacked sales table before final transformations*

7. Rename the query **sales**.

8. Select the *Source.Name* column and click **Home ➤ Replace Values**. Enter **.csv** as the *Value To Find* and leave the *Replace With* box empty. Click **OK**.

9. With the *Source.Name* column selected, click **Home ➤ Replace Values**. Enter - as the *Value To Find* and enter a **space** in the *Replace With* box. This replaces the hyphen (-) in the *north-east* and *north-west* region names. Click **OK**.

10. With the *Source.Name* column selected, click **Transform ➤ Format ➤ Capitalize Each Word**.

11. Rename the *Source.Name* column as **Region**.

12. Move the *Region* column to the **third** position between *Order Date* and *Product*.

13. Move the *Product* column to the **fifth** position between *Store* and *Units Sold*.

The *sales* table is complete (Figure 6-9). We will now load it to the data model.

Order ID	Order Date	Region	Store	Product	Units Sold	SP ID
1	11000	01/01/2019	East	9	R1005	30	SP3774
2	11001	01/01/2019	East	6	R1005	20	SP3774
3	10940	02/01/2019	East	8	R1004	12	SP2886
4	11339	04/01/2019	East	6	R1020	8	SP1131
5	11340	04/01/2019	East	8	R1020	14	SP1131
6	11341	04/01/2019	East	6	R1020	5	SP1131
7	12134	04/01/2019	East	6	R1014	8	SP2365
8	12135	04/01/2019	East	6	R1014	40	SP2365
9	10967	05/01/2019	East	9	R1004	5	SP3774
10	11184	05/01/2019	East	6	R1020	15	SP2365
11	11185	05/01/2019	East	6	R1020	50	SP2365

Figure 6-9. *Completed sales table*

14. Click **Home ➤ Close & Load** list ➤ **Close & Load To**. Select **Only Create Connection** and check the box to **Add this data to the Data Model** (Figure 6-10).

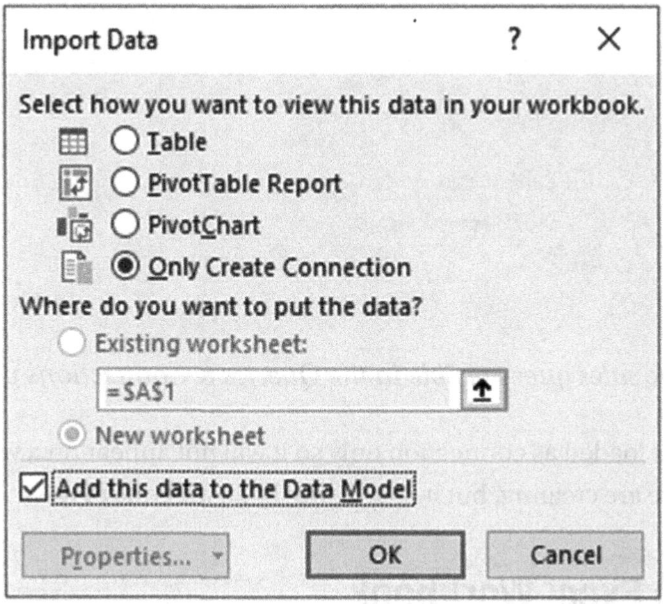

Figure 6-10. *Import as a connection only and add to the data model*

The *sales* query is loaded and displayed in the Queries & Connections pane with its 9020 rows. Other queries are shown that are required by the import from the folder process. We will not be working with these so they can be hidden (Figure 6-11).

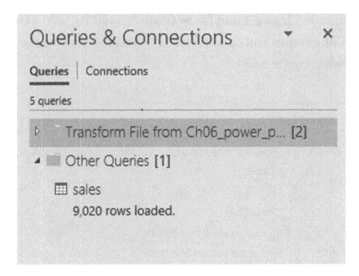

Figure 6-11. *The sales query visible in the Queries & Connections pane*

The query was loaded as connection only so it will not appear on a worksheet. This is a simple model we are creating, but it could have been millions of rows.

Import from Excel Workbook

With the sales data loaded, we have three more tables to import into the model. These three tables are coming from two different Excel workbooks.

1. Click **Data ➤ Get Data ➤ From File ➤ From Workbook**.

2. Locate the *lookup-tables.xlsx* workbook and click **Import**.

3. The Navigator window lists one table and two worksheets. Check the **Select multiple items** box and check the boxes for the **products** table and the **Reps** worksheet (Figure 6-12).

Figure 6-12 shows a preview of the Reps worksheet. As this is not in a table, there are no defined headers. We need to promote the first row to headers in this query.

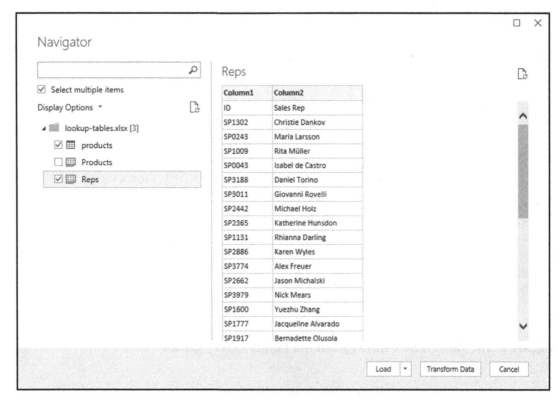

Figure 6-12. *Select the products table and the Reps worksheet*

4. Click **Transform Data**.

5. Select the *Reps* query and rename it **reps** to keep the query names in consistent case.

6. Click **Home ➤ Use First Row as Headers**.

7. Select the *products* query and change the data type of the *Price* column to **Currency**. Click **Replace Current** if you receive a message about changing the current changed type step or creating a new one.

Before we close and load these queries to the model, let us get the data we need from the other Excel workbook.

8. Right-click the *Queries* pane and select **New Query ➤ File ➤ Excel** (Figure 6-13).

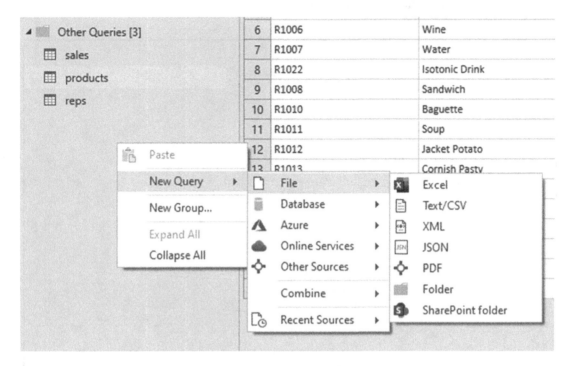

Figure 6-13. *Start a new query from the Power Query Editor*

9. Locate the *stores.xlsx* workbook and click **Import**.

10. In the Navigator window, select the **Store** worksheet. In the preview, you can see that there are some blank rows and a mistype in the header of the second column (Figure 6-14). Click **OK**.

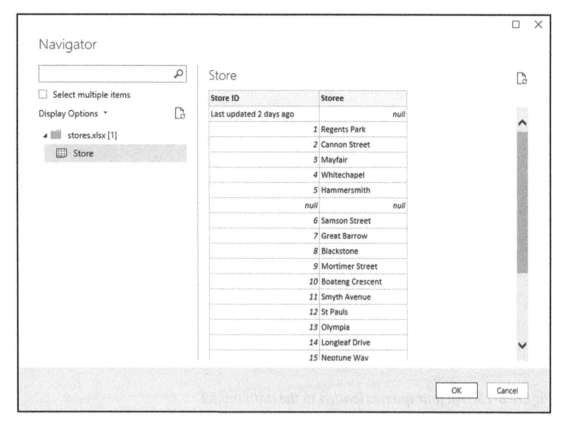

Figure 6-14. *Preview of the stores information in the Navigator window*

11. Rename the query **stores**.

12. Rename the *Storee* column to **Store**.

13. Filter the *Store* column to remove the **Null** rows.

14. Click **Home ➤ Close & Load** list ➤ **Close & Load To**. Select **Only Create Connection** and check the box to **Add this data to the Data Model**. Click **OK**.

All four queries are loaded as connection only and to the data model (Figure 6-15).

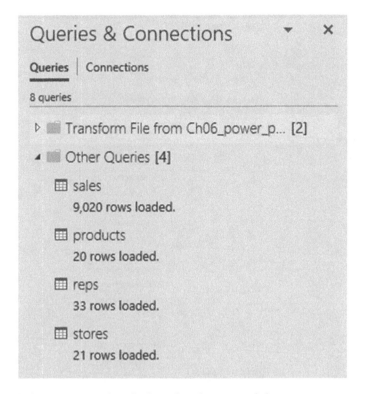

Figure 6-15. *All four queries loaded to the data model*

Create the Table Relationships

With the tables loaded into the data model, we can now create a PivotTable from the model. Let us create a PivotTable to show the total number of units sold for each product.

1. Click **Insert ➤ PivotTable**.

2. The PivotTable identifies that you have a data model in the workbook and automatically selects that option (Figure 6-16). If, for any reason, this has not happened, select **Use this workbook's Data Model**. Specify a location and click **OK**.

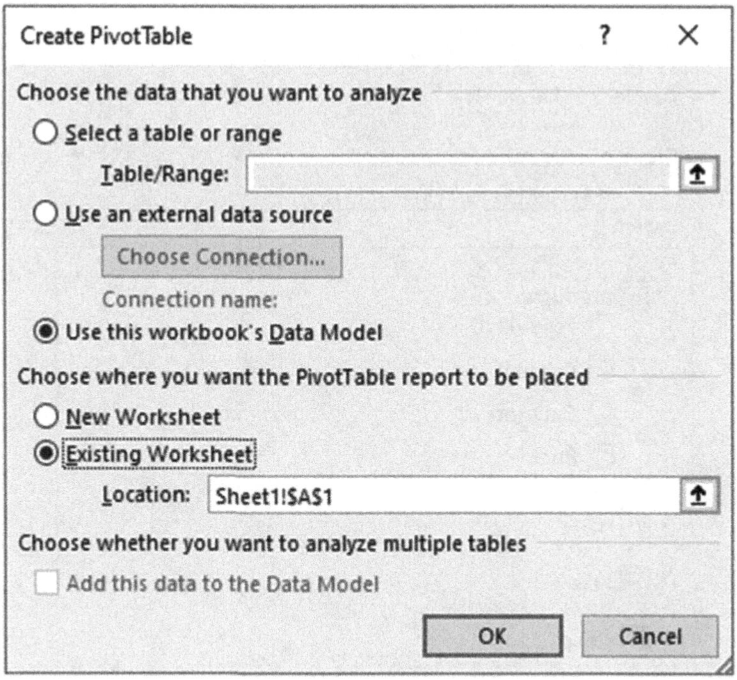

Figure 6-16. *Create a PivotTable from the data model*

The PivotTable Fields pane shows the four tables from the model (Figure 6-17). The cylinder icon next to their name indicates that they are from the data model.

Click the arrow next to their name to expand the table and access the fields.

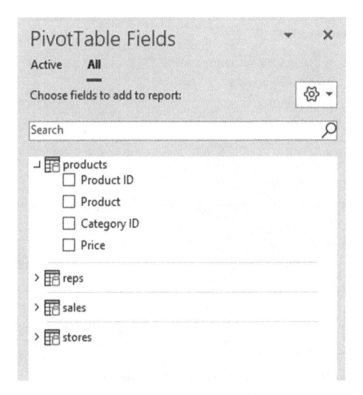

Figure 6-17. *PivotTable Fields pane with the four tables from the model*

3. Click and drag the **Product** field from the *products* table into the **Rows** area and click and drag the **Units Sold** field from the *sales* table into the **Values** area.

4. The resulting PivotTable is shown in Figure 6-18. This is clearly not correct as each product has sold the same number of units. Even the grand total has the same value.

We have not created relationships between our tables yet, and that is the issue. Without the relationship between the *products* table and the *sales* table, it is unable to filter the total units sold value by the product to get each product's total.

◢	A	B
1	**Row Labels** ▾	**Sum of Units Sold**
2	Baguette	215540
3	Beer	215540
4	Blueberry Muffin	215540
5	Caramel Shortbread	215540
6	Chocolate Chip Muffin	215540
7	Coffee	215540
8	Cornish Pasty	215540
9	Crisps	215540
10	Croissant	215540
11	Flapjack	215540
12	Hot Chocolate	215540
13	Jacket Potato	215540
14	Orange Juice	215540
15	Samosa	215540
16	Sandwich	215540
17	Sausage Roll	215540
18	Soup	215540
19	Tea	215540
20	Water	215540
21	Wine	215540
22	**Grand Total**	**215540**
23		

Figure 6-18. *This PivotTable is clearly wrong; it is not filtering by product*

We are alerted to this issue in the PivotTable Fields pane also (Figure 6-19). We could click the **Auto-Detect** button to set up the table relationships, but then we miss out on the fun. So, let us do it ourselves.

Figure 6-19. Missing relationships warning in the PivotTable Fields pane

---

Note   The light gray line separating the tables in the PivotTable Fields list indicates that they are not related.

---

1. Click the **Power Pivot** tab and then the **Manage** button.

2. The Power Pivot window opens and will probably take you to the *Data* view. This looks like Excel with tabs at the bottom for the four different tables. Click **Home ➤ Diagram View**.

   This view is the best for managing your table relationships as it is very visual. You can see the four blocks that resemble the tables and the fields/columns listed within them.

   You can move and resize the tables to organize them how you want.

3. Click and drag the **sales** table underneath the other three tables and space them out neatly (Figure 6-20).

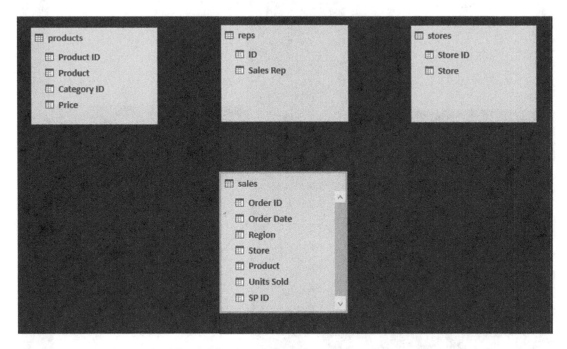

Figure 6-20. *Organize the tables to make the relationships easier to read*

The *sales* table is known as a fact table or a data table. It contains the information on the transactions, in this case, sales.

The *products*, *sales reps,* and *stores* tables are known as dimension or lookup tables. They contain the information about the subjects used in the transactions.

I like to think of the fact table being the story and the dimension tables as the characters in the story.

To create a relationship, click and drag between the key fields in each table. Click and drag from the fact table to the dimension table (just like the lookup value and lookup array of the XLOOKUP function).

4. Click and drag from the **Product** field in the *sales* table to the **Product ID** field of the *products* table (Figure 6-21).

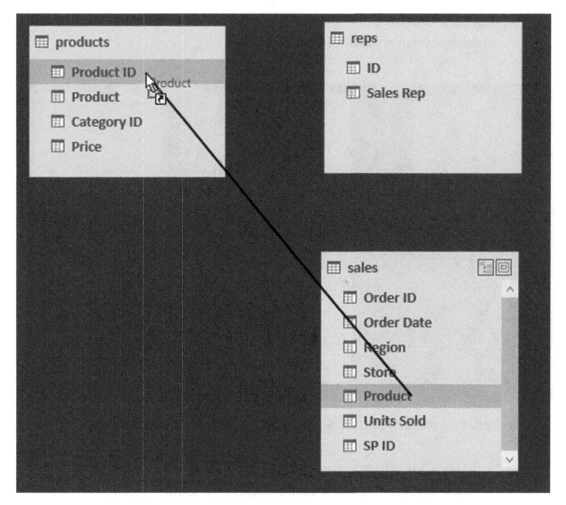

Figure 6-21. *Creating a relationship between the sales and the products tables*

5. Create a relationship between the *sales* and *reps* tables using the
   SP ID field in *sales* and the **ID** field in *reps*.

6. Create a relationship between the *sales* and *stores* tables using the
   Store field in *sales* and the **Store ID** field in *stores*.

The relationships are shown with lines linking the related tables (Figure 6-22). When a relationship line is selected (*sales* and *stores* in this image), the key fields from each table are identified with green rectangles.

The relationship lines have a one and an asterisk on each end indicating a many-to-one relationship. For example, one product can be sold many times. This is the only relationship (cardinality) we will discuss in this book.

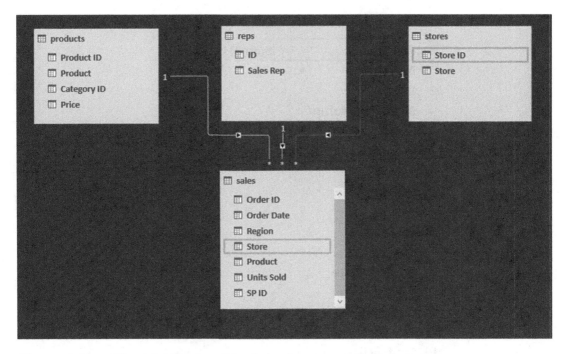

Figure 6-22. *All table relationships have been established*

There is also an arrow on the relationship line showing the filter direction. The tables have been arranged in this way as it visually shows the lookup tables filtering the fact table.

Switch to the Excel window, the PivotTable we created now works perfectly (Figure 6-23). The *products* table is filtered before it sums the total units of the *sales* table.

◢	A	B
1	**Row Labels** ▾	**Sum of Units Sold**
2	Baguette	26539
3	Beer	11912
4	Blueberry Muffin	14312
5	Caramel Shortbread	5623
6	Chocolate Chip Muffin	5941
7	Coffee	18291
8	Cornish Pasty	4469
9	Crisps	14520
10	Croissant	6204
11	Flapjack	5799
12	Hot Chocolate	4161
13	Jacket Potato	13303
14	Orange Juice	5175
15	Samosa	14898
16	Sandwich	5009
17	Sausage Roll	9886
18	Soup	8293
19	Tea	9565
20	Water	13326
21	Wine	18314
22	**Grand Total**	**215540**
23		

Figure 6-23. *PivotTable works perfectly when tables are related correctly*

In the Diagram view of Power Pivot, you can edit and delete existing table relationships by right-clicking the relationship line. The easiest way though is to click **Design ➤ Manage Relationships**.

This window lists the table relationships with columns showing the relationships tables, key fields, cardinality, and filter direction (Figure 6-24). As mentioned, this chapter focuses on a simple model that does not require knowledge in all these areas. But it is interesting to read.

There are buttons at the top of the window to create, edit, and delete relationships. Everything can be done from here.

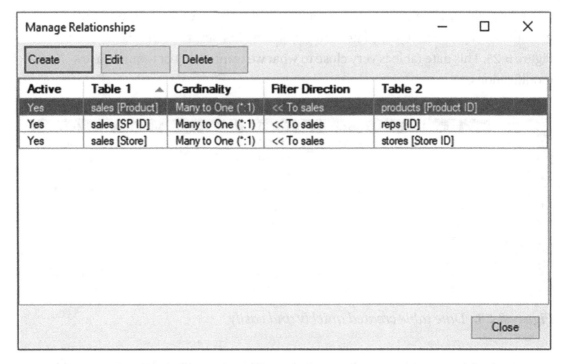

Figure 6-24. *The Manage Relationships window*

Create a Date Table

There is one more table that we will add to our Power Pivot model, and that is a date table. A date table is essential to work effectively with dates.

As part of our data analysis, we may want to compare different date periods such as years and months or show cumulative monthly sales. To get our model working efficiently, we need a table of dates.

Sometimes, you will have a date table as an import from an external source. In this example, we will need to create one ourselves.

There are a variety of techniques for creating a date table. These include using Power Query which is a dynamic and powerful approach.

In this example, we will use a feature in Power Pivot that creates a date table at the click of a button. It's very fast and very simple. We can then make some improvements to it.

1. In Power Pivot, click **Home ➤ Data View** to switch to data view.

2. Click **Design ➤ Date Table ➤ New**.

A date table is instantly created named *Calendar* and uses the columns and measures of a predefined template. You can see the first few rows of this table in Figure 6-25. This date table is very close to what we wanted; it just requires a few modifications.

Date	Year	Month Number	Month	MMM-YYYY	Day Of Week Number	Day Of Week
1 01/01/...	2019	1	January	Jan-2019	3	Tuesday
2 02/01/...	2019	1	January	Jan-2019	4	Wednesday
3 03/01/...	2019	1	January	Jan-2019	5	Thursday
4 04/01/...	2019	1	January	Jan-2019	6	Friday
5 05/01/...	2019	1	January	Jan-2019	7	Saturday
6 06/01/...	2019	1	January	Jan-2019	1	Sunday
7 07/01/...	2019	1	January	Jan-2019	2	Monday
8 08/01/...	2019	1	January	Jan-2019	3	Tuesday
9 09/01/...	2019	1	January	Jan-2019	4	Wednesday
10 10/01/...	2019	1	January	Jan-2019	5	Thursday

Figure 6-25. *Date table created quickly and easily*

It is important that the date table includes every date for every year that you plan to perform data analysis. In this table, the *Date* column is the base for all the other columns.

In this example, the sales data we are using is for the year of 2019 only. So, the *Date* column lists every date between 1 January and 31 December 2019.

Users may include the future or previous year's sales data by adding the CSV files to the source folder. In this case, we can update the range by clicking **Design ➤ Date Table ➤ Update Range** and specifying different start and end dates (Figure 6-26).

Date Table Range	✕
Start Date	01/01/2019
End Date	31/12/2019
	OK Cancel

Figure 6-26. *Update the date table range*

You can add, remove, and edit the columns in this table to ensure you have the fields you want to use in your PivotTable labels and Slicers or for use in other measures. For example, you might want to add fiscal years or quarters.

We will just make a few small modifications to this table. This will be our first glimpse at DAX, but we will cover it in more detail soon.

3. Select the **Month** column and edit the DAX formula to display the month as "**MMM**" (Figure 6-27). The shortened month name will use less space in our table and chart labels.

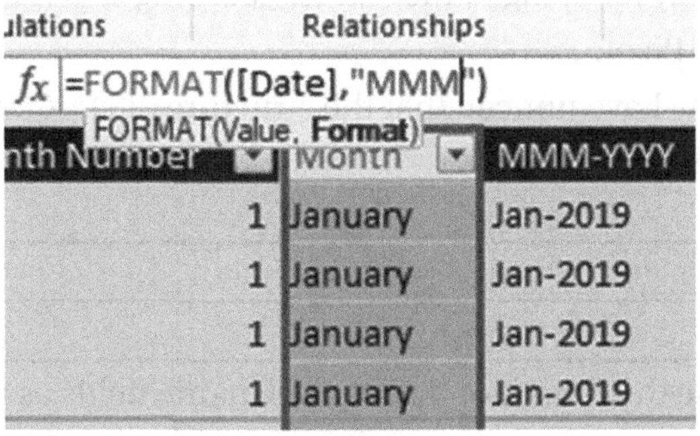

Figure 6-27. *Edit the DAX formula to display a shortened month name*

Note   The FORMAT function is the DAX alternative to the TEXT function we used in Chapter 4 for dynamic chart labels.

---

4. Select the **Day Of Week** column and edit the DAX formula to show the day of the week as "**DDD**".

   =FORMAT([Date],"DDD")

5. Select the **Day Of Week Number** column and edit the WEEKDAY function by adding **2** for the *Return Type* argument.

   =WEEKDAY([Date],2)

This changes the first day of the week from Sunday to Monday. It is important that the first day of the week is specified correctly, so they appear in this order in our PivotTable labels and Slicers.

The last few steps have provided a nice introduction to DAX formulas. You can only create columns in Power Pivot by using DAX. These are known as calculated columns.

The columns you need are normally imported from the source data or created in Power Query before loading to the model. Calculated columns are used to create additional columns in your lookup tables, if they are not provided by the queries. They should be avoided with your fact tables.

We will be seeing a lot more of DAX formulas shortly when we write measures. A measure is a DAX formula that is used in the Values area of a PivotTable, while calculated columns are used in the label and filter fields of a PivotTable. When we talk of DAX formulas, we are normally referring to measures. Learning to write measures unleashes the real power of Power Pivot.

Fortunately, you may have noticed that the structure of DAX formulas is very similar to Excel worksheet functions.

Sort by Column

At the moment, if we use the month or day of week name fields as a label, they are ordered incorrectly. Figure 6-28 shows them being used as row labels in a PivotTable.

Row Labels ▾			Row Labels ▾	
Apr			Fri	
Aug			Mon	
Dec			Sat	
Feb			Sun	
Jan			Thu	
Jul			Tue	
Jun			Wed	
Mar			**Grand Total**	
May				
Nov				
Oct				
Sep				
Grand Total				

Figure 6-28. *The month and day of week names are not ordered correctly*

They are both displayed in A to Z order, but month and day of week names have their own special order. In Excel, custom lists are used to order them, but in Power Pivot we do things differently.

By specifying their order in the model, we will not have to sort them each time they are used in our reports.

1. Select the **Month** column and click **Home ➤ Sort by Column**.

2. Select the **Month Number** column as the column to sort by (Figure 6-29). Click **OK**.

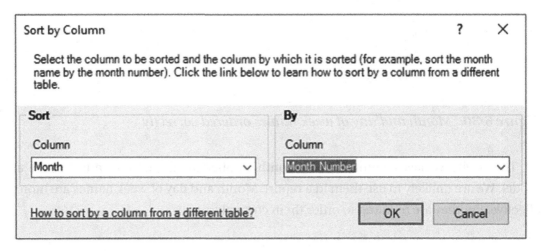

Figure 6-29. *Sort the month name by the month number column*

3. Select the **Day Of Week** column and click **Home ➤ Sort by Column**.

4. Select the **Day Of Week Number** column as the column to sort by. Click **OK**.

The month and day of week names are now ordered correctly in the PivotTables (Figure 6-30).

Row Labels ▼			Row Labels ▼
Jan			Mon
Feb			Tue
Mar			Wed
Apr			Thu
May			Fri
Jun			Sat
Jul			Sun
Aug			**Grand Total**
Sep			
Oct			
Nov			
Dec			
Grand Total			

Figure 6-30. *Month and day of week names ordered correctly*

This is why we have columns for the month number and day of week number in our model. We are unlikely to use them in a report. Month and day of week names are more effective. But they are required to order them correctly.

Note The day of week names begin with "Mon" because we edited the WEEKDAY function to start the week from Monday.

The sort by column functionality of Power Pivot provides great flexibility with how you order items. Month names do not have to begin with January, and other text labels do not need to be ordered A to Z. There may be a different order you want to use, for example, poor, good, great, excellent.

Mark the Table as a Date Table

This date table has already been marked as a date table to Power Pivot because we used the date table feature to create it. Marking it as a date table lets Power Pivot know where to find the dates when filtering the model.

Although this table has been marked already, let us go through the steps of how to do this.

1. Click **Design ➤ Mark as Date Table ➤ Mark as Date Table**.

2. Ensure that the **Date** column is selected as the column of unique dates in the table (Figure 6-31).

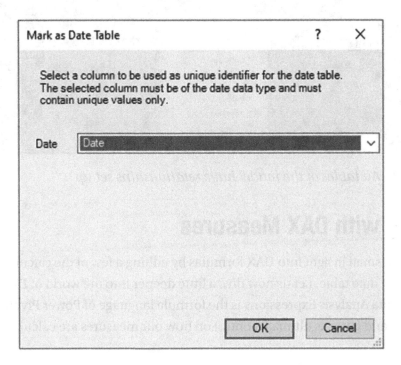

Figure 6-31. Specify the column of unique dates in your date table

Create the Relationship to the Date Table

The final stage in creating the date table is to establish its relationship in the model.

1. Click **Home ➤ Diagram View** to switch back to diagram view.

2. Click and drag from the **Order Date** column of the *sales* table to the **Date** column of the *Calendar* table.

The *Calendar* table is now related to the *sales* (fact) table, just like the other three lookup (dimension) tables (Figure 6-32).

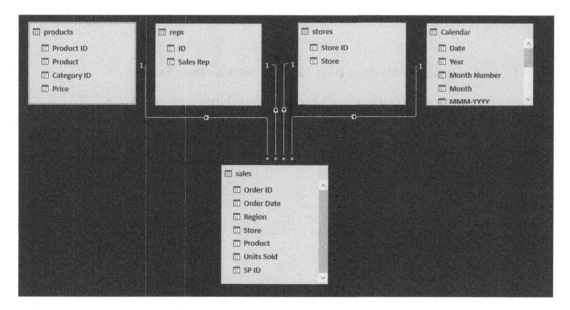

Figure 6-32. *All tables of the model have relationships set up*

Working with DAX Measures

We have had a small insight into DAX formulas by editing a few of the calculated columns of the date table. Let us now dive a little deeper into the world of DAX.

DAX or Data Analysis Expressions is the formula language of Power Pivot. It is vast and powerful and gives us ultimate control on how our measures are calculated.

What Are the Advantages of Using Measures?

When using PivotTables, and you drag a field into the *Values* area, an aggregation is performed (Figure 6-33). This defaults to sum if a numeric field is used and count if a text field is used. You can easily change how the data is summarized. This is great!

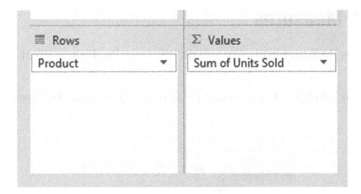

Figure 6-33. *The Units Sold field is summed when moved into the Values area*

However, these are known as implicit measures. Each time you drag a field into a PivotTable, you have another implicit measure. These work great, but there are many advantages to creating your own (explicit) measures.

The advantages of writing DAX measures include

- DAX measures can be reused but are only calculated once. They can be used in PivotTables and Slicers as many times as you want.

- Measures can also be used in other measures. This simplifies your DAX formulas. For example, you can sum a value in a measure and then use that in other measures, instead of having to sum it in each measure (we will perform this example soon).

- There are hundreds of DAX functions to take advantage of. PivotTables only offer 11 functions to summarize values (sum, average, count, etc.). So, DAX takes you far beyond the standard PivotTable (hence the name Power Pivot).

- Being able to reuse measures in other PivotTables, Slicers, and measures creates a fast and lean model that is much more efficient than one using implicit measures.

- DAX measures are formatted when they are created. This ensures a consistent format across all reports and prevents having to specify the format every time it is used.

Create DAX Measures

Let us create a few DAX measures. We will do this from the **Power Pivot** tab on the Ribbon in Excel.

Click the **Switch to Workbook** button (Figure 6-34) or close the Power Pivot window.

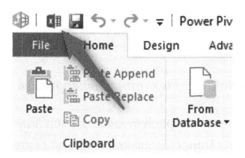

Figure 6-34. *Switch from the Power Pivot window to the Excel workbook*

Calculate the Number of Sales

For our first measure, we will calculate the number of sales. For this, we will use a DAX function named COUNTROWS to count the number of rows in the *sales* table.

1. Click **Power Pivot ➤ Measures ➤ New Measure**.

2. Select the **sales** table for the *Table name*.

3. Enter **No of Sales** for the *Measure name*.

4. Enter the following formula into the box provided. Click the **Check formula** button to check for syntax errors.

   ```
   =COUNTROWS(sales)
   ```

Note   You can press the **Ctrl** key and roll the mouse wheel to zoom in and out of the formula box.

---

5. Specify the format as a **Number ➤ Whole Number** and check the box to **Use 1000 separator**.

Figure 6-35 shows the completed Measure window. This window makes it easier to create measures and ensures we are less likely to miss a step such as formatting the measure.

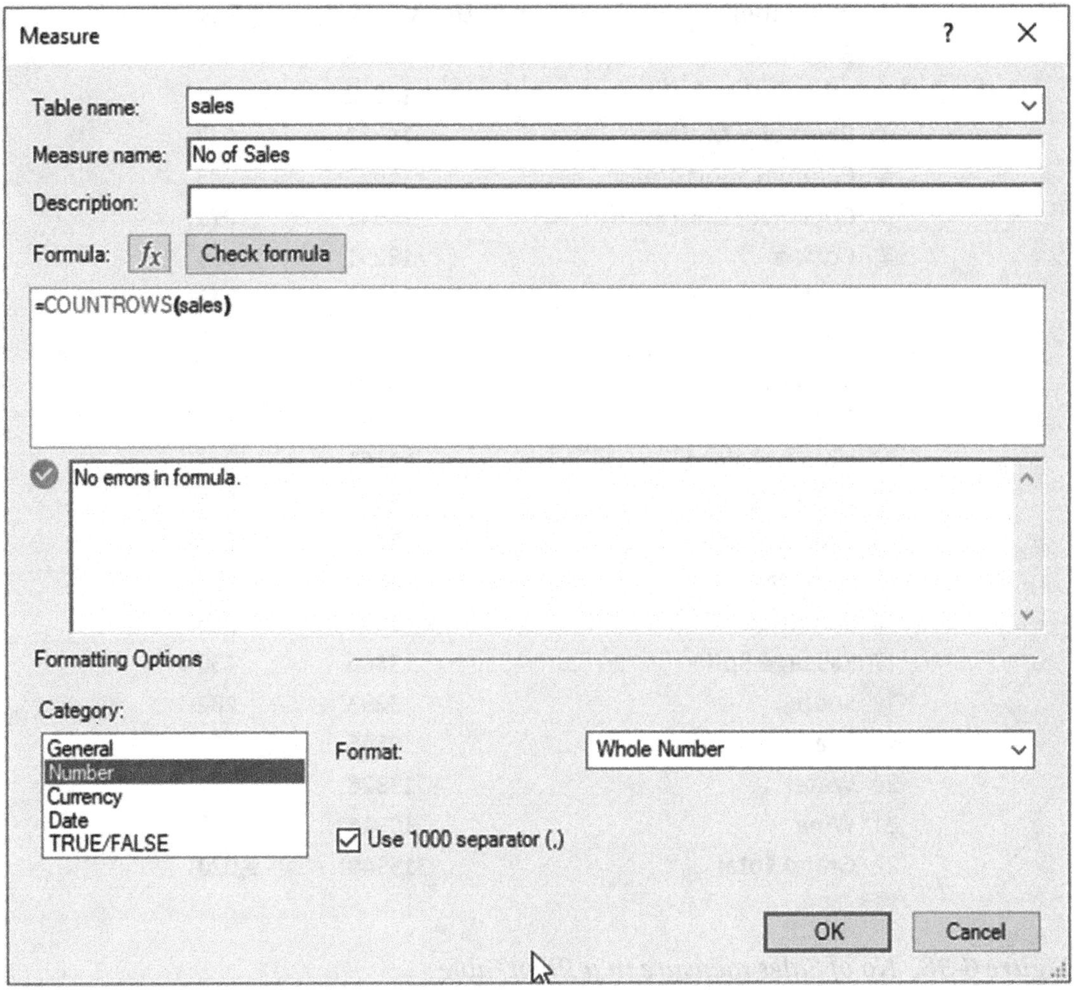

Figure 6-35. *Measure to calculate the number of sales*

Click **OK** to create the measure. If a PivotTable was active when you created the measure, it will automatically add the measure to the *Values* area.

It is a good idea whenever you create a measure to add it to a PivotTable. This gives you the chance to check it works and is formatted correctly before you go any further. Figure 6-36 shows this measure added to the PivotTable we created earlier in this chapter.

You can see the measure name used in the heading, the formatting is correct, and the grand total of 9,020 matches the number of rows loaded in the model.

	A	B	C
1	Row Labels	Sum of Units Sold	No of Sales
2	Baguette	26539	985
3	Beer	11912	541
4	Blueberry Muffin	14312	637
5	Caramel Shortbread	5623	283
6	Chocolate Chip Muffin	5941	271
7	Coffee	18291	759
8	Cornish Pasty	4469	213
9	Crisps	14520	585
10	Croissant	6204	262
11	Flapjack	5799	272
12	Hot Chocolate	4161	212
13	Jacket Potato	13303	506
14	Orange Juice	5175	294
15	Samosa	14898	567
16	Sandwich	5009	216
17	Sausage Roll	9886	450
18	Soup	8293	282
19	Tea	9565	429
20	Water	13326	477
21	Wine	18314	779
22	Grand Total	215540	9,020
23			

Figure 6-36. *No of Sales measure in a PivotTable*

When you are writing DAX formulas, think filtering. A large part of mastering DAX is understanding the filters on your model. This is something new to many Excel users and is the most important thing to understand when getting started.

When you write an aggregation formula such as count or sum in an Excel cell, you receive one number as a result. But with Power Pivot, that one result has different context depending on how we use it. In this example, it is in a PivotTable and is filtered by the row label of the product.

We can continue to use it in as many PivotTables as we want. And it can be filtered by a PivotTable's row, column, report filter, Slicer, and by table relationships.

The *No of Sales* measure can be found in the *sales* table in the PivotTable Fields pane (Figure 6-37). The fx icon next to its name identifies it as an explicit measure.

Figure 6-37. *No of Sales measure in the PivotTable Fields pane*

Total Sales Revenue

Let us now calculate the total sales revenue. This will be a more complex DAX formula.

It will be more complex because we do not have a column to sum. The *sales* table contains a column with the number of units sold, and the *products* table has a column with the product price. Before we can sum the total sales, we first need to multiply these two values to get the total for each sale.

Now, we could create a calculated column in the *sales* table with the total for each row. And then sum that column.

We want to avoid the use of calculated columns though. The *sales* table has 9020 rows, so we would have 9020 calculations we want to avoid, keeping our model lean. And imagine if the *sales* (fact) table was hundreds of thousands or even millions of rows.

To do this, there are DAX functions known as iterator functions. These functions move (iterate) down each row of a table and perform a calculation. And when finished, they aggregate the result. These functions have an X after their name, for example, SUMX, COUNTX, COUNTAX.

We will use the SUMX function to multiply the price by the number of units sold and then sum the resulting values (Figure 6-38).

1.   Click **Power Pivot ➤ Measures ➤ New Measure**.

2.   Select **sales** as the table name and enter **Total Sales** for the measure name.

3.   Enter the following formula in the box provided:

    =SUMX(sales,RELATED(products[Price])*sales[Units Sold])

4.   Specify the format as **Currency**, **£**, and **2 decimal places**.

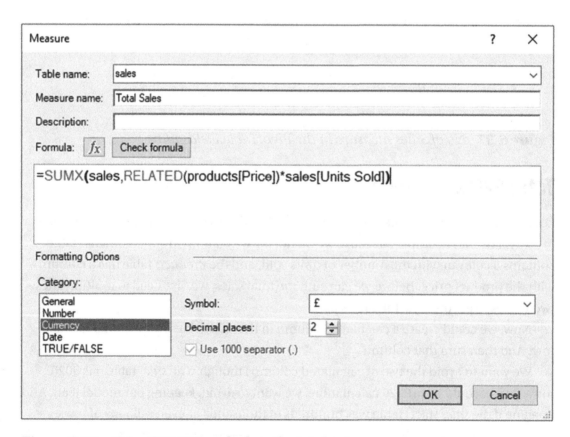

Figure 6-38. *Using SUMX to calculate the total sales revenue*

The SUMX function asks for a table and then an expression. The *sales* table is provided as the table to iterate down. The expression is the product price multiplied by the units sold.

The RELATED function returns the price from the products table using the table relationship. It's much easier than writing a VLOOKUP.

Even though the SUMX function is iterating down the *sales* table, the table is mentioned when referencing the *Units Sold* column. This is good practice to help distinguish table columns from measures. You should always use the table name before a column name.

Figure 6-39 shows the first few rows of the *Total Sales* measure being used in a PivotTable with the *Stores* field in row labels.

	A	B
1	Row Labels ▼	Total Sales
2	Baker Street	£33,276.60
3	Bartholomew Drive	£18,667.90
4	Blackstone	£18,363.90
5	Boateng Crescent	£63,354.30
6	Cannon Street	£30,135.50
7	Eastbourne Avenue	£17,402.00
8	Evans Street	£12,637.90

Figure 6-39. *First few rows of a PivotTable showing total sales by store*

Cumulative Sales Total

The next measure will be for the cumulative sales total. This measure will take advantage of the *dates* table and the *Total Sales* measure we just created.

1. Start a new measure and store it in the **sales** table with the name **Total Sales YTD**.

2. Use the following formula:

```
=CALCULATE([Total Sales],DATESYTD('Calendar'[Date]))
```

3. Specify the format as **Currency**, **£**, and **2 decimal places**.

This formula uses the CALCULATE function, the most important function in DAX. The CALCULATE function allows us to add, change, and remove filter context in a formula.

In this example, it uses the *Total Sales* measure as the expression, and the DATESYTD function is used to apply a filter to that expression.

Note   The Total Sales measure and the Date column look the same as they are both enclosed in square brackets []. Because the Calendar table is mentioned before Date, we can instantly tell that it is a column and not a measure.

Writing DAX can take a lot of practice before you get comfortable. The last two examples might be difficult to understand. Persevere, and after writing them a few times, you will understand them better.

Figure 6-40 shows the *Total Sales* and *Total Sales YTD* measures in a PivotTable with *Month* in row labels. It is good practice to test your measures in PivotTables, and this PivotTable demonstrates the *Total Sales YTD* measure is working perfectly.

	A	B	C
1	Row Labels ▾	Total Sales	Total Sales YTD
2	Jan	£31,756.70	£31,756.70
3	Feb	£27,430.20	£59,186.90
4	Mar	£48,971.20	£108,158.10
5	Apr	£41,667.20	£149,825.30
6	May	£47,816.70	£197,642.00
7	Jun	£63,621.10	£261,263.10
8	Jul	£62,942.90	£324,206.00
9	Aug	£64,256.40	£388,462.40
10	Sep	£82,726.90	£471,189.30
11	Oct	£38,350.50	£509,539.80
12	Nov	£17,220.80	£526,760.60
13	Dec	£26,027.50	£552,788.10
14	**Grand Total**	**£552,788.10**	**£552,788.10**
15			

Figure 6-40. *Total Sales and Total Sales YTD measures filtered by month*

% of Year Total

We will now create a measure to calculate the month's total sales as a percentage of the year total.

We will do this by creating two DAX formulas. First, we will calculate the total sales for all months. And then we can divide a month's total by the result of all months' measure.

1. Create a new measure in the **sales** table named **TS All Months**.

2. Use the following formula:

    ```
    =CALCULATE([Total Sales],ALL('Calendar'[Month]))
    ```

3. Specify the format as **Currency**, **£**, and **2 decimal places**.

This formula uses the ALL function within CALCULATE to remove the filter context. This is important! When we divide the total sales by the *TS All Months* measure, we know that it will be the total for all months and is unaffected by any month filters.

Figure 6-41 shows the *TS All Months* measure in a PivotTable with *Month* in the row labels. It does not look nice, but this proves that the month does not filter all months' total.

	A	B
1	Row Labels	TS All Months
2	Jan	£552,788.10
3	Feb	£552,788.10
4	Mar	£552,788.10
5	Apr	£552,788.10
6	May	£552,788.10
7	Jun	£552,788.10
8	Jul	£552,788.10
9	Aug	£552,788.10
10	Sep	£552,788.10
11	Oct	£552,788.10
12	Nov	£552,788.10
13	Dec	£552,788.10
14	**Grand Total**	**£552,788.10**
15		

Figure 6-41. *TS All Months measure removes the filter context from row labels*

Note Only the year 2019 is used in this data, so the DAX works perfectly. If your data contains multiple years, then you need to filter for a specific year to return the correct % of year total.

We will now calculate the month's percentage of year total.

1. Create a new measure in the **sales** table named **% of Year Total**.
2. Use the following formula:

```
=DIVIDE([Total Sales],[TS All Months],0)
```

3. Specify the format as **Number ➤ Percentage** and **2 decimal places**.

The DIVIDE function is a safe divide that offers an alternative action instead of producing #DIV/0! errors common in Excel. A zero has been entered as an alternative action here.

The formula [Total Sales]/[TS All Months] would also have worked, but it is good practice to use the DIVIDE function in Power Pivot.

Figure 6-42 shows the *% of Year Total* measure being used in a PivotTable report.

	A	B	C
1	Row Labels ▼	Total Sales	% of Year Total
2	Jan	£31,756.70	5.74%
3	Feb	£27,430.20	4.96%
4	Mar	£48,971.20	8.86%
5	Apr	£41,667.20	7.54%
6	May	£47,816.70	8.65%
7	Jun	£63,621.10	11.51%
8	Jul	£62,942.90	11.39%
9	Aug	£64,256.40	11.62%
10	Sep	£82,726.90	14.97%
11	Oct	£38,350.50	6.94%
12	Nov	£17,220.80	3.12%
13	Dec	£26,027.50	4.71%
14	Grand Total	£552,788.10	100.00%
15			

Figure 6-42. *Total sales and percentage of year total*

Difference and % Difference to Previous Month

In this example, we will create measures to calculate the difference and the percentage difference between the current and the previous month.

The Measures window we have used so far has been very helpful, but let us create these measures in the Power Pivot window to get more familiar with that environment.

Click **Power Pivot ➤ Manage** to switch to the Power Pivot window.

The measures that have been created so far can be seen in the *Calculation Area* at the bottom of the *Data View* (Figure 6-43). It also shows their unfiltered result.

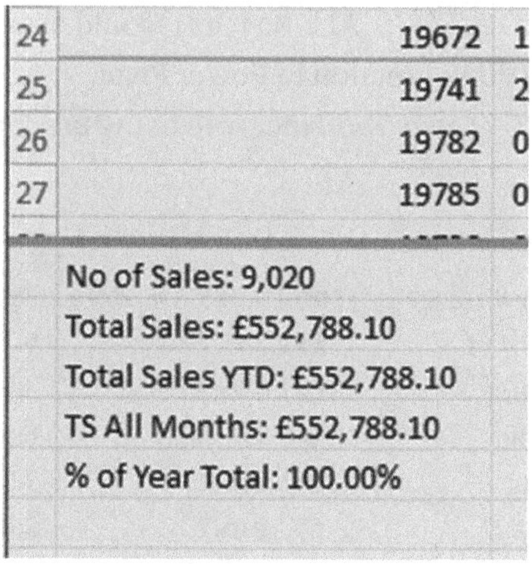

24		19672	1
25		19741	2
26		19782	0
27		19785	0

No of Sales: 9,020
Total Sales: £552,788.10
Total Sales YTD: £552,788.10
TS All Months: £552,788.10
% of Year Total: 100.00%

Figure 6-43. *Measures shown in the Calculation Area*

Note   Click **Home ➤ Calculation Area** if it is not visible.

To create a DAX measure in the Data View:

1. Click the next empty cell below the measures in the Calculation Area.

2. Enter the following formula in the Formula Bar:

    TS Prev Month:=CALCULATE([Total Sales],DATEADD('Calendar'
    [Date],-1,MONTH))

3. Specify the format **Currency**, **£**, and **2 decimal places** using the formatting buttons on the **Home** tab.

This formula uses CALCULATE to apply a filter to the *Total Sales* measure. The DATEADD function moves a given set of dates by a specified interval. In this example, they filter the total sales to one month previous.

The measure is named *TS Prev Month,* and this is written before the formula followed by a colon and an equals (:=).

Let us switch to the Excel workbook and test this measure out in a PivotTable. Using it side by side to the total sales is a simple method to check it is working correctly (Figure 6-44).

◢	A	B	C
1	Row Labels ▼	Total Sales	TS Prev Month
2	Jan	£31,756.70	
3	Feb	£27,430.20	£31,756.70
4	Mar	£48,971.20	£27,430.20
5	Apr	£41,667.20	£48,971.20
6	May	£47,816.70	£41,667.20
7	Jun	£63,621.10	£47,816.70
8	Jul	£62,942.90	£63,621.10
9	Aug	£64,256.40	£62,942.90
10	Sep	£82,726.90	£64,256.40
11	Oct	£38,350.50	£82,726.90
12	Nov	£17,220.80	£38,350.50
13	Dec	£26,027.50	£17,220.80
14	Grand Total	£552,788.10	£526,760.60
15			

Figure 6-44. *Using a PivotTable to check that TS Prev Month works correctly*

We can now create a measure named **Diff Prev Month** using the following formula:

```
Diff Prev Month:=[Total Sales]-[TS Prev Month]
```

Format the measure as **Currency**, **£**, with **2 decimal places**.
And then create a measure named **% Diff Prev Month** using the DIVIDE function.

```
% Diff Prev Month:=DIVIDE([Diff Prev Month],[TS Prev Month],0)
```

Format this measure as a **Percentage** to **2 decimal places**.
Figure 6-45 shows these two measures in a PivotTable.

▲	A	B	C	D
1	Row Labels ▼	Total Sales	Diff Prev Month	% Diff Prev Month
2	Jan	£31,756.70	£31,756.70	0.00%
3	Feb	£27,430.20	-£4,326.50	-13.62%
4	Mar	£48,971.20	£21,541.00	78.53%
5	Apr	£41,667.20	-£7,304.00	-14.91%
6	May	£47,816.70	£6,149.50	14.76%
7	Jun	£63,621.10	£15,804.40	33.05%
8	Jul	£62,942.90	-£678.20	-1.07%
9	Aug	£64,256.40	£1,313.50	2.09%
10	Sep	£82,726.90	£18,470.50	28.74%
11	Oct	£38,350.50	-£44,376.40	-53.64%
12	Nov	£17,220.80	-£21,129.70	-55.10%
13	Dec	£26,027.50	£8,806.70	51.14%
14	Grand Total	£552,788.10	£26,027.50	4.94%
15				

Figure 6-45. *Difference and % difference to previous month*

Note   The *Total Sales* measure has been used six times in other measures and also multiple times in the PivotTable examples. This measure is only created once, keeps our measures concise, and is formatted once on creation.

Hide Bad Measure Totals

The PivotTable grand totals for the *Diff Prev Month* and *% Diff Prev Month* measures in Figure 6-45 are not useful. There is no previous month to the grand total, so they are confusing and not relevant.

To hide the totals in the PivotTable, we will use a DAX function called HASONEFILTER. This is used to check if a filter (the month in this case) has been applied or not.

We will wrap this in an IF function to test the HASONEFILTER response. If the month filter has been applied, then keep the result. And for the totals where no filter is applied, we will show nothing.

1. In Excel, click **Power Pivot ➤ Measures ➤ Manage Measures**.

2. Select the *Diff Prev Month* measure in the list and click **Edit**.

3. Use the following formula in the box provided (Figure 6-46). Click **OK**.

```
=IF(HASONEFILTER('Calendar'[Month]),[Total Sales]-
[TS Prev Month],"")
```

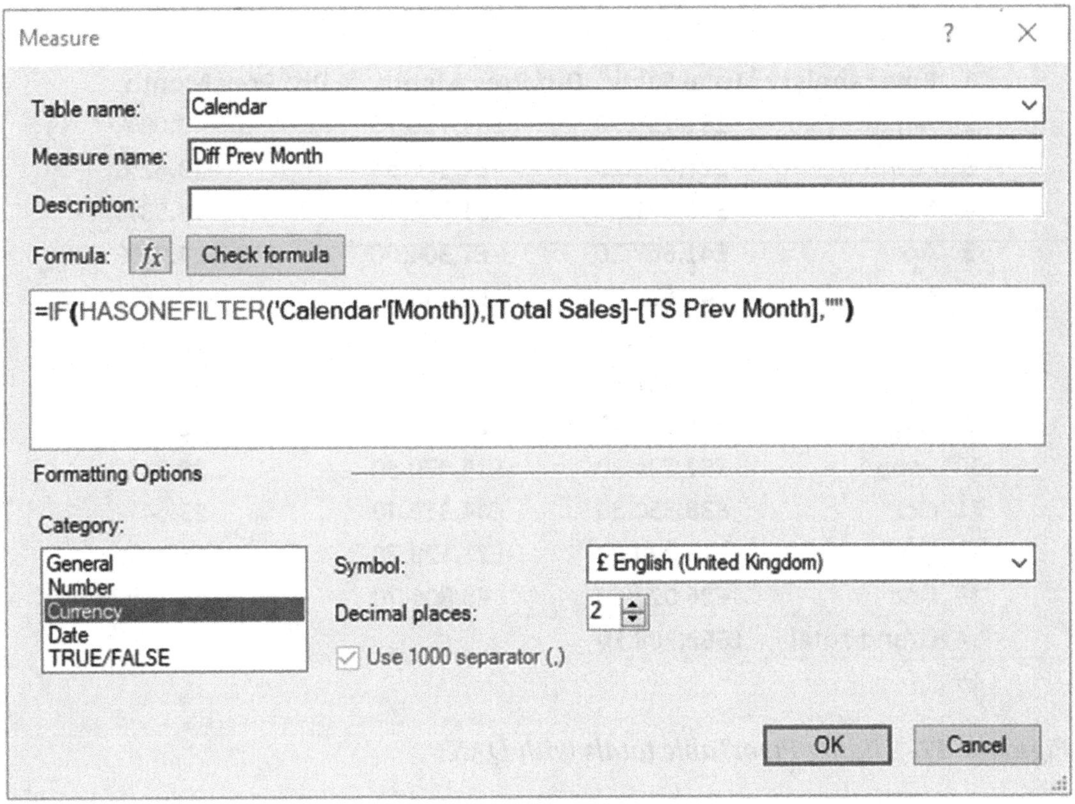

Figure 6-46. HASONEFILTER used to hide the value of an unfiltered measure

The HASONEFILTER function checks the *Month* column from the *Calendar* table to see if it is filtered and returns True if this is the case. The IF function then takes the appropriate response.

4. Select the *% Diff Prev Month* measure in the list and click **Edit**.

5. Use the following formula in the box provided and click **OK**:

```
=IF(HASONEFILTER('Calendar'[Month]),DIVIDE([Diff Prev Month],
[TS Prev Month],0),"")
```

Close the Manage Measures window. The grand totals have been hidden for those two measures (Figure 6-47).

	A	B	C	D
1	Row Labels ▼	Total Sales	Diff Prev Month	% Diff Prev Month
2	Jan	£31,756.70	£31,756.70	0.00%
3	Feb	£27,430.20	-£4,326.50	-13.62%
4	Mar	£48,971.20	£21,541.00	78.53%
5	Apr	£41,667.20	-£7,304.00	-14.91%
6	May	£47,816.70	£6,149.50	14.76%
7	Jun	£63,621.10	£15,804.40	33.05%
8	Jul	£62,942.90	-£678.20	-1.07%
9	Aug	£64,256.40	£1,313.50	2.09%
10	Sep	£82,726.90	£18,470.50	28.74%
11	Oct	£38,350.50	-£44,376.40	-53.64%
12	Nov	£17,220.80	-£21,129.70	-55.10%
13	Dec	£26,027.50	£8,806.70	51.14%
14	**Grand Total**	**£552,788.10**		
15				

Figure 6-47. *Hiding PivotTable totals with DAX*

Organizing Your Measures and Fields

As you create more measures, you can see the PivotTable Fields list start to get cluttered. It can be awkward to find and use the fields and measures that you want.

Let us look at a few techniques for organizing your measures and fields better.

View Fields and Areas Side by Side

This is a simple little trick that can help you work with your fields and measures in PivotTables. Instead of using the classic view of the areas below the fields and measures list, you can view them side by side.

In the PivotTable Fields pane, click the **Tools** button (gear icon) and select **Fields Section and Areas Section Side-By-Side** (Figure 6-48).

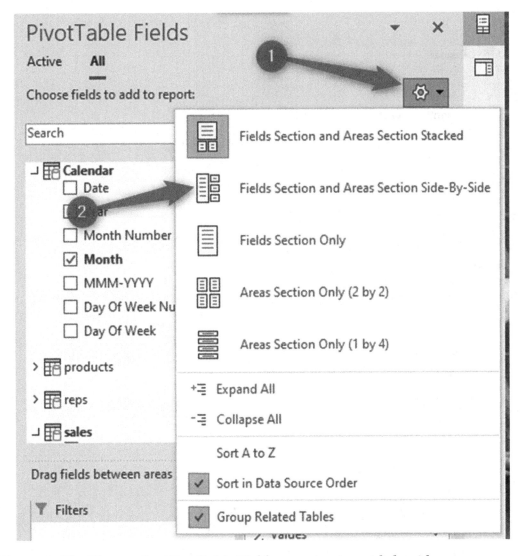

Figure 6-48. *Change the PivotTable Fields pane to view side by side*

This provides a larger area for the fields and measures list (Figure 6-49). I also find clicking and dragging to the right easier than dragging to below the list.

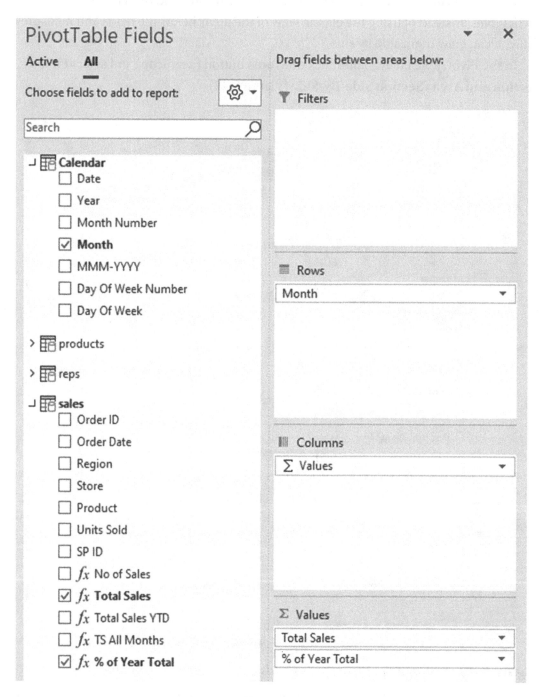

Figure 6-49. *Larger area to view and work with fields and measures*

Hide Fields from Client Tools

All the fields and measures in the model have a job, but not all of them will be used in the reports.

Some of the fields are key fields used to establish relationships, and we have no plans to use them in a reporting scenario. Some of the measures we created such as *TS Prev Month* and *TS All Months* were meant to be used in other measures, not in any reports.

We will hide these fields and measures, so they do not appear in the PivotTable Fields list. This will reduce the clutter in our working environment.

1. Open the Power Pivot window and switch to Diagram View.

2. Right-click the field or measure and click **Hide from Client Tools**. In Figure 6-50, the *ID* field from the *reps* table is being hidden.

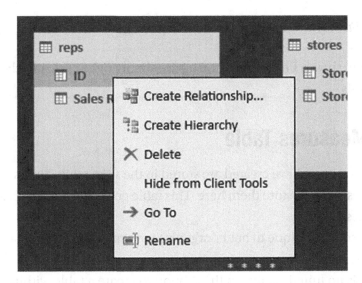

Figure 6-50. *Hide fields so they do not appear in the PivotTable Fields list*

3. Continue until all the unnecessary fields and measures are hidden. Figure 6-51 shows a few tables on the PivotTable Fields pane after hiding fields such as *Month Number, Day of Week Number, Product ID,* and reps *ID*.

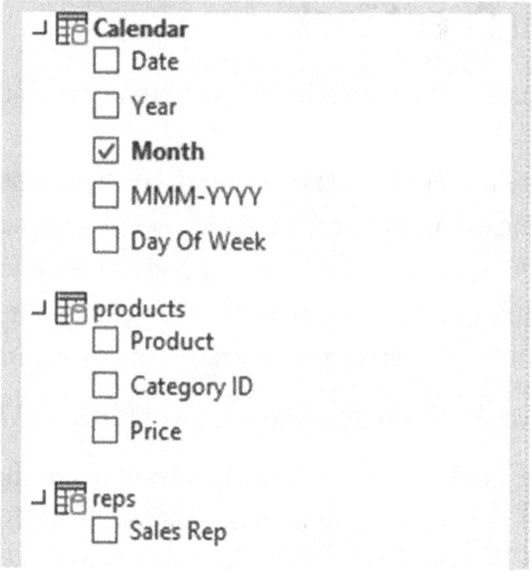

Figure 6-51. Fields hidden from the PivotTable Fields list

If you need to show a field or measure again, simply right-click and click **Unhide from Client Tools**.

Create a Measures Table

All the measures that we have created are stored in the *sales* table. This is the fact or data table, so it makes sense to store them here. This table generally has less fields than the dimension tables also.

However, a cool technique to better organize your measures is to create a measures table to store them in.

Now, there is no functionality on the Ribbon to create a table within Power Pivot. However, there is an awesome trick that I learned from my friend Mark Proctor to get this done.

1. Switch to an Excel worksheet and copy any blank cell.

2. Open the Power Pivot window, click **Home ➤ Paste**.

3. In the Paste Preview window, enter _**Measures** as the *Table Name* (Figure 6-52).

Paste Preview   ?   ✕

Preview the data that you are about to paste. You can modify the table name and specify
whether to use the first row as a header row in the destination table.

Table Name:

_Measures

Data to be pasted:

Column

☑ Use first row as column headers.

⚠ | One or more column headers will be replaced because they contain invalid characters. |
| --- |

| OK | Cancel |

Figure 6-52. *Create a table within Power Pivot*

The table is added to the data model and shown in the Data view
of the Power Pivot window.

The table is added to the model, and the Power Pivot window
opens. Rename the table **_Measures** (or whatever you want) by
right-clicking the tab at the bottom of the Data view and click
Rename ().

Note   The tables in the PivotTable Fields list are ordered A to Z. By naming the
table with an underscore as a prefix, we ensure it appears at the top of the list.

Unfortunately, we cannot move a batch of measures in one go;
we will need to move them one at a time. However, from now on,
when you create a measure, you can store it in this table.

4. Switch back to Excel and click **Power Pivot ➤ Measures ➤ Manage Measures**.

5. Select a measure and click **Edit**.

6. Change the table name to _**Measures** and click **OK** (Figure 6-53).

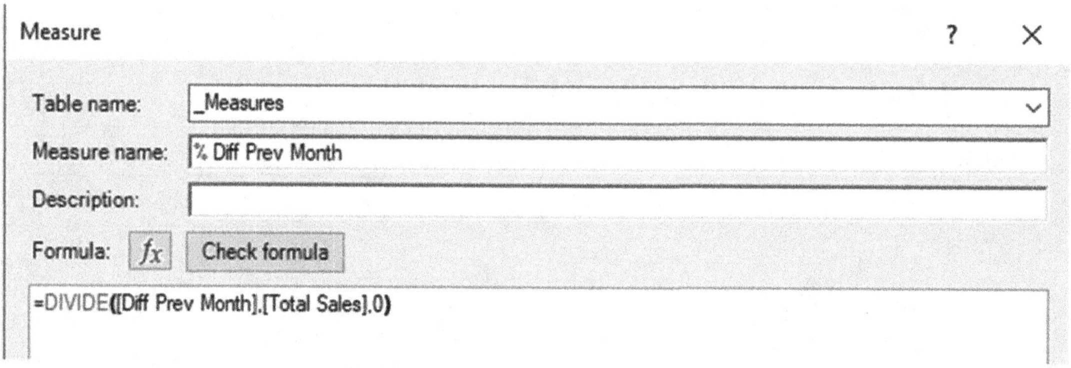

Figure 6-53. *Changing the table that your measures are stored in*

7. Repeat for all the measures you want to move.

Figure 6-54 shows the *_Measures* table in the PivotTable Fields list. A message is shown stating that relationships may be needed. This is because the *_Measures* table is not related to any other tables. This is fine so we can close that message.

The table still has the original *Column* column from the table we created within Power Pivot. We will hide this column.

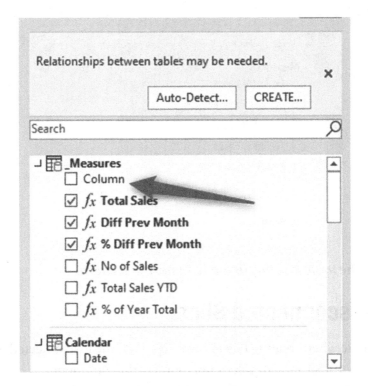

Figure 6-54. *Disconnected measures table still with the Column field*

8. Open the Power Pivot window, switch to Diagram View, right-click
    the **Column** column in the *_Measures* table, and click **Hide from
    Client Tools**.

Only the measures are now visible in the *_Measures* table, and the icon next to its
name has automatically changed from a table to a Sigma (Figure 6-55).

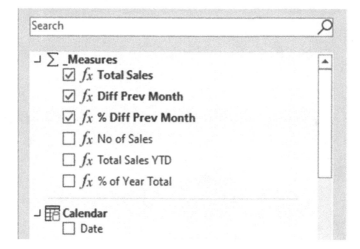

Figure 6-55. *The table has the Sigma icon next to its name*

Using a Disconnected Slicer

A useful technique when creating Power Pivot reports is the disconnected Slicer. It enables us to create a Slicer with values not found within our model.

In this example, we will create a Slicer with two different calculation options – the *Total Sales* or the *Total Sales YTD* measure. And this selection will change the calculation in the PivotTable.

1. Create a table on a worksheet like the one in Figure 6-56. This simple table has an *ID* column and a column with the calculations we will use in the Slicer. Name the table **CalcSlicer**.

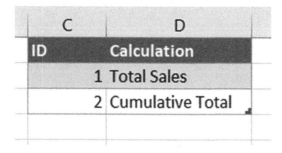

Figure 6-56. *Table with the calculations we will use in the Slicer*

2. Click the table and click **Power Pivot ➤ Add to Data Model**.

With the table now loaded to the data model, let us create the PivotTable and insert the Slicer.

3. Insert a PivotTable that uses the workbook's data model and move the **Month** field into the *Rows* area and the **Total Sales** measure into the *Values* area (Figure 6-57).

Row Labels ▼	Total Sales
Jan	£31,756.70
Feb	£27,430.20
Mar	£48,971.20
Apr	£41,667.20
May	£47,816.70
Jun	£63,621.10
Jul	£62,942.90
Aug	£64,256.40
Sep	£82,726.90
Oct	£38,350.50
Nov	£17,220.80
Dec	£26,027.50
Grand Total	**£552,788.10**

Figure 6-57. *PivotTable showing total sales by month*

Total Sales is being used as a placeholder and will soon be replaced by the measure that uses the selected calculation.

4. Click **Insert ➤ Slicer**.

5. Click the **All** tab and check the **Calculation** column of the *CalcSlicer* table (Figure 6-58). Click **OK**.

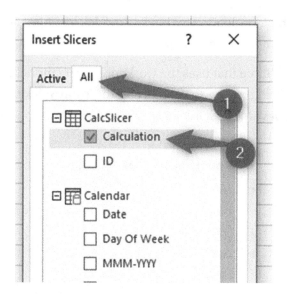

Figure 6-58. *Insert a Slicer with the different calculation options*

We now have the PivotTable and the Slicer (Figure 6-59), but currently when you click a Slicer option, nothing happens.

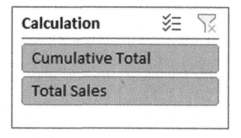

Row Labels ▾	Total Sales
Jan	£31,756.70
Feb	£27,430.20
Mar	£48,971.20
Apr	£41,667.20
May	£47,816.70
Jun	£63,621.10
Jul	£62,942.90
Aug	£64,256.40
Sep	£82,726.90
Oct	£38,350.50
Nov	£17,220.80
Dec	£26,027.50
Grand Total	**£552,788.10**

Figure 6-59. *Slicer with calculation options, but does not change the PivotTable*

We will create two measures: one to record the selected option from the Slicer and another to perform the correct calculation based on this selection.

6. Create a new measure named **Slicer Selection** and store it in the **_Measures** table.

7. The measure will use the following formula and will be formatted as a **Whole Number**:

```
=MIN(CalcSlicer[ID])
```

This formula returns the ID of the selected value on the Slicer.

8. Create a new measure named **Selected Calc** and store it in the **_Measures** table.

9. The measure will use the following formula and will be formatted as **Currency**, **£**, with **2 decimal places**:

```
=SWITCH([Slicer Selection],1,[Total Sales],2,[Total Sales YTD])
```

The SWITCH function is used to return the correct measure based on which ID was returned by the *Slicer Selection* measure.

10. The final step is then to replace the *Total Sales* measure in the *Values* area of the PivotTable with the **Selected Calc** measure (Figure 6-60).

Clicking a Slicer option changes the calculation in the PivotTable.

Row Labels ▼	Selected Calc
Jan	£31,756.70
Feb	£59,186.90
Mar	£108,158.10
Apr	£149,825.30
May	£197,642.00
Jun	£261,263.10
Jul	£324,206.00
Aug	£388,462.40
Sep	£471,189.30
Oct	£509,539.80
Nov	£526,760.60
Dec	£552,788.10
Grand Total	**£552,788.10**

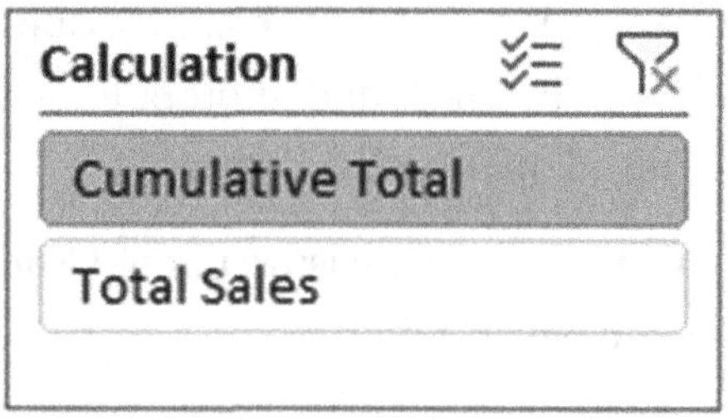

Calculation	⅏	▽ₓ
Cumulative Total		
Total Sales		

Figure 6-60. *PivotTable with a Slicer that changes the calculation used*

We can now take things further by creating a PivotChart from the PivotTable (**PivotTable Analyze ➤ PivotChart**) and making further modifications to the Slicer.

1. Select the Slicer and click the **Slicer** tab and then **Slicer Settings**.

2. Uncheck the **Display header** box (Figure 6-61). The header is unnecessary, and there is no reason for a user to clear the selection.

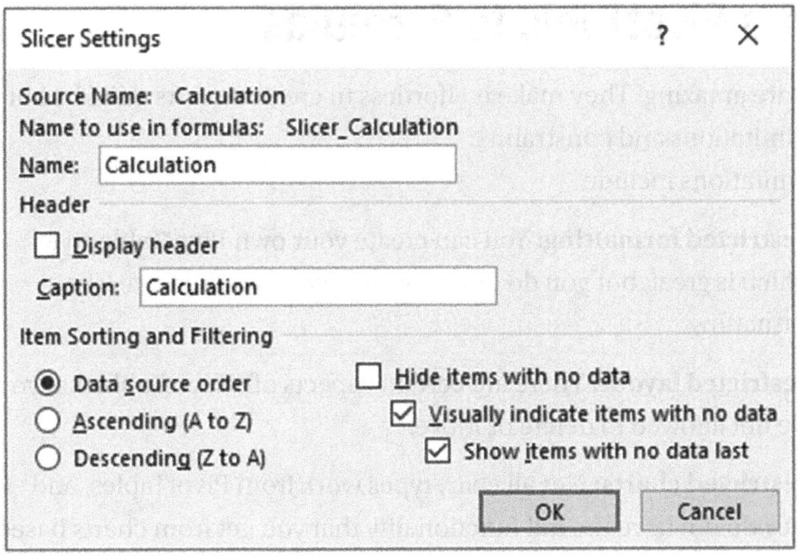
Slicer Settings
?
✕
Source Name: Calculation
Name to use in formulas: Slicer_Calculation
Name: Calculation
Header
☐ Display header
Caption: Calculation
Item Sorting and Filtering
◉ Data source order
○ Ascending (A to Z)
○ Descending (Z to A)
☐ Hide items with no data
☑ Visually indicate items with no data
☑ Show items with no data last
OK
Cancel

Figure 6-61. *Remove the header from the Slicer*

3. Select the Slicer and change the **Columns** setting on the *Slicer* tab to ***2***. This will display the two options horizontally instead of vertically (Figure 6-62).

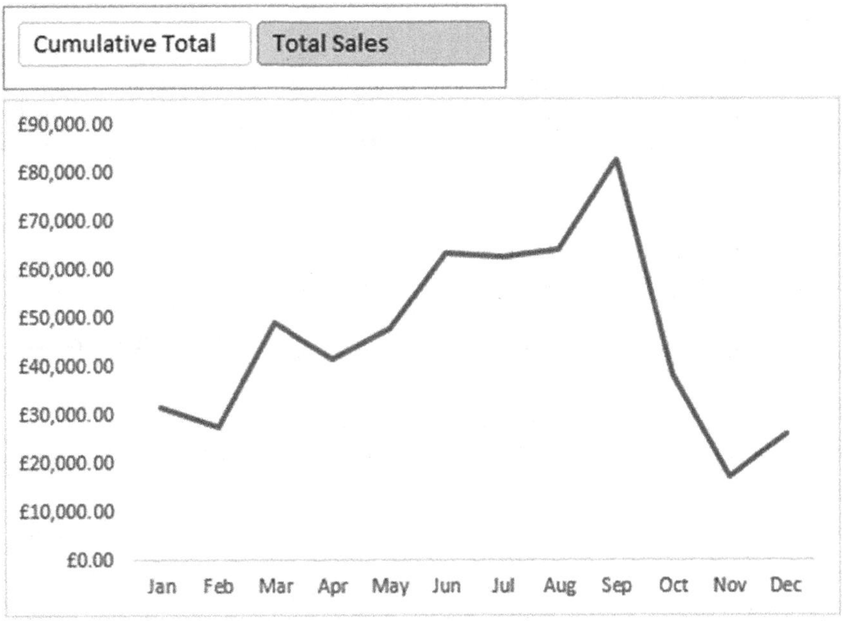
Cumulative Total
Total Sales
£90,000.00
£80,000.00
£70,000.00
£60,000.00
£50,000.00
£40,000.00
£30,000.00
£20,000.00
£10,000.00
£0.00
Jan
Feb
Mar
Apr
May
Jun
Jul
Aug
Sep
Oct
Nov
Dec

Figure 6-62. *PivotChart with the Slicer to change calculation*

Convert a PivotTable to Formulas

PivotTables are amazing! They make it effortless to create reports quickly, but they do have some limitations and constraints.

These limitations include

- **Restricted formatting:** You can create your own PivotTable styles, which is great, but you do not have complete freedom over the formatting.

- **Restricted layout:** There are certain aspects of a PivotTable that you are not allowed to delete or move.

- **Restricted charts:** Not all chart types work from PivotTables, and they do not have the full functionality that you get from charts based on ranges or tables.

So, it is cool that there is an option to convert your PivotTables to formulas. This gives you freedom over moving the cells, formatting, and charts.

Click the PivotTable and click the **PivotTable Analyze** tab (may be named Analyze or Options) ➤ **OLAP Tools** ➤ **Convert to Formulas** (Figure 6-63).

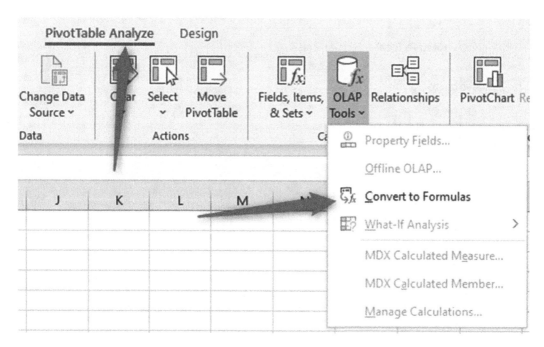

Figure 6-63.   *Convert your PivotTable to formulas*

The PivotTable has been converted into formulas. When you select a cell, you will see the formula in the formula bar (Figure 6-64).

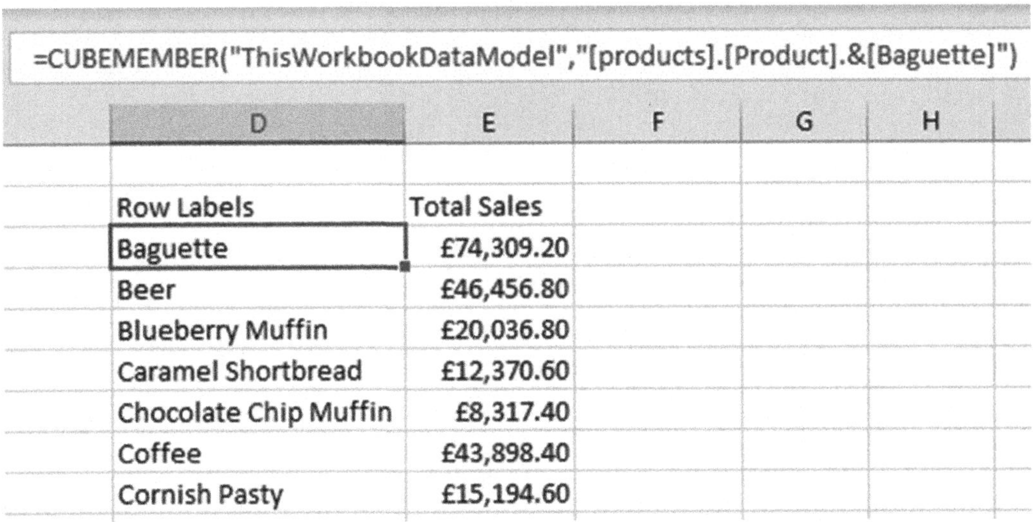

=CUBEMEMBER("ThisWorkbookDataModel","[products].[Product].&[Baguette]")

D	E	F	G	H
Row Labels	Total Sales			
Baguette	£74,309.20			
Beer	£46,456.80			
Blueberry Muffin	£20,036.80			
Caramel Shortbread	£12,370.60			
Chocolate Chip Muffin	£8,317.40			
Coffee	£43,898.40			
Cornish Pasty	£15,194.60			

Figure 6-64. *CUBE functions used to access the data model*

CUBE functions are used to access the data model without the PivotTable. Slicers will continue to work with the CUBE functions just as they did with the PivotTable results. You can learn more on how to use these CUBE functions and do some awesome things.

However, without getting involved with the formulas, you still have the advantage of being able to move cells around, format them, insert columns and rows, and more.

Index

A, B

Advanced formatting
    bar in bar chart, 219–221
    conditional formatting, 214–217
    line chart, 217–219
    target range, 222–225

C

Chart labels
    data labels, 208–212
    display symbols, 212–214
    title, 205–208
CHOOSE function
    Data Validation list, 113, 114
    formula, 112
    link options buttons, cell, 111, 112
    MATCH function, 114
    select formula, options
        buttons, 110, 111
    specific columns, filter, 115, 116
    syntax, 110
    user selection, 112, 113
Combined tables, 238, 239
    master Query, 240
    Master table, 241, 242
    worksheets, 240, 241
Conditional Formatting, 214–217
    compare lists, 151–153
    data bars

compare values, 156–158
    showing progress, goal, 158–161
dates
    between, 145, 146
    due/expired, 146
    format cells, 144
    formula, 144
    identifying, expired, 145
    table of names/expiry dates, 143
heat map, color scales, 161–163
icon sets
    arrow icons, 155, 156
    table, sales performance, 153, 154
    variance column, 154, 155
multiple columns, 141, 142
PivotTables, 164, 166, 167
rules
    entire row, 140
    members, Gold membership,
        140, 141
    selecting tables *vs.* sheet columns,
        138, 139
    single cells, 138
    table of members, 138
weekends/important dates
    COUNTIFS function, 149
    create rule, 148
    formula, 150
    table of product sales, 147, 149, 150
    WEEKDAY function, 148

© Alan Murray 2021
A. Murray, *Advanced Excel Success*, https://doi.org/10.1007/978-1-4842-6467-6

Printed in the United States
By Bookmasters